"In the last 20 years, studies investigating [psychopathy have increased] exponentially. Several theoretical frameworks [have been proposed], focusing on either social, psychological or biological explanations. Yet, there is a great deal of controversy and lack of replication among existing studies. If we manage to consider the unique and interactive influences among biological, psychological and social influences, as argued in this book, we may begin to offer a better explanation of the complicated phenomenon of psychopathy. Psychopathy is an exciting area of research, and Thomson offers an in-depth expert analysis of the latest research on the biopsychosocial mechanisms of psychopathy, providing an excellent resource for researchers and clinicians alike."

– **Dr. Kostas Fanti, PhD., Associate Professor of Psychology at the University of Cyprus and Director of the Developmental Psychopathology Lab**

"Thomson provides us with a highly readable volume on the multifarious nature of psychopathy. Having done the exhaustive scientific leg-work, he presents the evidence for a biopsychosocial understanding of psychopathy, and thus provides the topology, the banks of the river so to speak, for beginning the challenging journey of tracing the inter-connected multi-causal nature of this personality disorder. It may help address one of the most puzzling questions regarding the link between covert antisocial features of the disorder (deceitful, callous, manipulation of others) and the more overt features (impulsive, reckless, aggression), which can precede the covert features, and that both are components of a broad genetic factor."

– **Dr. Craig Neumann, PhD., Distinguished Research Professor of Psychology at the University of North Texas**

"*Understanding Psychopathy* provides a comprehensive review of the development and causal links of psychopathy. By integrating the latest research from the biological, psychological, and social sciences, the book extensively considers psychopathy from a biopsychosocial perspective. Thomson delivers an accessible and compelling resource for forensic practitioners, researchers, students, and laypersons."

– **Dr. Annette McKeown, PsyD., Principal Forensic Psychologist, Kolvin Service UK**

"This outstanding new book on psychopathy, focusing on the biopsychosocial model, offers a comprehensive and detailed overview of the most recent theoretical and empirical analyses. It is well written, easily accessible and clearly presented and the use of case examples in combination with thorough scientific discussion makes it a pleasure to read. It provides key insights for both readers who are new in the field as well as for more experienced professionals. In short, a must-read for everyone who wants to gain deeper understanding of psychopathy."

– **Vivienne de Vogel, Professor at the University of Applied Sciences Utrecht, and researcher De Forensische Zorgspecialisten, The Netherlands**

"Over the past 30 years, the construct of psychopathy has received unparalleled attention from researchers and scholars interested in the origins and maintenance of criminal behavior. Psychopathy is the subject of numerous empirical studies, theoretical articles, book chapters, and books, and the popularity of psychopathy in mainstream movies, television shows, podcasts, and books aimed at the general public has increased dramatically in recent years. The topic of psychopathy has also been written about from multiple perspectives, including psychological, biological, neurological, neuropsychological, and sociological.

Given the unprecedented attention devoted to psychopathy over the past few decades, it is rare to read anything "new" on the subject. But Thomson's *Understanding Psychopathy* offers a refreshingly novel treatment of psychopathy. Thomson examines the development of psychopathy from a biopsychosocial perspective, and *Understanding Psychopathy* provides up-to-date, insightful, and comprehensive coverage of the multidisciplinary research that has been conducted over the past 30 years. Although the book focuses primarily on the development of psychopathy using the biopsychosocial approach as a guiding framework, there are also chapters addressing the assessment of psychopathy and the relationship between psychopathy and crime. *Understanding Psychopathy* simultaneously serves as a comprehensive synthesis of existing research and a blueprint for current and future researchers interested in conducting meaningful science in this area. Thomson has succeeded in writing a scholarly and practical book that will be attractive to students, researchers, clinicians, and anyone else interested in this fascinating disorder."

– **David DeMatteo, JD, PhD, ABPP (Forensic), Drexel University, Department of Psychology and Thomas R. Kline School of Law**

"This remarkably comprehensive volume represents a landmark in the field of psychopathy research. As detailed throughout the book, the puzzle of psychopathy has often been approached in a piecemeal fashion. Theory and research tends to emphasize biological, psychological, and sociological accounts as relatively separate. Fortunately for the field, Thomson has organized a novel and pathbreaking account that successfully ties these separate threads together, to provide a comprehensive biopsychosocial perspective to contextualize and understand psychopathy. A remarkable accomplishment and a critical addition to the libraries of researchers, students, and front-line practitioners."

– **Dr. Robert F. Krueger, Ph.D., Distinguished McKnight University Professor, University of Minnesota, USA**

UNDERSTANDING PSYCHOPATHY

Understanding Psychopathy is an essential, accessible new guide on psychopathy and its development. Through the lens of the biopsychosocial model, Thomson explores a wide range of factors contributing to the development of psychopathy, from the genetic to the environmental, supported by the latest research into the disorder.

Thomson examines psychopathy from all angles, analysing social, psychological and biological factors, in addition to the history and assessment of psychopathy, and links to violent crime. Theory and research are supported throughout with fascinating case studies. These case studies provide accessible and relevant examples for readers who are new to the field, and to those more familiar with psychopathy and its implications.

Understanding Psychopathy is a brilliant resource for psychology students, researchers and practitioners in the criminal justice system alike, with grounding in forensic psychology, clinical psychology and criminology.

Nicholas D. Thomson, PhD., is Assistant Professor in the Department of Surgery at Virginia Commonwealth University (VCU), Program Evaluator for the Injury and Violence Prevention Program at VCU Health Trauma Center, and Honorary Fellow at the University of Durham. He is an accredited psychotherapist by the United Kingdom Council for Psychotherapy and has over a decade of clinical experience working in prisons and inpatient settings in both the US and UK, and currently runs a private practice. Formerly, he was the module leader for the Forensic Psychology and Psychopathy programs, and taught Abnormal Psychology at the University of Durham.

The author is donating his royalties in full to Project EMPOWER, UK, a multidisciplinary initiative dedicated to enhancing prevention and intervention services to individuals and their families who experience intimate partner violence, sexual violence, domestic violence, or human trafficking.

New Frontiers in Forensic Psychology
Edited by Graham J. Towl and Tammi Walker

Graham J. Towl is Professor of Forensic Psychology at Durham University. He is the recipient of the British Psychological Society Award for Distinguished Contributions to Professional Practice. He is widely published and, as Pro Vice Chancellor at Durham University, he chaired the sector-leading Sexual Violence Task Force, which has received widespread endorsements.

Tammi Walker is Deputy Director of the Centre for Applied Research in Health (CARH) and is a Reader in Forensic Psychology at the University of Huddersfield. She is a registered Chartered Psychologist and Fellow of the British Psychological Society and has published in this area for over 15 years.

New Frontiers in Forensic Psychology brings together the most contemporary research in core and emerging topics in the field, providing a comprehensive review of new areas of investigation in forensic psychology and new perspectives on existing topics of enquiry.

The series includes original volumes in which the authors are encouraged to explore unchartered territory, make cross-disciplinary evaluations and, where possible, break new ground.

The series is an essential resource for senior undergraduates, postgraduates, researchers and practitioners across forensic psychology, criminology and social policy.

Titles in the series:

Tackling Sexual Violence at Universities: An International Perspective by Graham J. Towl and Tammi Walker

Understanding Psychopathy: The Biopsychosocial Perspective by Nicholas D. Thomson

UNDERSTANDING PSYCHOPATHY

The Biopsychosocial Perspective

Nicholas D. Thomson

LONDON AND NEW YORK

First edition published 2019
by Routledge
2 Park Square, Milton Park, Abingdon, Oxon, OX14 4RN

and by Routledge
52 Vanderbilt Avenue, New York, NY 10017

Routledge is an imprint of the Taylor & Francis Group, an informa business

© 2019 Nicholas D. Thomson

The right of Nicholas D. Thomson to be identified as author of this work has been asserted by him in accordance with sections 77 and 78 of the Copyright, Designs and Patents Act 1988.

All rights reserved. No part of this book may be reprinted or reproduced or utilized in any form or by any electronic, mechanical, or other means, now known or hereafter invented, including photocopying and recording, or in any information storage or retrieval system, without permission in writing from the publishers.

Trademark notice: Product or corporate names may be trademarks or registered trademarks, and are used only for identification and explanation without intent to infringe.

British Library Cataloguing-in-Publication Data
A catalogue record for this book is available from the British Library

Library of Congress Cataloging-in-Publication Data
Names: Thomson, Nicholas D., author.
Title: Understanding psychopathy : the biopsychosocial perspective / Nicholas D. Thomson. Other titles: New frontiers in forensic psychology.
Description: First edition. | Abingdon, Oxon ; New York, NY : Routledge, 2019. | Series: New frontiers in forensic psychology | Includes bibliographical references and index.
Identifiers: LCCN 2018055403| ISBN 9781138570726 (hbk.) | ISBN 9781138570733 (pbk.) | ISBN 9780203703304 (ebk.)
Subjects: | MESH: Antisocial Personality Disorder—psychology | Psychopathology—methods | Forensic Psychology—methods | Risk Factors | Models, Psychological
Classification: LCC RC555 | NLM WM 190.5.A2 | DDC 616.85/820651—dc23
LC record available at https://lccn.loc.gov/2018055403

ISBN: 978-1-138-57072-6 (hbk)
ISBN: 978-1-138-57073-3 (pbk)
ISBN: 978-0-203-70330-4 (ebk)

Typeset in Bembo
by Swales & Willis Ltd, Exeter, Devon, UK

Printed and bound in Great Britain by
TJ International Ltd, Padstow, Cornwall

For Adelaide and Hugo

CONTENTS

List of figures and tables   *x*
Acknowledgments   *xi*
Biography   *xii*
Foreword by David P. Farrington   *xiii*

1   Psychopathy and the biopsychosocial model   1

2   History and assessment of psychopathy   17

3   Psychopathy and violent crime   38

4   Genetics and the environment   57

5   Biological factors   78

6   Psychological factors   100

7   Social factors   124

8   The biopsychosocial model of psychopathy   143

Index   *153*

FIGURES AND TABLES

Figures

2.1	Factor and facet structure of the Psychopathy Checklist – Revised	22
2.2	Construct of the Comprehensive Assessment of Psychopathic Personality (CAPP)	24
8.1	The biopsychosocial model of psychopathy	147

Tables

2.1	Adult psychopathy self-report measures	25
2.2	Youth psychopathic trait measures	32

ACKNOWLEDGMENTS

To be given the platform to share research on psychopathy is a great honor and a humbling experience. This volume would not have been possible if it were not for Professor Graham J. Towl and Dr. Tammi Walker. I am also fortunate, by the kindness of others, to have these chapters reviewed by experts in the field. For that I would like to thank each of you, David Farrington, Joel Paris, Daniel Boduszek, Scott Lilienfeld, Michael Lewis, Annette McKeown, Dennis Reidy, Matt DeLisi, Christopher Patrick, Joseph McClay, Kent Kiehl, Arielle Baskin-Sommers, Kostas Fanti, Jasmin Vassileva, Michael Vitacco, Henriette Bergstrøm, Hue San Kuay, Craig Neumann and Michel Aboutanos. Allie Thomson, you are the backbone of my work, thank you for all that you do.

BIOGRAPHY

Dr. Nicholas D. Thomson is Assistant Professor in the Department of Surgery, Division of Acute Care Surgical Services at Virginia Commonwealth University (VCU), Program Evaluator for the Injury and Violence Prevention Program at VCU Health Trauma Center, and Honorary Fellow at the University of Durham. He is an accredited psychotherapist by the United Kingdom Council for Psychotherapy and has over a decade of clinical experience working in prisons and inpatient settings in both the US and UK, and currently runs a private practice. Dr. Thomson has a master's degree in clinical psychology and a PhD in developmental psychopathology. As a Teaching Fellow at the University of Durham, he taught abnormal psychology and led the forensic psychology program. In 2018, his research was nominated for the Award for Outstanding Doctoral Research Contributions to Psychology. His research interests include a multidisciplinary approach to understanding mechanisms of violence, violence prevention and intervention, and sex differences in psychopathy and violent behavior.

FOREWORD

I am delighted to welcome the publication of this clearly written book on the important topic of psychopathy. Whereas biological explanations of psychopathy tend to have been emphasized in the past, Nicholas Thomson makes the persuasive argument that biological, psychological and social influences all need to be considered. I am very pleased that the biopsychosocial approach to offending, antisocial behaviour and personality disorders is becoming more popular, as shown for example by the founding in 2017 of the Division of Biopsychosocial Criminology of the American Society of Criminology. The biopsychosocial approach to psychopathy is not new; as an example, Joel Paris propounded it in 1998, and Adrian Raine has always emphasized the need to study interactions between biological, psychological and social factors (see e.g. Raine, Brennan & Farrington, 1997). However, Nicholas Thomson's book is the most up-to-date, comprehensive and well-researched statement of this approach. I learned a lot!

Psychopathy encompasses a large number of intercorrelated personality features, including an arrogant, deceitful interpersonal style (e.g. superficial charm, self-centredness, lying and manipulation), deficient affective experience (e.g. low empathy, low guilt, callousness, a weak conscience) and an impulsive or irresponsible behavioural style (e.g. failing to think before acting, excitement-seeking, a parasitic lifestyle; see e.g. Farrington, 2005). Not surprisingly, psychological traits are correlated with various types of offending (e.g. assault, robbery, sex offending, intimate partner violence) – although, apparently, not with homicide – as Thomson describes in great detail in Chapter 3.

A key issue is whether the definition and measurement of psychopathy should include offending and antisocial behaviour, as Robert Hare argues (e.g. Hare & Neumann, 2010), or whether psychopathy should be viewed purely as a personality factor, excluding offending and antisocial behaviour, as David Cooke argues (e.g. Skeem & Cooke, 2010). Thomson discusses the definition and measurement of psychopathy in Chapter 2, and points out the problem that it would be tautological to include antisocial behaviour in the definition of psychopathy and then use psychopathy in the explanation of antisocial behaviour. In my opinion, psychopathy should be defined and measured based purely on its personality features (see e.g., Bergstrom, Larmour & Farrington, 2018). Chapter 2 reviews the history of psychopathy and contains very useful descriptions of assessment instruments.

Chapter 4 presents a very clear exposition of behaviour genetics research, together with a review of emerging molecular genetics findings and even a discussion of psychopathic traits in chimpanzees! Chapter 5 reviews a remarkably wide array of biological topics, including neuroimaging, the prefrontal cortex, the amygdala, heart rate, skin conductance, cortisol and testosterone. I learned a lot from these well-researched reviews. Chapter 6 reviews childhood factors such as callous-unemotional traits, personality, impulsivity, executive functioning, intelligence, emotion recognition, moral attitudes and moral decision-making. Again, this chapter presents very good summaries of research. Chapter 7 reviews social and environmental factors, including prenatal and postnatal factors, parenting, child maltreatment, antisocial parents and peer delinquency. This book is a wonderful source of references for anyone who is carrying out systematic reviews of factors that are related to psychopathy!

Chapter 8 concludes with a strong argument about the need to consider biological, psychological and social factors in explaining the development of psychopathic traits. Thomson highlights the need to study interaction effects and mediating factors (see e.g. Auty, Farrington & Coid, 2015). He also mentions Adrian Raine's (2002) "social push" hypothesis, namely that biological factors will be less important for individuals who come from adverse social environments and more important for those who do not possess social risk factors. In my opinion, this hypothesis deserves more testing. Thomson also mentions protective factors, suggesting that a genetic vulnerability to psychopathy might be counteracted by psychological and social factors, but much more research is needed on factors that might be protective against the development of psychopathy. The discovery of protective factors (see e.g. Farrington, Loeber & Ttofi, 2012) should have important implications for interventions, and Thomson also discusses cognitive-behavioural treatment in Chapter 8. The main message is the need for the biopsychosocial model!

This book is made more appealing by its inclusion of case histories of psychopaths and of informative summary figures. There are many existing books on psychopathy, including the very useful primer on biological factors by Glenn and Raine (2014) and the massive comprehensive handbooks edited by Patrick (2018) and Felthous and Sass (in press). However, Nicholas Thomson's book contains the best available and accessible reviews of biological, psychological and social factors in psychopathy.

In psychopathy research, a major problem is the paucity of major longitudinal studies; almost the only ones are the Cambridge Study in Delinquent Development (e.g. Bergstrom & Farrington, in press) and the Pittsburgh Youth Study (e.g. Lynam, Caspi, Moffitt, Loeber & Stouthamer-Loeber, 2007). Clearly, more prospective longitudinal studies of psychopathy are needed, based on community samples, in order to advance knowledge about the role of biological, psychological, and social factors in the development of psychopathy. More research is also needed on the development of dynamic, unbiased, valid and reliable instruments to measure psychopathy, that do not measure antisocial behaviour and that are based not only on self-reports but also on other information. The Comprehensive Assessment of Psychopathic Personality (Cooke, Hart, Logan & Michie, 2012) is a good start, but it needs to be tailored to and used more with community samples.

In addition, there needs to be more interplay between explanatory and intervention research. More randomized experiments are needed to evaluate interventions, with outcome measures of psychopathy. In principle, a great deal can be learned from these experiments about the causal effects of explanatory factors. With better assessment, longitudinal research, and intervention experiments, the promise of the biopsychosocial model, which is excellently set out in this book, can be realized more effectively.

David P. Farrington
Emeritus Professor of Psychological Criminology
Cambridge University

References

Auty, K. M., Farrington, D. P. & Coid, J. W. (2015). Intergenerational Transmission of Psychopathy and Mediation via Psychosocial Risk Factors. *British Journal of Psychiatry*, 206, 26–31.

Bergstrom, H. & Farrington, D. P. (in press). "The Beat of My Heart": The Relationship between Resting Heart Rate and Psychopathy in a Prospective Longitudinal Study. *Journal of Criminal Psychology*.

Bergstrom, H., Larmour, S. R. & Farrington, D. P. (2018). The Usefulness of Psychopathy in Explaining and Predicting Violence: Discussing the Utility of Competing Perspectives. *Aggression and Violent Behavior*, 42, 84–95.

Cooke, D. J., Hart, S. D., Logan, C. & Michie, C. (2012). Explicating the Construct of Psychopathy: Development and Validation of a Conceptual Model, the Comprehensive Assessment of Psychopathic Personality (CAPP). *International Journal of Forensic Mental Health*, 11, 242–252.

Farrington, D. P. (2005). The Importance of Child and Adolescent Psychopathy. *Journal of Abnormal Child Psychology*, 33, 489–497.

Farrington, D. P., Loeber, R. & Ttofi, M. M. (2012). Risk and Protective Factors for Offending. In B. C. Welsh & D. P. Farrington (Eds.), *The Oxford Handbook of Crime Prevention* (pp. 46–69). Oxford: Oxford University Press.

Felthous, A. R. & Sass, H. (Eds.) (in press). *International Handbook on Psychopathic Disorders and the Law, vol. 1: Diagnosis and Treatment* (2nd ed.). New York: Wiley.

Glenn, A. L. & Raine, A. (2014). *Psychopathy: An Introduction to Biological Findings and Their Implications*. New York: New York University Press.

Hare, R. D. & Neumann, C. S. (2010). The Role of Antisociality in the Psychopathy Construct: Comment on Skeem and Cooke (2010). *Psychological Assessment*, 22, 446–454.

Lynam, D. R., Caspi, A., Moffitt, T. E., Loeber, R. & Stouthamer-Loeber, M. (2007). Longitudinal Evidence that Psychopathy Scores in Early Adolescence Predict Adult Psychopathy. *Journal of Abnormal Psychology*, 116, 155–165.

Paris, J. (1998). A Biopsychosocial Model of Psychopathy. In T. Millon, E. Simonsen, M. Birket-Smith & R. D. Davis (Eds.), *Psychopathy: Antisocial, Criminal and Violent Behavior* (pp. 277–287). New York: Guilford.

Patrick, C. J. (Ed.) (2018). *Handbook of Psychopathy* (2nd ed.). New York: Guilford.

Raine, A. (2002). Biosocial Studies of Antisocial and Violent Behavior in Children and Adults: A Review. *Journal of Abnormal Child Psychology, 30*, 311–326.

Raine, A., Brennan, P. A. & Farrington, D. P. (1997). Biosocial Bases of Violence: Conceptual and Theoretical Issues. In A. Raine, P. A. Brennan, D. P. Farrington & S. A. Mednick (Eds.), *Biosocial Bases of Violence* (pp. 1–20). New York: Plenum.

Skeem, J. L. & Cooke, D. J. (2010). Is Criminal Behavior a Central Component of Psychopathy? Conceptual Directions for Resolving the Debate. *Psychological Assessment, 22*, 433–445.

1
PSYCHOPATHY AND THE BIOPSYCHOSOCIAL MODEL

"You stabbed him [Slaboszewski] once through the heart", and only two days earlier Slaboszewski had texted his friend to the effect "that life was beautiful now that he had you as his girlfriend" (Justice Spencer, 2014, p. 2). This was the first of a series of murders that Joanne Dennehy would go on to commit during a 10-day cold-blooded violent spree. According to court transcripts, Dennehy manipulated and lured her victims, as well as committing villainous random violence. Although Dennehy committed the acts for her own hedonistic pleasure, she used the help of Gary Stretch, a seven-foot-three-inch ex-convict, who had become infatuated with Dennehy, so much so he would do anything to help her satisfy her taste for violence. After luring and stabbing Slaboszewski in the heart, Dennehy temporarily stored his body in a wheelie bin, until she had the means to rid of it permanently. Dennehy could not keep her murder a secret, boastfully inviting Georgina Page, a 14-year-old neighbor she had recently befriended, to see the body in the wheelie bin. Recounting to psychiatrists why she had committed the first murder, Dennehy ruthlessly stated, "I wanted to see if I was as cold as I thought I was. Then it got moreish and I got a taste for it" (Spencer, 2014, p. 17). In order to dump the body, Dennehy needed a car. She convinced and borrowed money from her landlord who would soon become her third victim. Two days had passed since the first killing. Dennehy and Stretch took a taxi to purchase a car so they could dump Slaboszewski's body on the outskirts of Peterborough in England. After dumping Slaboszewski's body, Dennehy killed her housemate John Chapman by stabbing him once in the neck and five times in the chest. Dennehy later reported that she killed Chapman because he walked in on her while she was in the bath. Chapman's carotid artery was severed, and his heart was penetrated with severe force. None of the sustained injuries indicated Chapman made any attempt to defend himself, and with a blood alcohol level four times greater than the driving limit it was likely Dennehy attacked Chapman as he lay asleep in the early hours of Good Friday morning.

Next, Dennehy killed her landlord, Kevin Lee, a 48-year-old husband and father. Over the period of several months, Dennehy had befriended Lee, telling him how she had been severely abused as a child, and served many years in prison for killing her father. This was false. There is no evidence that Dennehy was abused as a child, and her father is still alive today. Out of compassion and desire, Lee employed Dennehy at his property letting business and provided her accommodation. Lee and Dennehy became close over the months, and reportedly engaged in sadomasochistic sex games. The two were so close that Dennehy confided in Lee about her first murder. After inviting Lee to engage in sexual activities, Dennehy stabbed Lee five times in the chest, puncturing both lungs and his heart. Now having two bodies to dispose of, Dennehy recruited Stretch and another infatuated admirer, Leslie Layton, to help get rid of the bodies. As a final act of humiliation, Dennehy dumped Lee's body dressed in a black sequined dress and positioned the body so that the buttocks lay bare and exposed facing upwards. After killing three men and dumping their bodies, Dennehy and Stretch fled the area. Several days later, the two were in East Anglia on the prowl for Dennehy's next victims. Spotting a man walking his dog, Stretch asked Dennehy, "Will he do?" (Spencer, 2014). Dennehy jumped out of the car and approached Robin Bereza from behind, stabbing him in the back and then in the right upper arm. When Bereza turned, Dennehy said, "I want to hurt you, I am going to fucking kill you". After Bereza had put up some resistance to the attack, and with another car approaching, Dennehy calmly retreated and left the scene. Feeling unsatisfied with the failed attack, Dennehy sought out another victim, again an older man walking his dog, 56-year-old John Rogers. Dennehy approached Rogers from behind, stabbing him in the back, as he turned around Dennehy continued to repeatedly stab him. As Rogers fell to the ground, the stabbing continued. Rogers lay on the ground, dying from 30 stab wounds. Dennehy picked up the dog and left the scene. Fortunately, both Rogers and Bereza survived the attacks, and minutes after leaving the scene Dennehy and Stretch were caught by police. On February 24, 2013, before sentencing Dennehy to life in prison, Justice Spencer stated:

> I bear in mind that it is a feature of your psychopathic personality that you are a pathological liar . . . Joanne Dennehy, within the space of 10 days at the end of March last year you murdered three men in cold blood. Although you pleaded guilty you have made it quite clear that you have no remorse for those murders. With the help of one or more of your co-defendants you dumped the bodies of your three victims in remote rural areas around Peterborough hoping they would not be found. Only a matter of days later you attempted to murder two more men, this time openly on the streets of Hereford, victims chosen entirely at random. Miraculously they survived. You claim to feel remorse for stabbing those two men nearly to death. I have no hesitation in rejecting that suggestion. You are a cruel, calculating, selfish, and manipulative serial killer.
>
> *(Spencer, 2014, p. 1)*

To which Dennehy shouted from the docks while laughing, "Bollocks!" (Hamilton, 2014; Spencer, 2014; Wansell, 2016). Dr. Farnham's psychiatric assessment showed Dennehy suffered from paraphilia sadomasochism (giving or receiving pleasure through acts of pain or humiliation) and was a psychopath, characterized by superficial charm, callous disregard for others, pathological lying and diminished capacity for remorse (Spencer, 2014, p. 16).

Dennehy encapsulates what it means to be psychopathic; however, not all serial killers are psychopathic, and not all psychopaths are serial killers. It is estimated that the prevalence of psychopathy in the general population is 1.2% (0.3–0.7% in women and 1–2% in men; Neumann & Hare, 2008; Patrick & Drislane, 2015). Although small in number, psychopaths are responsible for 30–40% of all violent crimes, and their violence is more sadistic and severe. There is no surprise then that 93% of psychopaths are either in prison or on parole/probation (Kiehl & Hoffman, 2011). This propensity to violence and criminality makes psychopathy one of the costliest psychiatric disorders, with estimates in the US nearing $460 billion every year; twice the cost of smoking or obesity (Kiehl & Hoffman, 2011; Kiehl & Sinnott-Armstrong, 2013, p. 1). Once caught and incarcerated, psychopaths continue to pose a high risk of prison violence and general misconducts, often emerging as inmate leaders (DeLisi, 2016; Schrag, 1954; Thomson, Towl & Centifanti, 2016). Once released from prison, psychopaths are more likely than other criminals to recidivate (Olver & Wong, 2015). There is no wonder then that psychopathy has become one of the most widely valued clinical constructs in the criminal justice system, and often used in conjunction with violence risk assessments, as well as being central to theories of crime (see DeLisi, 2016; Vaughn & DeLisi, 2008).

Psychopathy is characterized by a constellation of personality and behavioral traits that offer many advantages to perpetrating crime. For instance, the psychopath is able to use others by conning and manipulating them, using her self-centered confidence, superficial charm and charismatic personality. Getting someone to do what she wants is the tip of the iceberg. Without the ability to feel empathy or remorse, and the callous equanimity and desire to hurt others, she is truly an extraordinarily damaging perpetrator. Not only does she display personality traits that help deceive her victims and accomplices, and the inability to let emotions stand in the way of her goal, she is willing to take risks without the concern of consequences, these may be impulsive risks, but always motivated by a self-indulgent goal. There is no surprise, then, that she has a long record of criminal activity and an extensive history of juvenile behavioral problems, and without remorse or guilt and an incapacity to take responsibility for her actions, she will go on to be a lifetime career criminal, regardless of being imprisoned. Even during court and parole hearings, the psychopath continues her manipulative and charming parade. Psychopaths are more likely to attempt malingering (Gacono, Meloy, Sheppard, Speth & Roske, 1995) and to receive a shorter sentence for their crime (Häkkänen-Nyholm & Hare, 2009), and twice as likely to convince parole boards to grant them conditional release (Porter, ten Brinke & Wilson, 2009).

Given that this fairly small population are responsible for almost half the violent crimes committed, understanding the disorder to treat psychopaths has become a pivotal endeavor towards decreasing the number of victims and the massive financial burden on society. A great body of research has been conducted since the 1980s, with biological sciences showing rapid development in the past 15 years. This research has yielded momentous information on the understanding of psychopathy – etiology, correlates and treatment. Unfortunately, the study of psychopathy is mostly discipline-specific, and interdisciplinary research is sparse. Yet, it is widely recognized that interdisciplinary research is vital to increasing our understanding of psychopathy. Therefore, exploring the individual and interactive effects of biological, psychological and social factors will provide a more refined knowledge of the etiology, development and correlates of psychopathy, which will ultimately lead to improvement in treatment efficacy.

The biopsychosocial model

The biopsychosocial model is broad and ambitious, applying a multidisciplinary view that mental illness is attributed to the individual and interactive contribution of biological, psychological and social factors. The biopsychosocial model employs a truly integrative approach to understanding psychiatric disorders for forensic practitioners and researchers. However, even though there has been support for multidisciplinary research (Stoff & Susman, 2005), there has been little discussion or research on the biopsychosocial model since its development (Farrington, 2006). Part of the failure of the biopsychosocial model to take hold is the lack of specificity in the combination of social, psychological and biological factors that contribute to a disorder. Even with this limitation, at present, the biopsychosocial model remains influential to most mental health practitioners (Davies & Roache, 2017), albeit with little clarity. Despite it being over 10 years since Farrington (2006) proposed that the time is "ripe for Western countries to mount an ambitious coordinated program of research on psychopathy, focusing on international multidisciplinary collaboration and aiming to train a new generation of biopsychosocial researchers" (p. 331), there is still very little discussion on the role and importance of the biopsychosocial model in understanding and treating psychopathy.

The aim of this book is to draw together a coherent summary of psychopathy research from multiple disciplines that has occurred over the last 30 years. This research is scattered among handbooks and scientific journals, with only a handful integrating the findings using a biopsychosocial approach. Chapter 1 will deliver an outline of the biopsychosocial model, its history, strengths and critiques, and a case study application for forensic psychology. Chapter 2 provides the reader with a background of the history, the main theories, and methods of assessment of psychopathy. To grasp the value of psychopathy as a construct in forensic psychology, Chapter 3 will critically evaluate the link between psychopathy and crime. An ideal starting point to recognize that psychopathy is a disorder of complex biopsychosocial interactions, Chapter 4 will review the genetic and environmental link in the development of psychopathy. The subsequent chapters each cover a comprehensive review of the biological (Chapter 5), psychological (Chapter 6), and social (Chapter 7) risk factors for psychopathy, as well as its correlates. These chapters highlight the importance of multidisciplinary research and the use of the biopsychosocial approach to understanding psychopathy. Lastly, Chapter 8 will discuss the limited amount of research that has integrated at least two of the biopsychosocial domains, and provides a discussion on the importance of applying the biopsychosocial approach in treatment.

The development of the biopsychosocial model

Before the biopsychosocial model was introduced, the biomedical model was used in full swing. The biomedical model is neatly packaged for the practitioner – disease is fully accountable by measurable biological (physiochemical) deviations from the norm. Further, disease is managed independent of social behavior, and atypical behavior is understood by biochemical or neurophysiological processes. Using the biomedical framework, psychological and social factors were not considered important for understanding and treating disease. Although proponents of the biomedical model focus on the physical scientific principles as the model's unwavering strength, Engel (1977) pointed out that the biomedical model was likely rooted in theology as much as it was with science.

Over 500 years ago, the Christian church first allowed the dissection of the human body for scientific reasons, with one important caveat – no associations could be made between the human body and the human mind or behavior. In the view of the church, the human mind and behavior were the responsibility of the church because they were more to do with the soul and religion (Engel, 1977), whereas the body was a weak and imperfect vessel for the soul, and therefore allowed to be subjected to scientific inquiry. Engel (1977) suggests this early encouragement of dualism (separation of body and mind) may have propelled Western medicine into a purely anatomically driven science. However, many physicians at the time recognized the importance of emotions in understanding the development and course of disease.

During the 1960s, the anti-psychiatry movement started to gain traction. Thomas Szasz (2001) argued that mental illness was a myth because it fell outside of the biomedical model of disease – no psychiatric disorder met the scientific definition of "disease" because it could not be recognized by a pathologist. Further, Szasz argued that a psychiatric diagnosis was used by members of the profession to solidify and bolster their social status, rather than to help the patient (Berlim, Fleck & Shorter, 2003; Wurtzburg & Thomson, 2014). At the time, psychiatry became under-siege by both the public and its practitioners. Two types of critics emerged – the reductionist, who argued that disease was completely explainable by biological underpinnings, and the exclusionist, who believed that whatever cannot be explained should be excluded from the category of disease.

Shortly before these times, and not receiving much attention, Roy Grinker first introduced the biopsychosocial view in his 1954 lecture and later argued for a unified model to understand human behavior and mental illness in his book, *Toward a Unified Theory of Human Behavior* (Grinker, 1956). However, Grinker was to go unrecognized as the founder of the biopsychosocial model, and much credit has been awarded to George Engel. Engel was an intern physician who published a paper challenging the biomedical model of disease for its reductionist view of mental illness, calling for a more person-centered and integrative scientific approach. Engel's (1977) central argument of disagreement in the biomedical model was that it relied solely on somatic causes to disease, and discredited the value of psychological and social factors. Ignoring such important contributors of disease, Engel considered the biomedical model as dogma rather than a model (Benning, 2015). Instead, Engel (1977) made a simple conclusion, drawing from his observation as an intern physician, that biological, psychological, and social factors were interrelated in both the progression of disease and treatment outcome. George Engel (1981, p. 114) provided an example of the application of the biopsychosocial model for physicians, of which the following is my own synopsis:

> A middle-aged man begins to experience chest pain. Six months ago he had a heart attack. The man becomes afraid that he could be having another heart attack and goes to accident and emergency (A&E). The attending physician, who is an intern, believes the man is having an infarction. The physician attempts to insert an intravenous line but fails several times. After failing to insert the intravenous line the physician goes to get help from a senior doctor. The man's chest pain continues, and he is afraid. He now fears that the care providers are incompetent, and to make things worse he is now feeling alone and abandoned. At this point the man suffers from cardiac arrest. Fortunately, he is resuscitated by the medical staff.

Using a purely biomedical approach to understand the case example, the resuscitation can be considered a success in treating the pathophysiological event (Frankel, Quill & McDaniel, 2003). However, at the person-level, it is clear there were social and psychological antagonists of the man's condition. If the intern physician paid attention to these risk factors (e.g., not leaving the patient unattended, easing the man's worries), the man's risk of cardiac arrest may have been reduced and/or prevented. These psychosocial risk factors, being afraid, feeling alone, abandoned and concerned about the competence of the attending physician, may have directly interacted and influenced the biological risk factor for cardiac arrest (e.g., increase in catecholamine levels, such as epinephrine [adrenaline]). The key point here is that the biopsychosocial approach does not imply the man's condition was a direct result of the psychosocial risk factors, but that they were additive to the worsening condition and contributed to the outcome (Frankel et al., 2003).

An important consideration is understanding that the development of mental illness is not all about risk factors, but equally important is the influence of protective factors, which may come from any domain of the biopsychosocial model. For instance, if an individual has a biological risk factor for psychopathy, the link may be broken by a protective factor from any of the psychosocial domains. For example, having a father scoring high on psychopathic traits predicts higher psychopathy levels in female and male offspring. However, this link is reduced if the father had not experienced difficulties with employment (e.g., currently unemployed, low occupational class, low wages; Auty, Farrington & Coid, 2015). Thus, the development or cessation of psychopathy is contingent on a specific contribution of biopsychosocial risk or protective factors.

Since Engel published his 1977 paper, the biopsychosocial model became popular but faced many challenges in being empirically tested and validated, which led to a loss of traction within psychiatry. Even with these challenges and setbacks, today health organizations have recognized the value of the biopsychosocial model. For instance, in the most recent National Offender Management Service Practitioners Guide published by the National Health Service, the biopsychosocial approach is used for understanding the development, assessment and management of personality disordered offenders (National Offender Management Service, 2015). It is here that I propose the biopsychosocial approach be reinstated and bolstered as the gold-standard for research practice in understanding the etiology and development of psychopathy, as well as a central approach for clinical practice.

Criticisms and strengths of the biopsychosocial model

Ghaemi (2009) stated the biopsychosocial approach has an incorrect perception of biology, as more recent models of biology include environmental–biological interactions, and therefore the biopsychosocial model does not offer anything new. In addition, there is little distinction compared to Osler's medical model, which works from the bases of the biomedical model but includes a humanistic approach. Thus, when competing with other models that exist, how does the biopsychosocial approach offer anything more? Unlike the biomedical model, the biopsychosocial model is not rooted in a single discipline. Thus, forensic practitioners and researchers who use the biopsychosocial model are not restrained to biology as a starting point for psychopathology. Instead, it is understood that biology is contributive for both the risk and protective factors of psychopathology. Therefore, the uniqueness and benefit of the biopsychosocial model in forensic psychology is that it is an unrestrained and dynamic working model.

To comprehend the scope of the biopsychosocial model is a huge undertaking. As Ghaemi (2009) points out, there are no boundaries to the model. Without boundaries, the predictive models of violence risk or understanding psychopathy could, in essence, be endless. But, this should be viewed as a strength rather than a flaw. Not only does the research being conducted today provide overwhelming support that each domain of the biopsychosocial model plays an important role in the development of psychopathy, but it urges for more exploration in applying an integrative nonpartisan approach to science. This overwhelming support for multidisciplinary research does not disquiet critics, and as Ghaemi (2012) states, "if everything causes everything, one cannot fail to be right, while at the same time nothing informative is really being said" (p. 4). This is absolutely true; if a model states that "everything causes everything" then we certainly have a problem with our models of treatment, risk assessment, and understanding the development of psychopathology. However, the biopsychosocial approach does not imply that "everything causes everything", only that we should consider the role of each domain (and their combination) and apply empirically proven factors within the domain to understand the target variable (e.g., psychopathy). For example, the Historical Clinical Risk Management-20 (HCR-20), is one of the most widely used and validated violence risk assessment tools in the forensic setting. The HCR-20 includes 20 items, predominantly psychological and social factors, that have been independently shown to influence the risk of violence, and when each of these items is considered in conjunction the measure becomes more refined and its predictive ability of violence increases (Douglas et al., 2014). The HCR-20 does not consider "everything as causal" of violence because it recognizes that "everything" is not a risk factor. Instead, it considers that each empirically driven risk factor *contributes* to risk. The HCR-20 relies on empirical evidence to support the use of each item which is then considered into the final construct. The biopsychosocial model applies the very same principle.

Thus, moving away from a pure unidimensional model for understanding psychopathy is important for this very reason. As researchers and clinicians, we should not be tied to finding a single causal factor of psychopathy and based on the evidence to date, expecting this would be irrational. For example, reduced amygdala activation while viewing negative images is a consistent finding among youth high on psychopathic traits (Jones, Laurens, Herba, Barker & Viding, 2009; Marsh et al., 2008) and psychopathy in adults (Decety, Skelly, Yoder & Kiehl, 2014). One could therefore propose that amygdala dysfunction is the underlying cause of psychopathy, because amygdala dysfunction interferes with affective processing. However, the same has also been found for patients with anorexia nervosa (Leppanen et al., 2017) and Williams Syndrome (Haas et al., 2009; Swartz et al., 2017). Instead, it is more likely that low amygdala reactivity to aversive imagery *contributes* to the development of psychopathy. Psychopathy is a multidimensional construct and consists of a variety of different personality and behavioral traits. In the same way that psychopathy consists of these various traits, it is only logical to expect that various biopsychosocial factors collectively contribute to psychopathy. Some of the most compelling findings from molecular and behavioral genetics suggest psychopathy is dependent on the contributive and interactive effects of biopsychosocial factors. Thus, using a single measure or scientific discipline, whether it be psychological, social, or biological, will result in understanding a less significant proportion of psychopathy. Further, to complicate matters, there are variations of risk factors depending on the presenting psychopathy symptomatology (e.g., higher levels of behavioral traits versus higher levels of personality traits). Therefore, the strength of the biopsychosocial approach is that it provides a dynamic framework that encourages multidisciplinary research to develop a truly person-centered data-driven model.

As any practitioner and researcher appreciates, a simplistic organization of what causes psychopathology is very appealing but ignoring the evidence to maintain a simple model endangers understanding the complexity of a patient/client. Instead of retreating to the biomedical model to understand psychopathy for ease and fear of trudging through "contamination and disorganization", we should be aiming to provide clarity to the model rather than ignoring its potency for individualized patient care.

Opponents of the biopsychosocial model state there is a difficulty in identifying where one domain (bio, psycho, or social) begins and the other ends. However, this is probably the strongest argument in favor for the biopsychosocial approach. Strict classification of the domains is only a problem with unidimensional models (e.g., the biomedical) because these are restricted to one domain (e.g., biology) as the bases for disease. Recognizing that there is no clear line between each of the domains highlights that a more integrative and dynamic model, such as the biopsychosocial model, is needed to fully understand the complexity of psychopathy.

Unlike traditional models of psychopathology and building on psychobiological theory, the biopsychosocial approach is unique because it may or may not give preference to a domain based on the evidence. A biomedical model is restricted to physiochemical explanations, and the psychobiological is limited to psychological and biological, whereas the biopsychosocial is not restricted. For instance, if an offender who has no history of depression or anxiety begins to display these symptoms within the first month of being incarcerated, we can identify that there are biological (e.g., increase in cortisol levels), social (e.g., lack of family contact) and psychological (e.g., feeling isolated and vulnerable) factors at play, and that these are all interacting with one another. However, because the inmate has not experienced symptoms of this magnitude before we could suppose that being incarcerated has triggered these risk factors, therefore, while the neurochemicals may generate the anxiety, this may be a result of being incarcerated – particularly the bidirectional effect of not having contact with family or friends and feeling alone and isolated. Therefore, it is well within the right of the biopsychosocial practitioner to prioritize one domain over another based on the evidence, because the biopsychosocial model acknowledges the interactive effects, and by effecting one domain will have a knock-on effect to the overall risk. In this instance, having the inmate involved in prison-based community activities or inmate service roles to increase social interaction may reduce him feeling isolated and alone, having a direct impact on the biological production of cortisol. Thus, the biopsychosocial approach is an ideal model providing flexibility for both researchers and clinical forensic practitioners.

A case example of the biopsychosocial model

On September 29, 1941, Frederick West was born to a poor family in a Herefordshire village in England. West was the second oldest of six children.

Accounts from the Wests' neighbors suggest West was a typical child – nice but occasionally cheeky and mouthy, like most children are. However, behind closed doors, things were far from typical. West later revealed that incest was an accepted part of his family life, with his father sexually abusing his daughters and teaching West bestiality. West recounted his father teaching him how to have sex with sheep (Simpson, 2017). West later gave an account in a police interview that his father told him, "do what you want, just don't get caught doing it". West looked up to his father, later telling the police that growing up he wanted to be like his dad, and admired what he stood for (Simpson, 2017). From the age of 12, West was sexually abused by his mother. At aged 15, West dropped out of high school and worked as a farm hand. During mid-adolescence, West aggressively harassed women and girls, irrespective of consent (Boduszek & Hyland, 2012). West would approach and sexually fondle a girl he liked, without a word being exchanged.

Two years after leaving high school West was in a motorbike accident, putting him into an eight-day coma, and he suffered from a fractured skull, and a broken arm and leg (Simpson, 2017). It is reported that after the accident West displayed a volatile temper (Flowers, 1995), and his family described to police that he had a change in personality – fits of rage, bragging incessantly, habitually lying and becoming a chronic thief (Simpson, 2017). At aged 19, West was involved in another accident. After putting his hand up a women's skirt he was pushed off of a fire escape, resulting in a head injury and losing consciousness for 24 hours. There is a strong likelihood that in either (or both) of these two accidents, West suffered from traumatic brain injury. At 20 years old, West impregnated a 13-year-old girl and was arrested for child molestation. However, a physician testified that West suffered from epileptic seizures, and the victim refused to testify, both of which saved West from a prison sentence. This close call with imprisonment would deter most people, but it had little impact on West. When confronted about his crime, West stated, "doesn't everyone do it?" (Schechter, 2003, p. 70). Based on the available information, it seems likely that the victim was his sister; however, there are sources which suggest the teen was a close family friend. Later he was sent to live with his Aunt and disowned by the rest of his family. West briefly began working in construction before he was fired for stealing from his employer. At 21, his family took him back and he returned to his parents' home in Herefordshire. West rekindled a past romantic relationship with Catherine "Rena" Costello, a troubled teen with a history of prostitution and theft. At age 22, West and Rena decided to get married and move to Scotland; however, Rena was pregnant with another man's child. Because the biological father was a Pakistani man, West urged Rena to write to their parents that the child was stillborn, and because of this, they decided to adopt a "mixed-race replacement" (Newton, 2006, p. 281).

Shortly after "adopting" their first child, West and Rena had a child together. During this time, West drove an ice cream van. West took advantage of his job, luring girls and reportedly abusing them. However, this came to a shattering end for two reasons. One of the girls West abused was a sister of a gang leader. Hearing this news, the gang pursued West, causing him a third head injury, narrowly escaping possible death. Shortly after this, West accidentally ran over a 4-year-old boy in his ice cream van (Boduszek & Hyland, 2012; Newton, 2006). West and Rena left Scotland and moved to a caravan park in Gloucestershire. At this point West started working in a slaughterhouse; it seems that as a butcher West developed a morbid obsession with corpses, blood and dismemberment (Creswell, 2015; Wilson, 1998). In 1967, Rena left West because she grew tired of his perverse sexual demands. Shortly after this, West and teenager Anna McFall began dating, and Anna soon became pregnant. Anna reportedly pressured West to marry her, and in response to this West committed his first documented murder – killing Anna and their unborn child, dismembering her, and keeping Anna's fingers and toes as souvenirs, an act he would later repeat. With Anna no longer in West's life, Rena and West shortly dated again, before she left him for good. This time Rena left her children with West, and they would become the victims of extensive sexual abuse (Schechter, 2003).

At age 28 West met Rosemary Letts, a 16-year-old daughter of a schizophrenic father and depressed mother. Rosemary was sexually promiscuous and engaged in incestuous acts with her younger brother. After moving in with Fred West, Rose had become pregnant and gave birth to their daughter Heather. During this time West was incarcerated for 10 months for dishonesty offenses, leaving Rose to look after West's child. It was not long after the birth of Heather that Rose killed West's eldest child, Charmaine. West dismembered Charmaine's body, keeping the fingers and toes, and buried her in the back garden. When Rena became worried about her child, she confronted West about her whereabouts. West sexually assaulted, murdered and dismembered Rena. Fred and Rosemary West went on to severely sexually abuse their daughter for many years to come in their homemade torture chamber basement. In 1972, West imprisoned, stripped and raped Caroline Owens, a 17-year-old nanny. Despite the Wests' threatening to kill Caroline if she were to go to the police, she managed to escape and get charges brought against the Wests. Even though Fred West had an extensive criminal history, he was able to convince the court magistrate that Caroline had consented in the sexual activities.

Over the period of 20 years, while living seemingly normal lives, the Wests continued to lure, torture and murder at least 12 women.

In this brief case study of Fred West, there are notable factors which may have contributed to his development of psychopathy and becoming a serial killer. From a biological perspective, there are several indicators that put West at risk of being a psychopathic serial killer (Boduszek & Hyland, 2012). Firstly, both his mother and his father demonstrated callous and antisocial behavior; his father showed no remorse for his violent ways, and promoted this behavior to West. His mother sexually abused him. Given that both behavioral and personality psychopathic traits are heritable, it is possible that West inherited some of these traits from his parents. In 2004, West and Rosemary's son, Stephen West, aged 31 years, was also imprisoned for nine months after pleading guilty to seven counts of sexual intercourse with a 14-year-old girl. Only nine years earlier he said to reporters:

> I've sat down and thought, Jesus Christ, what if it entered my mind one day to hurt someone? I know I'm so much like my dad in his nature. Not his bad nature, mind, but certain things. Sometimes I say something and it's like he said it. Then I get worried.
>
> *(Aitkenhead, 1995)*

Another important biological factor that may have contributed to West's deviant and explosive personality was the inflicted traumatic brain injury, which occurred three times during his adolescence and early adulthood, an integral time for neurological development. Notably, psychopathy is marked by atypical brain function, and brain injury is linked to violent and antisocial behavior. Dr. Ashcroft from the Centre for Forensic Psychophysiology suggests that West's head injuries put him at greater risk for the crimes he committed (Cawthorne, 2007). Therefore, inheriting psychopathic traits from his parents and suffering from brain injury may have increased the risk of developing, or at least, exacerbated his levels of psychopathic traits. However, we know that not all individuals who come from antisocial parents and/or suffer from traumatic brain injury develop psychopathy or go on to commit cold-blooded violence.

Fred West's case study reveals a devastating childhood history, which could suggest social factors had an integral role in the development of his psychopathic personality. From an early age, West was witness to an incestuous relationship between his father and his sisters. This did not take place in secret but was very apparent in West's upbringing. Sexual abuse was so rampant in West's life that his own father told him that "anything goes as long as you can get away with it". This depraved sexual activity showed no limits and extended to his father teaching him bestiality. In police reports, West recounted how he admired his father and wished to grow up like him. Even so, his father would physically abuse him. Entrenched in an environment where sexual abuse and incestuous relationships were normalized, this may have altered West's perception of what typical behavior and relationships were, as evidenced by his future behavior with female peers during adolescence. In addition, similar to his father, West preyed on young girls, and when he had his own daughter he would sexually abuse and torture her. As West grew up through adolescence and into adulthood he would surround himself with like-minded peers. For instance, West would have relationships with women known to be deviant, sexually promiscuous and involved in prostitution. West would take pleasure in watching other men having sex with his girlfriend(s). When married to Rosemary, the two of them would torture and rape their daughter in the company of close friends and family. There is clear evidence that West sought out relationships with the people that encouraged his behavior, creating a culture where callous sexual abuse was normalized.

The final factor of the biopsychosocial model is psychological. West displayed many psychological risk factors during his childhood. Based on the available evidence, there is a strong indication that as a child West displayed high levels of callous-unemotional traits, as evidenced by a persistent disregard for others, lack of empathy, shallow affect and callous perpetration for his own personal gain. Callous-unemotional traits have been considered a precursor to adult psychopathy. In line with fledgling psychopathic traits, neighbors saw West as "just an ordinary little lad, nothing that would stand out in your mind". But even the cruelest psychopaths are able to present themselves in a likable form. Indeed, West demonstrated skill in impression management; while some thought he was a typical lad, he was sexually assaulting girls without remorse and engaging in illegal activity from a young age. Impression management is a key feature of a psychopath and frequently observed in children with psychopathic traits who engage in severe violence, such as 11-year-old Andrew Golden who was responsible for the 1998 Arkansas school shooting, killing five pupils and wounding ten (Langman, 2009). A neighbor reported that Andrew was "a sweet child whenever his parents were around . . . but whenever he was away from his parents he was a little demon" (Newman, 2004, p. 40). Essentially, the same was found for West. While neighbors considered West as ordinary, from a young age he engaged in petty theft and aggressive behavior, and was frequently in trouble at school, as a result, West eventually left high school at the age of 15. In his adulthood, West applied his impression management, superficial charm and pathological lying to convince the Court Magistrate that his imprisonment, torture and raping of Caroline was consensual.

Summary

Using the case study of Fred West, we can see that there are many risk factors that may have contributed to the development of his psychopathic personality, and there were undoubtedly many more risk factors that were not available to draw from (e.g., neuropsychological assessment). What this case study shows, and this book will demonstrate, is that psychopathy is best understood from a multidisciplinary model. Although this case study provided a very brief overview of Fred West, we are still able to identify the importance of considering risk factors using the biopsychosocial approach (see Boduszek & Hyland, 2012 for a full review). Again, it is important to highlight that not one of the biopsychosocial factors can be solely responsible for his development of psychopathic traits. Instead, it is the interaction of sexual and physical abuse, poor parenting, immoral role models, viewing others as objects for his own pleasure, a genetic predisposition, traumatic brain injury, low intelligence and positive impression management, at the very least, which are responsible in the development of his psychopathic traits and the killing of at least 12 innocent women and girls. However, what this case study also brings to light is the scope in which the model works. The biopsychosocial model is truly a person-centered approach to understanding psychopathy.

Acknowledgments

Thank you to Dr. Joel Paris and Dr. Daniel Boduszek for their valuable review of this chapter. Dr. Paris is Professor of Psychiatry at McGill University and Research Associate in the Department of Psychiatry at Jewish General Hospital. Dr. Paris serves as the Editor-in-Chief of the *Canadian Journal of Psychiatry*, and his research specialty includes biopsychosocial risk factors of personality disorders and the study of culture and personality. Dr. Boduszek is Professor of Criminal Psychology and Co-Director of the None in Three Research Centre at the University of Huddersfield. Dr. Boduszek is the founding Editor of the *Journal of Criminal Psychology* and Associate Editor of the journal *Deviant Behavior*. His research specialty includes psychopathy, homicidal behavior, criminal thinking styles, and recidivism and prisonization.

References

Aitkenhead, D. (1995). I'm So Like My Dad, Says Stephen West. *Independent*, December 17. Retrieved from www.independent.co.uk/news/uk/home-news/im-so-like-my-dad-says-stephen-west-1526097.html.

Auty, K. M., Farrington, D. P. & Coid, J. W. (2015). Intergenerational Transmission of Psychopathy and Mediation via Psychosocial Risk Factors. *The British Journal of Psychiatry: The Journal of Mental Science*, *206*(1), 26–31.

Benning, T. B. (2015). Limitations of the Biopsychosocial Model in Psychiatry. *Advances in Medical Education and Practice*, *6*, 347–352.

Berlim, M. T., Fleck, M. P. A. & Shorter, E. (2003). Notes on Antipsychiatry. *European Archives of Psychiatry and Clinical Neuroscience*, *253*(2), 61–67.

Boduszek, D. & Hyland, P. (2012). Fred West: Biopsychosocial Investigation of Psychopathic Sexual Serial Killer. *International Journal of Criminology and Sociological Theory*, *5*(1), 864–870.

Cawthorne, N. (2007). *Serial Killers & Mass Murderers: Profiles of the World's Most Barbaric Criminals*. Berkeley, CA: Ulysses Press.

Creswell, K. (2015). *Garden of Bones: The Story of Fred and Rosemary West*. [no location]: KC Publishing.

Davies, W. & Roache, R. (2017). Reassessing Biopsychosocial Psychiatry. *The British Journal of Psychiatry: The Journal of Mental Science*, *210*(1), 3–5.

Decety, J., Skelly, L., Yoder, K. J. & Kiehl, K. A. (2014). Neural Processing of Dynamic Emotional Facial Expressions in Psychopaths. *Social Neuroscience*, *9*(1), 36–49.

DeLisi, M. (2016). Psychopathy, Its Etiology, and the Nature of Crime. In M. DeLisi, *Psychopathy as Unified Theory of Crime* (pp. 15–60). New York: Palgrave Macmillan.

Douglas, K. S., Hart, S. D., Webster, C. D., Belfrage, H., Guy, L. S. & Wilson, C. M. (2014). Historical-Clinical-Risk Management-20, Version 3 (HCR-20^{V3}): Development and Overview. *International Journal of Forensic Mental Health*, *13*(2), 93–108.

Engel, G. (1977). The Need for a New Medical Model: A Challenge for Biomedicine. *Science*, *196*(4286), 129–136.

Engel, G. (1981). The Clinical Application of the Biopsychosocial Model. *The Journal of Medicine and Philosophy*, *6*(2), 101–123.

Farrington, D. P. (2006). Family Background and Psychopathy. In C. J. Patrick (Ed.), *Handbook of Psychopathy* (pp. 229–250). New York: Guilford.

Flowers, R. (1995). *The Sex Slave Murders True Crime Bundle: Serial Killers*. [no location]: R. Barri Flowers.

Frankel, R. M., Quill, T. E. & McDaniel, S. H. (2003). *The Biopsychosocial Approach: Past, Present, and Future*. New York: University of Rochester Press.

Gacono, C. B., Meloy, J. R., Sheppard, K., Speth, E. & Roske, A. (1995). A Clinical Investigation of Malingering and Psychopathy in Hospitalized Insanity Acquittees. *The Bulletin of the American Academy of Psychiatry and the Law, 23*(3), 387–397.

Ghaemi, S. N. (2009). The Rise and Fall of the Biopsychosocial Model. *British Journal of Psychiatry, 195*(1), 3–4.

Ghaemi, S. N. (2012). The Biopsychosocial Model in Psychiatry: A Critique. *American Journal of Psychiatry, 121*, 451–457.

Grinker, R. R. (1956). *Toward a Unified Theory of Human Behavior*. Oxford: Basic Books.

Haas, B. W., Mills, D., Yam, A., Hoeft, F., Bellugi, U. & Reiss, A. (2009). Genetic Influences on Sociability: Heightened Amygdala Reactivity and Event-Related Responses to Positive Social Stimuli in Williams Syndrome. *The Journal of Neuroscience: The Official Journal of the Society for Neuroscience, 29*(4), 1132–1139.

Häkkänen-Nyholm, H. & Hare, R. D. (2009). Psychopathy, Homicide, and the Courts. *Criminal Justice and Behavior, 36*(8), 761–777.

Hamilton, F. (2014). Sadistic Woman Serial Killer Will Die in Jail. Retrieved from www.thetimes.co.uk/article/sadistic-woman-serial-killer-will-die-in-jail-25nwct2dcc5

Jones, A. P., Laurens, K. R., Herba, C. M., Barker, G. J. & Viding, E. (2009). Amygdala Hypoactivity to Fearful Faces in Boys with Conduct Problems and Callous-Unemotional Traits. *The American Journal of Psychiatry, 166*(1), 95–102.

Kiehl, K. A. & Hoffman, M. B. (2011). The Criminal Psychopath: History, Neuroscience, Treatment, and Economics. *Jurimetrics, 51*, 355–397.

Kiehl, K. A. & Sinnott-Armstrong, W. P. (2013). *Handbook on Psychopathy and Law*. New York: Oxford University Press.

Langman, P. (2009). Rampage School Shooters: A Typology. *Aggression and Violent Behavior, 14*(1), 79–86.

Leppanen, J., Cardi, V., Paloyelis, Y., Simmons, A., Tchanturia, K. & Treasure, J. (2017). Blunted Neural Response to Implicit Negative Facial Affect in Anorexia Nervosa. *Biological Psychology, 128*, 105–111.

Marsh, A. A., Finger, E. C., Mitchell, D. G. V. V, Reid, M. E., Sims, C., Kosson, D. S., . . . Blair, R. J. R. R. (2008). Reduced Amygdala Response to Fearful Expressions in Children and Adolescents with Callous-Unemotional Traits and Disruptive Behavior Disorders. *The American Journal of Psychiatry, 165*(6), 712–20.

National Offender Management Service. (2015). *Working with Offenders with Personality Disorder A Practitioners Guide*. [no location]: NHS England Publications. Retrieved from www.england.nhs.uk/commissioning/wp-content/uploads/sites/12/2015/10/work-offndrs-persnlty-disorder-oct15.pdf

Neumann, C. S. & Hare, R. D. (2008). Psychopathic Traits in a Large Community Sample: Links to Violence, Alcohol Use, and Intelligence. *Journal of Consulting and Clinical Psychology, 76*(5), 893–899.

Newman, K. (2004). *Rampage: The Social Roots of School Shootings*. New York: Basic Books.

Newton, M. (2006). *The Encyclopedia of Serial Killers*. New York: Facts on File.

Olver, M. E. & Wong, S. C. P. (2015). Short- and Long-Term Recidivism Prediction of the PCL-R and the Effects of Age: A 24-Year Follow-Up. *Personality Disorders: Theory, Research, and Treatment*, 6(1), 97–105.

Patrick, C. J. & Drislane, L. E. (2015). Triarchic Model of Psychopathy: Origins, Operationalizations, and Observed Linkages with Personality and General Psychopathology. *Journal of Personality*, 83(6), 627–643.

Porter, S., ten Brinke, L. & Wilson, K. (2009). Crime Profiles and Conditional Release Performance of Psychopathic and Non-psychopathic Sexual Offenders. *Legal and Criminological Psychology*, 14(1), 109–118.

Schechter, H. (2003). *The Serial Killer Files: The Who, What, Where, How, and Why of the World's Most Terrifying Murderers*. New York: Ballantine Books.

Schrag, C. (1954). Leadership among Prison Inmates. *American Sociological Review*, 19(1), 37.

Simpson, P. (2017). *The Serial Killer Files*. London: Robinson.

Spencer, J. (2014). *The Queen v. Joanne Christine Dennehy, Gary John Stretch, Leslie Paul Layton, Robert James Moore*. Judiciary of England and Wales.

Stoff, D. & Susman, E. J. (2005). Integrated Perspective for Psychobiological Research in Aggression: An Introduction. In D. M. Stoff & E. J. Susman (Eds.), *Developmental Psychobiology of Aggression* (pp. 3–11). New York: Cambridge University Press.

Swartz, J. R., Waller, R., Bogdan, R., Knodt, A. R., Sabhlok, A., Hyde, L. W. & Hariri, A. R. (2017). A Common Polymorphism in a Williams Syndrome Gene Predicts Amygdala Reactivity and Extraversion in Healthy Adults. *Biological Psychiatry*, 81(3), 203–210.

Szasz, T. (2001). Mental Illness: Psychiatry's Phlogiston. *Journal of Medical Ethics*, 27(5), 297–301.

Thomson, N. D., Towl, G. J. & Centifanti, L. C. M. (2016). The Habitual Female Offender Inside: How Psychopathic Traits Predict Chronic Prison Violence. *Law and Human Behavior*, 40(3), 257–269.

Vaughn, M. G. & DeLisi, M. (2008). Were Wolfgang's Chronic Offenders Psychopaths? On the Convergent Validity between Psychopathy and Career Criminality. *Journal of Criminal Justice*, 36(1), 33–42.

Wansell, G. (2016). *Lifers, Inside the Minds of Britain's Most Notorious Criminals*. London: Penguin.

Wilson, C. (1998). *The Corpse Garden*. London: True Crime Library.

Wurtzburg, S. J. & Thomson, N. D. (2014). Anti- Psychiatry Perspective of Mental Illness. In W. C. Cockerham, R. Dingwall & S. Quah (Eds.), *The Wiley Blackwell Encyclopedia of Health, Illness, Behavior, and Society*. New York: John Wiley & Sons.

2
HISTORY AND ASSESSMENT OF PSYCHOPATHY

Theophrastus (371–287 BCE) was an Ancient Greek Peripatetic philosopher and colleague of Aristotle, who published some of the earliest works in psychology, biology, metaphysics and ethics. In his book named *Characters* (Ἠθικοὶ χαρακτῆρες), Theophrastus depicted 30 (im)moral characters from Athenian life, reporting in the preface:

> I shall never cease to marvel, why it has come about that, albeit the whole of Greece lies in the same clime and all Greeks have a like upbringing, we have not the same constitution of character . . . having observed human nature a long time. . . have thought it incumbent upon me to write in a book the manners of each several kind of men both good and bad.
> *(Theophrastus, 1714, pp. 21–38)*

Within the 30 characters, the Shameless Man (also interpreted as the Unscrupulous Man) draws parallel features to modern clinical descriptions of psychopathy, which demonstrates that psychopaths have long wreaked havoc across cultures and societies throughout time:

> He breaks through all the rules of decency for the sake of a villainous theft . . . He turns his hand to anything, is sometimes a vintner, sometimes a pimp, and sometimes an excise-man. You see him today a cryer, tomorrow a cook, and the day following a gamester . . . He has neither a mask to disguise him, nor the pretense of drunkenness to excuse him . . . he is incapable of blushing. . . He is always up to his ears in law; sometimes plaintiff, sometimes defendant. Thievery is one of his particular infirmities; and a jail his ordinary abode; in which he sojourns a great part of his life . . . If he has a mother living 'tis odds she starves . . . In a word, he is always brawling and wrangling, throwing out ill-language to those that come in his way, and makes the whole market-place echo with his scurrilities.
> *(Theophrastus, 1714, pp. 155–159)*

The equivalences between the Shameless Man and a modern-day psychopath are striking. In the case of the Shameless Man, he acts without restraint or concern for whom he hurts, even if his behavior impacts his own mother. He is frequently involved with the law, engages in conning and manipulative behavior and thievery. He is a social and entrepreneurial chameleon and is incapable of feeling shame for his actions. The personality characteristics of the Shameless Man mirror the theories of psychopathic personality from the past 200 years, and many of these traits remain central to the current construct of the disorder.

Two thousand years after the publishing of *Characters*, French physician Dr. Philippe Pinel termed a cluster of personality and behavioral traits as *manie sans délire* (translated to insanity/mania without delirium). Pinel's patients who displayed *manie sans délire* had diminished emotional affect, poor impulse control, did not suffer from intellectual functioning deficits or psychosis, and engaged in chronic antisocial behavior (Gacono, 2000; Pinel, 1806, p. 152). Influenced by Pinel, English physician Dr. Prichard (1835) termed a similar cluster of personality traits as "moral insanity" and "moral imbecility", individuals with this disorder also displayed "affections and feelings that stand contradistinction to understanding and intellect" (Henderson, 1939, p. 11). These early pioneers recognized that psychopaths could understand, intellectually, what behaviors were wrong and right, but they were content and favorable to acting against this knowledge and were able to commit wrongful acts without being influenced by emotional states (e.g., guilt, empathy). Pinel (1806), Rush (1812), Esquirol (1838), Prichard (1835) and Maudsley (1874) each described these individuals as being antisocial not because of cognitive deficits but because of immorality and being emotionally disordered. Between the 1800s and 1920s, most clinical descriptions focused on the combination of immoral and criminal behaviors, as well as impulsivity, hedonistic drive and deficits in emotions (Kraepelin, 1915; Morel, 1839; Schneider, 1923). During the 1900s, descriptions of psychopathy started to turn their focus away from antisocial behavior and more emphasis was placed on core personality features that distinguished the psychopath.

Psychopathic states

Scottish psychiatrist Sir David Henderson was one of the first to succinctly categorize psychopaths based on their behavior and personality features. Henderson (1939) stated that past works on psychopathy were partly misled because of the focus on disordered behavior. Henderson (ibid.) proposed that in some cases psychopathy is the predominating feature in delinquency, but not in all cases – psychopathy and delinquency "are not in any way synonymous or equivalent terms" (ibid., p. 17). Instead, the psychopath can be best described as "moral blindness" (ibid.). In his 1939 book titled *Psychopathic States*, which was published after giving a lecture in New York, Henderson formulated and described three typologies of psychopathic states drawing from his clinical observations. The first psychopathic state is called the "predominately aggressive" and is considered the most violent and dangerous of the three psychopathic manifestations. Despite this state being the most aggressive, this individual may be successful in life. The second state, "predominately passive or inadequate", parasitically lives off of society and suffers from neuroticism and instability. The third state is the "predominately creative psychopath", who Henderson describes as an erratic and moody person but brilliant and "near genius" (ibid., p. 112), likening the creative psychopath to Lawrence of Arabia and Joan of Arc. Henderson suggests the social distinction between psychopaths and non-psychopaths is that non-psychopaths gravitate towards the "herd" for confidence, safety and overall prosperity (ibid., p. 133), whereas psychopaths do not need to seek social affiliation for these benefits. Henderson claimed psychopaths cannot function in society because their personality traits inevitably lead them to "fatalism or despair, the reaction to which may be aggressive" (ibid.). Henderson remained optimistic, believing that psychopathy was a treatable disorder.

Primary and secondary psychopathy

Karpman (1941) described two subtypes of psychopath: primary and secondary, which are still popularly referenced to in today's research. The primary psychopath suffers from hereditary affective deficits, whereas the secondary ("neurotic") psychopath suffers from affective disturbances because of harmful environmental influences. Karpman believed the secondary psychopath was treatable because the behavior was acquired and not inherited. Unlike the primary psychopath, the secondary psychopath has intact empathy and suffers from high internalizing symptoms, such as anxiety or depression. There are times when the secondary psychopath, as with someone with Antisocial Personality Disorder (ASPD), may present with a lack of empathy, such as hurting others in response to provocation and then blaming the victim, or the justification for stealing. But at other times, secondary psychopaths display typical levels of empathy, being protective and loyal to their family or peer group, or distraught because of the loss of a friend or partner. In contrast, the primary psychopath displays a lack of affective empathy and emotional connectedness, but may pretend to feel empathy, if it furthers his cause. The primary psychopath is driven by hedonism – he uses whatever means necessary to achieve his goal, such as violence, manipulation and domination, even if the victim is a family member, whereas the secondary psychopath is sensitive to his environment, often acting on impulse and in reaction to real or perceived provocations. Indeed, a great deal of research has found the primary psychopath to display low arousal to threat, while secondary psychopaths display heightened arousal.

Although he described psychopathy using two subtypes, Karpman (1948) argued that "true" psychopathy was the primary psychopath, whereas the secondary psychopath was represented across many disorders because of the universal symptoms that predispose people to antisocial behavior (e.g., neuroticism, problematic childhood). Karpman strongly urged researchers to be more stringent in their classification of psychopathy, and to not fall victim to viewing antisocial behavior as identical to psychopathy (ibid., p. 523).

Karpman distanced himself from Henderson, stating that Henderson's perception of psychopathy was too inclusive, and that any person who deviated morally or ethically from the norm, including if the individual was antisocial, could be classified as psychopathic. In some ways, this argument mimics the modern-day debate on the role of antisocial behavior in the construct of psychopathy, which is discussed later in this chapter. Karpman's model of subtyping psychopathy can be considered one of the most important contributions to the field of psychopathy, truly refining the clinical description of what it means to be psychopathic rather than antisocial. However, the nomenclature of Karpman's psychopathy variants are misleading and often misconstrued in today's literature, as in Karpman's view, the only psychopath was the primary psychopath, whereas the secondary "psychopath" was a person who displayed psychopathic *behavior* (e.g., aggressiveness), rather than a psychopathic *personality*.

The Mask of Sanity

Arguably one of the most notorious and important works in the field of psychopathy is the 1941 book called *The Mask of Sanity* by American psychiatrist Hervey Cleckley. Since the first edition in 1941, the book was updated five times during Cleckley's lifetime, and once more posthumously (1984). Cleckley's observations and clinical formulations hold validity and significance for current research, and have played a major role in current constructs of psychopathy. Although many of Cleckley's case studies included patients who exhibited aggressive behavior, Cleckley suggested that psychopaths tended to avoid the most serious forms of violence, "despite their continually repeated transgressions against the law and the rights of others and their apparent lack of moral compunction, [they] seem to avoid murder and other grave felonies that remove them indefinitely from free activity in the social group" (Cleckley, 1941: pp. 265–266). Cleckley's (1941) clinical profiles included patients with chronic histories of criminal behavior, indicating psychopaths are prolific offenders and display versatility in their offending styles. Cleckley's final edition in 1984 detailed 16 characteristics of the psychopath, covering affective, interpersonal, behavioral, cognitive and criminal traits:

1. Superficial charm and good "intelligence".
2. Absence of delusions and other signs of irrational thinking.
3. Absence of "nervousness" or psychoneurotic manifestations.
4. Unreliability.
5. Untruthfulness and insincerity.
6. Lack of remorse or shame.
7. Inadequately motivated antisocial behavior.
8. Poor judgment and failure to learn by experience.
9. Pathologic egocentricity and incapacity for love.
10. General poverty in major affective reactions.
11. Specific loss of insight.

12 Unresponsiveness in general interpersonal relations.
13 Fantastic and uninviting behavior with and without drink.
14 Suicide rarely carried out.
15 Sex life impersonal, trivial, and poorly integrated.
16 Failure to follow any life plan (Cleckley, 1984, pp. 338–339).

Most of these characteristics are still used today as the bases of self-report and clinical measures of psychopathy (Furnham, Daoud & Swami, 2009).

Clinical assessments: adults

Psychopathy Checklist – Revised

In 1985, Robert Hare built on Cleckley's work and drafted the semi-structured clinical assessment of psychopathy: The Psychopathy Checklist, which was revised in 1991 and 2003 (Hare & Neumann, 2006). The latest version, the PCL-R (Hare, 2003), is designed to be used for clinical, forensic and research purposes. The PCL-R and its derivatives require the administrator to hold an advanced degree (e.g., MD, PhD), have extensive clinical/forensic experience and to be well-versed in the psychopathy literature and research (Brazil & Forth, 2016; Hare & Neumann, 2006). To formulate a client's psychopathy score using the PCL-R, data is collected from a semi-structured clinical interview and a review of historical files/records. The PCL-R includes 20 items (see Figure 2.1), which are rated on a three-point scale from, "item does not apply" (0) to "item definitely applies" (2). The PCL-R provides a total score with a maximum of 40. A diagnosis of psychopathy in the US is made using a score of 30 or above, although lower scores have been used in European countries, as well as for women (PCL-R > 25).

In addition to total scores, factor analyses have found a superordinate two-factor model, three-facet model and four-facet model. For the dimensional models of the PCL-R, two of the PCL-R items were removed ("promiscuous sexual behavior" and "many short-term marital relationships"). Figure 2.1 shows how each item contributes to the factor or facet models. Notice the term "factor" is only used for the two-factor model, while the term "facet" is used for the three- and four-facet models. This is because the facet models do not differ from each other except that the four-facet model includes facet 4 (the Antisocial facet), whereas the three-facet model does not. Thus, the Interpersonal, Affective and Lifestyle facets are the same for the three- and four-facet models. To complicate the terminology further, prior research has used a variety of terms when talking about the same and/or different constructs. The two-factor model includes factor 1 and factor 2. Factor 1 is sometimes referred to as "primary" psychopathic traits, and because factor 1 includes the Interpersonal (e.g., superficial charm) and Affective facets (e.g., callousness), researchers more recently refer to this as the "Interpersonal-Affective" factor. Factor 2 is sometimes termed "secondary" psychopathic traits and includes the Lifestyle (e.g., impulsivity) and Antisocial facets (e.g., criminal versatility). Factor 2 is also more recently termed as the "impulsive-antisocial" factor. In order to unify the terminology for the reader, I will refer to each factor/facet in accordance with Figure 2.1 for PCL-R based measures and for self-report measures using a similar construct. For non-PCL-R derived measures I will refer to the dimensions based on the original publications.

The PCL-R has two derivatives: the screening version (PCL:SV) and youth version (discussed later in the chapter). The PCL:SV includes 12 of the original PCL-R items and is scored using the same 3-point system. With a maximum score of 24, a score of 18 or higher is indicative of a diagnosis of psychopathy for research purposes (Hare & Neumann, 2006). Consistent with the PCL-R, the same two-factor, three-facet and four-facet structure can be used for the PCL:SV. Since its development, the PCL-R and its derivatives have been recognized as the gold standard for measuring psychopathic traits, and as a result has become one of the most widely used and highly regarded clinical constructs in the criminal justice system.

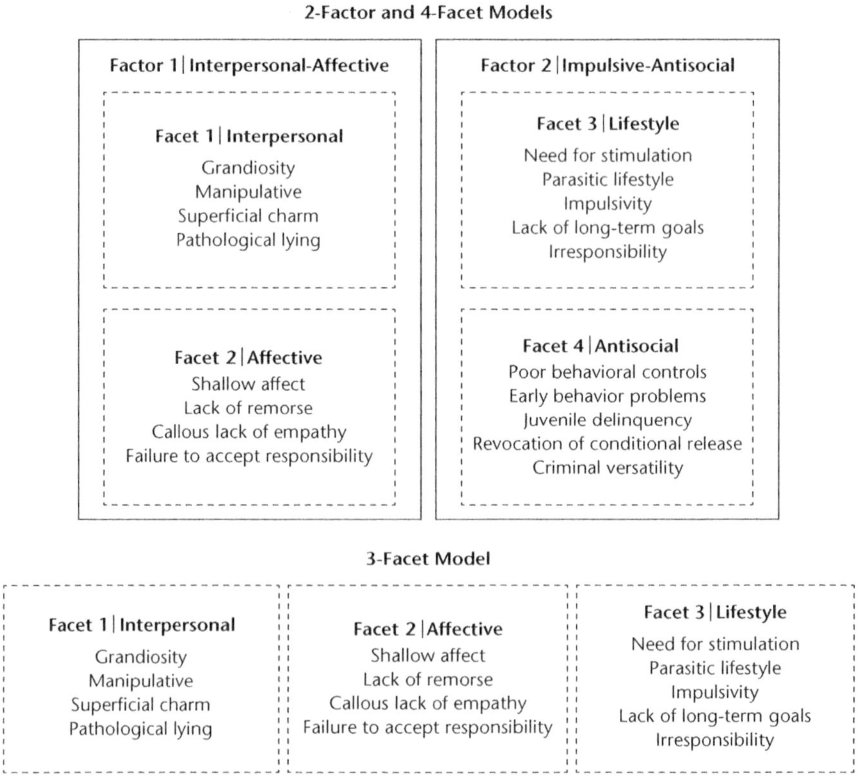

2-Factor and 4-Facet Models

Factor 1 | Interpersonal-Affective

Facet 1 | Interpersonal
Grandiosity
Manipulative
Superficial charm
Pathological lying

Facet 2 | Affective
Shallow affect
Lack of remorse
Callous lack of empathy
Failure to accept responsibility

Factor 2 | Impulsive-Antisocial

Facet 3 | Lifestyle
Need for stimulation
Parasitic lifestyle
Impulsivity
Lack of long-term goals
Irresponsibility

Facet 4 | Antisocial
Poor behavioral controls
Early behavior problems
Juvenile delinquency
Revocation of conditional release
Criminal versatility

3-Facet Model

Facet 1 | Interpersonal
Grandiosity
Manipulative
Superficial charm
Pathological lying

Facet 2 | Affective
Shallow affect
Lack of remorse
Callous lack of empathy
Failure to accept responsibility

Facet 3 | Lifestyle
Need for stimulation
Parasitic lifestyle
Impulsivity
Lack of long-term goals
Irresponsibility

FIGURE 2.1 Factor and facet structure of the Psychopathy Checklist – Revised
Source: adapted from Hare (2003) and Cooke & Michie (2001)

Comprehensive assessment of psychopathic personality

In response to criticisms of the PCL-R (discussed later in this chapter), Cooke, Hart, Logan and Michie (2012) developed the Comprehensive Assessment of Psychopathic Personality (CAPP). When developing the CAPP, the authors were intent on creating a measure of psychopathic *personality*, rather than moral and cultural deviations from the norms, such as criminality (Skeem & Cooke, 2010a, 2010b). Further, the authors wanted to develop a construct that was dynamic and could detect changes in symptoms over time and across a variety of settings (e.g., community, forensic psychiatric facilities, prisons). The CAPP captures the range and depth of psychopathic features by using a semi-structured clinical interview, as well as written information from clinical and/or institutional records, interviews with people who have known the client well for at least six months (e.g., mental health practitioner, probation practitioner, prison officer). The authors instruct users of the CAPP that scores must be derived from numerous sources of information, and the assessment should not be based on client self-report alone (Cooke et al., 2012). The CAPP consists of 33 symptoms over six domains: attachment, behavioral, cognitive, dominance, emotional and self. Figure 2.2 displays the symptoms for each domain. The CAPP is scored from 0 to 6 (not present, very mild, mild, moderate, moderately severe, severe and very severe), with a maximum score of 198. The CAPP was developed to be understood by both clinicians and laypeople, to help increase the specificity and clarity of psychopathic symptoms. Further, because the CAPP symptoms are described using trait-descriptive adjectives instead of behavioral examples (e.g., "Irritability and aggressiveness, as indicated by repeated physical fights or assaults"; APA, 2013, p. 659), the symptom definitions are not dependent on context (e.g., community, prison), populations (e.g., sex, age, or culture), or occurring within a specific timeframe (e.g., within 6-month, lifetime). This method of assessment makes the CAPP a more dynamic assessment of psychopathic traits.

Self-report measures

Self-report measures are often considered less desirable than clinical assessments. Psychopaths are notorious liars and frequently do it for "the sheer fun of it" (Lilienfeld & Fowler, 2006, p. 109). Kelsey, Rogers and Robinson (2014) found that when male inmates were encouraged to "appear to be a safe, caring person, who is sorry [for their crime]" in order to receive a shorter sentence, they were successfully able to mask their psychopathy levels on self-report scales – scoring lower than college and community samples. The authors found those with the highest psychopathy scores on the PCL-R achieved the largest reductions on self-report scales. Indeed, impression management (the intention to influence others' perception of self) is a behavior that is common to psychopaths. However, Lilienfeld and Fowler (2006) suggest that self-report scales are able to detect for impression management based on reporting patterns. Further, it is possible that self-reports

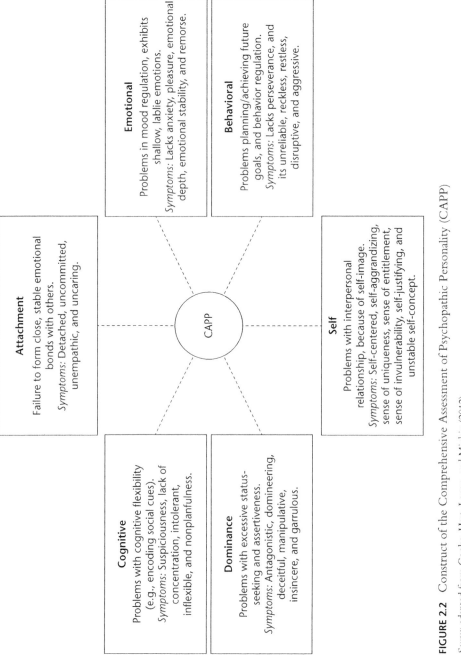

FIGURE 2.2 Construct of the Comprehensive Assessment of Psychopathic Personality (CAPP)

Source: adapted from Cooke, Hart, Logan, and Michie (2012)

may be less influenced by impression management because there is no audience or incentive to lie to as there is with a clinical assessment. Indeed, a meta-analytic review including 45 studies found self-report psychopathic traits are related to lower social desirability scores, suggesting those with higher psychopathy scores do not "fake good" (Ray et al., 2013). Probably the most significant benefit of administering self-report assessments is resource efficiency. Clinical assessments, such as the PCL-R, can take 90–120 minutes for the interview and 60 minutes for a file review, and require advanced clinical skills, education and training. This makes achieving larger sample sizes more challenging. An additional challenge to clinical assessments in non-forensic populations is that historical records for file review are not available. In contrast, self-reports can be administered in less than 25 minutes, and do not require extensive administrator training/experience, or file reviews. When compared to clinical assessments, self-reports are consistently found to be valid and reliable for measuring psychopathic traits across ages, sexes, cultures and contexts (Evans & Tully, 2016; Murphy, Lilienfeld, Skeem & Edens, 2016; Poythress et al., 2010; Ruchensky, Edens, Donnellan & Witt, 2017). Thus, self-report psychopathy scales make an ideal substitution for clinical assessment in diverse and larger populations. Table 2.1 provides a brief overview of the most common self-report assessments of psychopathy in adults and Table 2.2 includes the most frequently used youth assessments for psychopathic traits.

TABLE 2.1 Adult psychopathy self-report measures

	Dimensions	*Populations*	*No. of items*
Self-Report Psychopathy Scale (SRP-4; Paulhus, Neumann & Hare, 2016)	2-factor: – Interpersonal-Affective – Impulsive-Antisocial 4-facet: – Interpersonal – Affective – Impulsive – Antisocial	Community, college and offender	Full version: 64 Short form: 29
Levenson Self-Report Psychopathy Scale (LSRP; Levenson, Kiehl & Fitzpatrick, 1995)	2-factor: – Interpersonal-Affective – Impulsive-Antisocial 3-facet: – Egocentric – Callousness – Antisocial	Community, college, and offender	Expanded: 36[††] Full version: 26 Short form: 19

(continued)

TABLE 2.1 *(continued)*

	Dimensions	*Populations*	*No. of items*
Psychopathic Personality Inventory – Revised (PPI-R; Lilienfeld & Widows, 2005)	– Self-Centered Impulsivity (e.g., Machiavellian egocentricity, rebellious nonconformity, blame externalization, carefree nonplanfulness) – Fearless Dominance (e.g., social influence, fearlessness, stress immunity) – Coldheartedness	College; community; prison; psychiatric inpatient[†]	Full version: 154 Short form: 40
The Psychopathic Personality Traits Scale (PPTS; Boduszek, Debowska, Dhingra & DeLisi, 2016)	– Affective Responsiveness (e.g., low empathy, emotional shallowness). – Cognitive Responsiveness (e.g., understand others' emotional states, emotional processes, and engage with others' emotionally at a cognitive level). – Interpersonal Manipulation (e.g., superficial charm, grandiosity and deceitfulness). – Egocentricity (e.g., tendency to focus on one's own interests, beliefs and attitudes).	Students; community; prison	Full version: 20
Triarchic Psychopathy Measure (TriPM; C J Patrick, 2010)	– Boldness (e.g., high dominance, low anxiousness, Venturesomeness). – Meanness (e.g., callousness, cruelty, predatory aggression, excitement seeking) – Disinhibition (e.g., impulsiveness, irresponsibility, oppositionality, ager/hostility).	Students; community; prison; psychiatric inpatient	Full version: 58
The Psychopathic Processing and Personality Assessment (PAPA; Lewis, Ireland, Abbott, Ireland, 2017)	– Dissocial tendencies – Emotional detachment – Disregard for others – Lack of sensitivity	Students; prison; forensic psychiatric inpatient	Full version: 29

[†]Evidence of the construct validity in psychiatric inpatient samples is promising, but more provisional/preliminary than in student, community, or prison samples.
[††]Christian & Sellbom (2016) expanded the LSRP to 36 items improving the psychometric properties of the original scale.

Misnomers in psychiatry

One of the most common clinical misconceptions is that antisocial personality disorder, sociopathy, dissocial personality disorder and psychopathy are the same disorder, and can be used interchangeably (Werner, Few & Bucholz, 2015). To complicate matters, some researchers and books on the etiology of psychopathy also use these disorders interchangeably without informing the reader. This is problematic for many reasons, but the main focus here is that it is simply inaccurate based on overwhelming biological, social and psychological science. To address this, this section will provide an overview of the most widely used diagnostic manuals (DSM-5, ICD-10 and PDM-2) to illustrate the variation between them, as well as to illustrate to the emerging psychologist and criminologist that these are not interchangeable disorders if one understands the basic criteria. Moving forward from this section, the research presented in this book is specific to the construct of psychopathy and does not use the same "catch-all" approach in the dissemination of research.

Antisocial Personality Disorder with Psychopathic Features

The *Diagnostic and Statistical Manual of Mental Disorders* (DSM-5) is a taxonomic diagnostic tool for almost 300 disorders, published by the American Psychiatric Association (APA, 2013). Officially, the DSM-5 does not consider psychopathy as a stand-alone personality disorder (Few, Lynam, Maples, MacKillop & Miller, 2015), and rather embeds psychopathy within the construct of Antisocial Personality Disorder (ASPD). ASPD is a disorder characterized as a "pattern of disregard for, and violation of, the rights of others" (APA, 2013, p. 645), and because of descriptive similarities ASPD falls into Cluster B along with Borderline Personality Disorder, Histrionic Personality Disorder and Narcissistic Personality Disorder. In order to receive a diagnosis of ASPD, the adult (18 years or older) must meet at least three of the following criteria for behavior problems since the age of 15: (i) unlawful behavior, (ii) deceitfulness, (iii) impulsivity, (iv) irritability and aggressiveness, (v) reckless and dangerous behavior (to self and others), (vi) irresponsibility, and (vii) lack of remorse. Even though there are overwhelming epidemiological and etiological differences (e.g., genetic and neurobiological, as well as different correlates of psychological and social factors), the APA states that ASPD is the same as psychopathy, going as far as saying that the essential features of ASPD "have also been referred to as *psychopathy, sociopathy,* or *dissocial personality disorder*" (ibid., p. 659). Yet, the APA further states that individuals diagnosed with ASPD can also receive a specifier of "with psychopathic features" if the individual displays a lack of anxiety and fear, a bold interpersonal style, high levels of attention seeking, stress immunity, and assertiveness and dominance (ibid., p. 765). In the view of the APA, then, the diagnosis of psychopathy is not possible without receiving a diagnosis of ASPD. Using the DSM-5 formulation suggests criminality is *the* central feature of psychopathy. This is a contentious view of psychopathy (see Skeem & Cooke, 2010a), given that antisocial behavior is more likely a "downstream" product of the core personality features of psychopathy (e.g., callousness, lack of guilt; ibid.). Lumping psychopathy as a specifier of ASPD rejects a great deal of literature drawing etiological distinctions between ASPD and psychopathy.

There is no doubt that psychopathy and ASPD share many similarities, and reportedly have high comorbidity rates in forensic samples. For example, in a forensic inpatient sample 65% of patients scoring high on the PCL-R also had an ASPD diagnosis (Ogloff, Campbell & Shepherd, 2016); of note, only 5.5% of those with a diagnosis of ASPD scored high on the PCL-R. Given that antisocial behavior roughly constitutes at least a quarter of the PCL-R this is somewhat unsurprising. Comorbidity is not unique to ASPD and psychopathy, as many personality disorders overlap with one another and with psychopathy, and this varies for men and women (e.g., psychopathy is more strongly related to borderline personality disorder in women than men; Sprague, Javdani, Sadeh, Newman & Verona, 2012). The comorbidity may also be exacerbated because Cluster B personality disorders all share behavioral outcomes – dramatic, overly emotional or unpredictable thinking or behavior (APA, 2013, p. 646). Similarly, psychopathy and ASPD share observable behaviors (e.g., aggressiveness and criminality), which are included as diagnostic features and criteria in factor 2 of the PCL-R and ASPD (e.g., childhood behavior problems, criminality).

It should also be noted for the emerging clinician, criminologist and researcher that while sociopathy shares many characteristics with ASPD and factor 2 on the PCL-R, sociopathy is *not* the same as psychopathy (see Mokros et al., 2015). Over the years the term sociopathy has assumed several meanings leading to confusion, for example it has been used to describe a pattern of antisocial/criminal behavior which develops from psychosocial risk factors (Partridge, 1930), and has been used to describe high functioning psychopathy. However, both ASPD and sociopathy are marked by heightened emotional dysregulation (e.g., frustration, anger), whereas psychopathy is marked by emotional hyporesponsivity. Thus, even though both disorders share overlap, which is mostly related to antisocial behavior, psychopathy and ASPD/sociopathy represent two ends of emotional responsivity spectrum, which are related to unique neurobiological differences and developmental origins (see Yildirim & Derksen, 2013 for review).

Dissocial Personality Disorder

The World Health Organization publishes the International Classification of Diseases (ICD) which provides universal taxonomies of diseases, including mental and behavioral disorders (World Health Organization, 1992). The ICD-10 includes Dissocial Personality Disorder (F60.2), which is described as a "gross disparity between behavior and the prevailing social norms" (p. 204), as characterized by (a) callousness, (b) irresponsibility and disregard for others and rules, (c) ability to establish relationships but the inability to maintain them, (d) easily frustrated (as evidenced by aggression and violence), (e) absence of guilt and failure to learn from punishment, and (f) a tendency to blame others/society for their behavior (ibid., p. 204). Consistent with the DSM-5, the ICD-10 clusters amoral, antisocial, asocial, sociopathic and psychopathic personality disorder. The ICD-10 states that psychopathy is a more extreme form of dissocial personality disorder. Based on the diagnostic criteria of the ICD-10, dissocial personality disorder shares many symptoms with ASPD but does not capture the full criteria of psychopathy. As with ASPD in the DSM-5, dissocial personality disorder includes many of the deviant behaviors associated with psychopathy but does not account for many of the interpersonal or affective traits that are central to psychopathy.

Psychopathic personality

The Psychodynamic Diagnostic Manual (PDM-2; Alliance of Psychoanalytic Organizations, 2017) is grounded in psychodynamic clinical models and theories developed for case formulation and treatment planning. The PDM-2 can be used in conjunction with the DSM-5 or ICD-10, or as an alternative. Unlike the DSM-5 and ICD-10, the PDM-2 recognizes that psychopathy is different from ASPD, explicitly stating that "we prefer the earlier term psychopathic (Cleckley, 1941; Hare, 1991; Meloy, 1988), to the current antisocial" (Alliance of Psychoanalytic Organizations, 2017, p. 50). Further, the PDM-2 directly states, "obviously" not all people with psychopathy are antisocial (ibid.). Instead, the PDM-2 proposes that some people with psychopathic personalities have "successful" lives receiving social approval and admiration. Also, the PDM-2 highlights that while many people with psychopathic personalities become involved in the criminal justice system, others manage to escape justice. This notion makes the study of psychopathy in community populations integral to understanding psychopathy. The PDM-2 identifies psychopathic personality as characteristically similar to Cleckley's description (e.g., lack of anxiety, low empathy, manipulative, insincere, charming, etc.), as well as Henderson's typologies (e.g., not all aggressive or violent, some are passive). Within the PDM-2, psychopathy falls under the Personality Syndromes section (also called the P Axis). Rather than using taxonomies like the ICD-10 and DSM-5, the PDM-2 is designed to portray "kinds of people" across a spectrum, from healthy to unhealthy (ibid., p. 16).

In order to measure psychopathy, the PDM-2 endorses the assessment of psychopathic personalities using the PCL-R and its derivatives. The PDM-2 identifies five key features to understand psychopathic personality. The first is called the "contributing constitutional-maturational patterns", which is described as having a high tolerance to emotional stimulation, and in some cases congenital aggressiveness. The second feature is "central tension/preoccupation", which is described as the tendency to dominate others to avoid being exploited and manipulated. The third feature is called the "central affects", which is evident by rage and envy that are not context-specific. Fourth, "characteristic pathogenic belief about self" is the belief that the psychopathic individual can do whatever he wants because he has been wronged in the past. Fifth, "characteristic pathogenic belief about others" is the attitude that everyone else is dishonorable, selfish, weak and manipulative, therefore, the psychopath feels justified to take advantage of people. Sixth, "central ways of defending" is having contempt for others and aiming for unlimited power and control over people. Expectedly, then, clients with psychopathic personalities are reportedly the most likely for psychotherapists to experience the highest levels of countertransference when compared to other personality disorders (Gordon, 2017).

Clinical assessments for youth

Psychopathy Checklist: Youth Version

The Psychopathy Checklist: Youth Version (PCL:YV; Forth, Kosson & Hare, 2003) is an age-appropriate version of the PCL-R for youth aged between 12 and 18 years. Although adolescents are not diagnosed as psychopaths, the PCL:YV is valuable as an indicator of levels of psychopathic traits. The PCL:YV two-factor, three-facet and four-facet structures have been widely used in forensic adolescent samples (Vincent, Odgers, McCormick & Corrado, 2008; Vitacco, Neumann, Caldwell, Leistico & Van Rybroek, 2006). As with the PCL-R, the PCL:YV requires file review and one-on-one interview by an individual with a license to conduct psychological assessments with an advanced degree (e.g., MD, PhD). Overall, the PCL:YV has been shown to be a reliable and valid measure for psychopathic traits in male and female adolescents (Brazil & Forth, 2016).

Conduct Disorder with Limited Prosocial Emotions

In the most recent version of the DSM-5, the APA recognized that youth with conduct problems were different based on the presence of psychopathic traits, specifically the personality features of psychopathy. Conduct Disorder (CD) shares many similar criteria with ASPD in adults, and as with ASPD it is focused on deviant behavior: (1) aggression towards people and animals (e.g., fighting, bullying); (2) destruction of property (e.g., fire setting, vandalism); (3) deceitfulness (e.g., conning, shoplifting); and (4) serious violations of rules (e.g., truancy, running away from home; APA, 2013). Depending on the age of onset, CD can be diagnosed as "childhood onset" (<10 years old), "adolescent onset" (>10 years old), or unspecified (when the age of onset is not verifiable). When compared to adolescent onset, CD with childhood onset is associated with more severe long-term outcomes, including cognitive deficits, mental health problems and more violent behavior in adulthood (Johnson, Kemp, Heard, Lennings & Hickie, 2015). Depending on the number of symptoms and the severity, CD can be further classified as "mild" (few symptoms and/or causes minor harm; e.g., lying, truancy), to "severe" (many more symptoms than required for a diagnosis and considerable harm to others is caused; e.g., forced sex, use of a weapon).

A subgroup of youth with CD may be further diagnosed on the presence of affective psychopathic traits, with the specifier called Limited Prosocial Emotions (LPE). LPE is most popularly termed as Callous-Unemotional (CU) traits. To meet the diagnostic criteria for LPE, the individual should present with at least two of the four characteristics: (1) a lack of remorse or guilt, (2) callous lack of empathy, (3) shallow or deficient affect, or (4) lack of concern about performance (Blair, Leibenluft & Pine, 2014). Besides a lack of concern about performance, LPE characteristics are almost identical to the affective facet on the PCL-R for adults (see Figure 2.1). For consistency with the vast majority of research on this topic, this book will refer to LPE as CU traits. Research has shown children with conduct problems and CU traits pose the greatest risk of continually high levels of conduct problems, delinquency and police contacts (Frick, Stickle, Dandreaux, Farrell & Kimonis, 2005). Consistent with adult psychopathy, children with CU traits have a lack of concern for the welfare and safety of others, often engaging in physical and emotional cruelty to others in order to achieve a goal (Pardini & Byrd, 2012). Youth with CU traits have a lack of emotionality (Essau, Sasagawa & Frick, 2006), making them fearless perpetrators of harmful and delinquent behavior without consideration of the consequences of their actions (Fanti, Panayiotou, Lazarou, Michael & Georgiou, 2016). As discussed above, adults with ASPD demonstrate emotion dysregulation and adults with psychopathy display hypoarousal, both of which may be a catalyst for their associated maladaptive behaviors. Similarly, youth with CD display emotion dysregulation, whereas youth with CD *and* CU traits display hypoarousal (Frick & Viding, 2009; Sebastian et al., 2015).

Clinical Assessment of Prosocial Emotions

For many years CU traits has been measured using self-and informant-report on the Inventory of Callous-Unemotional Traits (ICU; see Table 2.2), which captures three dimensions: Callousness, Uncaring and Unemotional. Currently in development, the Clinical Assessment of Prosocial Emotions (CAPE; Frick, 2013) is the first clinician-administered measure of CU traits. The CAPE was developed in accordance with the DSM-5 LPE specifier, as well as the construct of the ICU. Although the PCL:YV measures affective psychopathic traits, which complement the diagnostic procedure for LPE, unlike the PCL-R, the CAPE can be administered from children as young as 3 years up to emerging adulthood at age 21 years. Ratings are based on at least two interviewees, typically the child and the parent/caregiver or teacher. If the child is younger than 9 years old, a second informant is needed instead of the child (e.g., teacher and parent). The CAPE is a semi-structured interview, with stem questions (e.g., "Does [name of child] seem to feel bad or guilty if s/he does something wrong or hurts someone?"), the respondent is asked to provide specific examples pertaining to the question, and information about the context of the behavior. The clinicians rate the descriptiveness of the response, from 0 (not descriptive) to 2 (highly descriptive), as well as reporting the accuracy and honesty of the informant. Scores for each of the four domains can be

TABLE 2.2 Youth psychopathic trait measures

	Dimensions	Informant	No. of items
Inventory of Callous-Unemotional Traits (ICU; Kimonis et al., 2008)	– Callousness – Unemotional – Uncaring	Self; caregiver; teacher	Full version: 24
Antisocial Process Screening Device (APSD; Frick & Hare, 2001)	3-facet: – Narcissism – Callousness – Impulsivity	Self; caregiver; teacher	Full version: 20
Youth Psychopathic Traits Inventory (YPI; Andershed, Kerr, Stattin & Levander, 2002)	3-facet: – Interpersonal (incl. dishonest charm, grandiosity, lying and manipulation) – Affective (incl. callousness, unemotionality and remorselessness) – Behavioral (incl. impulsiveness, thrill-seeking and irresponsibility)	Self	Full version: 50 Short form: 18
Childhood Psychopathy Scale (CPS; Lynam, 1997)	2-factor: – Callous-Unemotional – Antisocial Behavior 3-facet: – Interpersonal – Affective – Behavioral	Self;caregiver	Full version: 50
The Child Problematic Traits Inventory (CPTI; Colins et al., 2014)	3-facet: – Grandiose-Deceitful – Callous-Unemotional – Impulsive-Need for Stimulation	Teacher; caregiver	Full version: 28

summed; however, to meet the diagnostic threshold the youth must receive at least two "highly descriptive" examples of the specific behavior. Because the CAPE is still in development, the psychometric properties have not yet been published.

Psychopathy as a construct: the role of antisocial behavior

The construct of psychopathy is one of the most hotly debated topics in the field of psychopathy. Most researchers agree that the interpersonal-affective traits are the core features of psychopathy. However, there are strong arguments questioning the place of antisocial behavior in the construct of psychopathy. On one side of the debate, scholars have stated "an integral part of psychopathy is the emergence of an early and persistent pattern of problematic behaviors"

(Hare & Neumann, 2005, p. 58), going as far as saying antisocial behavior as "critical" (Vitacco, Neumann & Jackson, 2005, p. 473) and "central" to psychopathy (Hare & Neumann, 2005, p. 58). On the other side, proponents of a personality-focused psychopathy construct suggest antisocial behavior cannot be a diagnostic feature of psychopathy because antisocial behavior is a product of the psychopathic personality (Boduszek & Debowska, 2016; Cooke, Hart, Michie & Clark, 2004; Cooke & Logan, 2015; Cooke & Michie, 2001; Corrado et al., 2015; Preszler, Marcus, Edens & McDermott, 2018). Antisocial behavior, past and present, is not unique to psychopathy. Disorders that are related to higher levels of antisocial behavior, such as Borderline Personality Disorder (BPD), do not have antisociality as the central diagnostic feature. Instead, antisocial behavior is a product of the core personality features (e.g., emotion dysregulation increase risk of physical fights).

Essentially, scholars in the field of psychopathy argue that including antisocial behavior as a diagnostic feature of psychopathy is considered a "tautological" measure (Cooke & Logan, 2015; Skeem & Cooke, 2010a). In line with Meehl's maxim (1954), past behavior is one of the best predictors of future behavior (Camp et al., 2013; Gendreau, Goggin & Smith, 2002). Of course, then, it is only logical to expect past antisocial behavior (as indexed by antisocial psychopathic traits) predict future antisocial behavior. As a result of the repetitious measure of antisocial behavior, it has been suggested that the robust links between psychopathy and criminality are mostly due to the antisocial facet of psychopathy, and not because of the core personality features of psychopathy. Indeed, this is somewhat contradictory to the proposed argument but nevertheless is a valid point. Whether or not antisocial behavior should be included in the psychopathy construct, studies have found time and time again that psychopathy is predictive of future criminality and violence even while accounting for past criminality, delinquency and the presence of antisocial personality disorder and antisocial psychopathic traits, and many of the associations between psychopathy and violence are driven by the personality features of psychopathy (see Chapter 3).

Summary

Regardless of the perspective that one takes – either that antisocial behavior should be included in the construct, or the construct of psychopathy should be purely personality focused – this level of academic debate is important for the development of a refined model of psychopathy. As we have seen in this chapter, psychopathy has been observed and depicted in writings throughout history and across cultures, yet, it is the active debate over the past 30 years that has spurred the development of several psychopathy measures, with some choosing to focus less on antisocial behavior and prioritizing personality features, such as the Triarchic Psychopathy Measure. Even with the increasing number of psychopathy scales being published and tested, these measures are more closely related than they are different, which suggests the central features of psychopathy are being captured and provide a robust construct across various populations and measures.

Acknowledgments

Thank you to Dr. Scott Lilienfeld, Dr. Michael Lewis and Dr. Annette McKeown for their valuable input to this chapter. Dr. Lilienfeld is a clinical psychologist and Professor of Psychology at Emory University, and serves as the Editor-in-Chief for the journal *Clinical Psychological Science* and Associate Editor for the journal *Archives of Scientific Psychology*. He is recent past president of the Society for the Scientific Study of Psychopathy, and has extensive research expertise in the field of psychopathy and assessment. Dr Michael Lewis is a chartered psychologist and Lecturer in Forensic Psychology at University of Central Lancashire. He is the Editor-In-Chief for the *Journal of Criminological Research, Policy and Practice*, and holds an honorary contract with Mersey Care NHS Trust, High Secure Psychiatric Services. His research specialty includes the clinical assessment and treatment of psychopathy. Dr Annette McKeown is a Principal Forensic Psychologist at Kolvin Service, and her research specialism includes, risk assessment, female offenders, personality disorder and domestic violence.

References

Alliance of Psychoanalytic Organizations. (2017). *Psychodynamic Diagnostic Manual, Version 2 (PDM-2)*. New York: Guilford Press.

APA. (2013). *Diagnostic and Statistical Manual of Mental Disorders* (5th ed.). Washington, DC: American Psychiatric Association.

Blair, R. J. R., Leibenluft, E. & Pine, D. S. (2014). Conduct Disorder and Callous-Unemotional Traits in Youth. *New England Journal of Medicine, 371*(23), 2207–2216.

Boduszek, D. & Debowska, A. (2016). Critical Evaluation of Psychopathy Measurement (PCL-R and SRP-III/SF) and Recommendations for Future Research. *Journal of Criminal Justice, 44*, 1–12.

Brazil, I. A. & Forth, A. E. (2016). Psychopathy Checklist: Screening Version (PCL:SV). In V. Zeigler-Hill & T. K. Shackelford (Eds.), *Encyclopedia of Personality and Individual Differences* (pp. 1–4). Berlin: Springer International Publishing.

Camp, J. P., Skeem, J. L., Barchard, K., Lilienfeld, S. O. & Poythress, N. G. (2013). Psychopathic Predators? Getting Specific about the Relation between Psychopathy and Violence. *Journal of Consulting and Clinical Psychology, 81*(3), 467–480.

Christian, E. & Sellbom, M. (2016). Development and Validation of an Expanded Version of the Three-Factor Levenson Self-Report Psychopathy Scale. *Journal of Personality Assessment, 98*(2), 155–168.

Cleckley, H. (1941). *The Mask of Sanity*. St. Louis, MO: Mosby.

Cleckley, H. (1984). *The Mask of Sanity: An Attempt to Clarify Some Issues About the So-Called Psychopathic Personality*. St. Louis, MO: Mosby.

Cooke, D. J., Hart, S. D., Logan, C. & Michie, C. (2012). Explicating the Construct of Psychopathy: Development and Validation of a Conceptual Model, the Comprehensive Assessment of Psychopathic Personality (CAPP). *International Journal of Forensic Mental Health, 11*(4), 242–252.

Cooke, D. J., Hart, S. D., Michie, C. & Clark, D. A. (2004). Reconstructing Psychopathy: Clarifying the Significance of Antisocial and Socially Deviant Behavior in the Diagnosis of Psychopathic Personality Disorder. *Journal of Personality Disorders, 18*(4), 337–357.

Cooke, D. J. & Logan, C. (2015). Capturing Clinical Complexity: Towards a Personality-Oriented Measure of Psychopathy. *Journal of Criminal Justice, 43*(4), 262–273.

Cooke, D. J. & Michie, C. (2001). Refining the Construct of Psychopathy: Towards a Hierarchical Model. *Psychological Assessment, 13*(2), 171–88.

Corrado, R. R., DeLisi, M., Hart, S. D., McCuish, E. C., Corrado, R. R., DeLisi, M., . . . McCuish, E. C. (2015). Can the Causal Mechanisms Underlying Chronic, Serious, and Violent Offending Trajectories Be Elucidated Using the Psychopathy Construct? *Journal of Criminal Justice, 43*(4), 251–261.

Esquirol, E. (1838). *Des Maladies Mentales Consideerees sous les Rapporrs Medical, Hygienique er Medico-Legal [Mental Diseases under Medical, Hygienic and M edico-Legal Aspects]*. Paris: Bailliere.

Essau, C. A., Sasagawa, S. & Frick, P. J. (2006). Callous-Unemotional Traits in a Community Sample of Adolescents. *Assessment, 13*(4), 454–469.

Evans, L. & Tully, R. J. (2016). The Triarchic Psychopathy Measure (TriPM): Alternative to the PCL-R? *Aggression and Violent Behavior, 27*(27), 79–86.

Fanti, K. A., Panayiotou, G., Lazarou, C., Michael, R. & Georgiou, G. (2016). The Better of Two Evils? Evidence that Children Exhibiting Continuous Conduct Problems High or Low on Callous-Unemotional Traits Score on Opposite Directions on Physiological and Behavioral Measures of Fear. *Development and Psychopathology, 28*(1), 185–198.

Few, L. R., Lynam, D. R., Maples, J. L., MacKillop, J. & Miller, J. D. (2015). Comparing the Utility of DSM-5 Section II and III Antisocial Personality Disorder Diagnostic Approaches for Capturing Psychopathic Traits. *Personality Disorders: Theory, Research, and Treatment, 6*(1), 64–74.

Forth, A. E., Kosson, D. S. & Hare, R. D. (2003). *The Psychopathy Checklist: Youth Version Manual*. Toronto: Multi-Health Systems.

Frick, P. J. (2013). *Clinical Assessment of Prosocial Emotions: Version 1.1 (CAPE 1.1)*. Unpublished Rating Scale, University of New Orleans.

Frick, P. J., Stickle, T. R., Dandreaux, D. M., Farrell, J. M. & Kimonis, E. R. (2005). Callous–Unemotional Traits in Predicting the Severity and Stability of Conduct Problems and Delinquency. *Journal of Abnormal Child Psychology, 33*(4), 471–487.

Frick, P. J. & Viding, E. (2009). Antisocial Behavior from a Developmental Psychopathology Perspective. *Development and Psychopathology, 21*(4), 1111–1131.

Furnham, A., Daoud, Y. & Swami, V. (2009). "How to Spot a Psychopath": Lay Theories of Psychopathy. *Social Psychiatry and Psychiatric Epidemiology, 44*(6), 464–472.

Gacono, C. B. (2000). *The Clinical and Forensic Assessment of Psychopathy: A Practitioner's Guide*. Hillsdale, NJ: Lawrence Erlbaum Associates.

Gendreau, P., Goggin, C. & Smith, P. (2002). Is the PCL-R Really the "Unparalleled" Measure of Offender Risk? A Lesson in Knowledge Cumulation. *Criminal Justice and Behavior, 29*(4), 397–426.

Gordon, R. M. (2017). A Concurrent Validity Study of the PDM-2 Personality Syndromes. *Current Psychology*, doi: 10.1007/s12144-017-9644-2

Hare, R. D. (1991). *The Hare Psychopathy Checklist – Revised: Manual*. Toronto, Canada: Multi-Health Systems.

Hare, R. D. (2003). *The Hare Psychopathy Checklist – Revised* (2nd ed.). Toronto, Canada: Multi-Health Systems.

Hare, R. D. & Neumann, C. S. (2005). Structural Models of Psychopathy. *Current Psychiatry Reports, 7*(1), 57–64.

Hare, R. D. & Neumann, C. S. (2006). The PCL-R Assessment of Psychopathy: Development, Structural Properties, and New Directions. In C. J. Patrick (Ed.), *Handbook of Psychopathy* (pp. 58–90). New York: Guilford Press.

Henderson, D. K. (1939). *Psychopathic States.* New York: W. W. Norton & Company.
Johnson, V. A., Kemp, A. H., Heard, R., Lennings, C. J. & Hickie, I. B. (2015). Childhood- versus Adolescent-Onset Antisocial Youth with Conduct Disorder: Psychiatric Illness, Neuropsychological and Psychosocial Function. *PloS ONE, 10*(4), e0121627.
Karpman, B. (1941). On the Need of Separating Psychopathy into Two Distinct Clinical Types: the Symptomatic and the Idiopathic. *Journal of Criminal Psychopathology, 3,* 112–137.
Karpman, B. (1948). The Myth of the Psychopathic Personality. *American Journal of Psychiatry, 104*(9), 523–534.
Kelsey, K. R., Rogers, R. & Robinson, E. V. (2014). Self-Report Measures of Psychopathy: What is their Role in Forensic Assessments? *Journal of Psychopathology and Behavioral Assessment, 37*(3), 380–391.
Kraepelin, E. (1915). *Psychiatrie: Eine Lehrbuch für Studierende und Artze* (8th ed.). Leipzig: Barth.
Lilienfeld, S. O. & Fowler, K. A. (2006). The Self-Report Assessment of Psychopathy. In C. J. Patrick (Ed.), *Handbook of Psychopathy* (pp. 107–132). New York: Guilford Press.
Maudsley, H. (1874). *Responsibility in Mental Disease.* London: King.
Meloy, J. R. (1988). *The Psychopathic Mind: Origins, Dynamics, and Treatment.* New Jersey: Aronson.
Mokros, A., Hare, R. D., Neumann, C. S., Santtila, P., Habermeyer, E. & Nitschke, J. (2015). Variants of Psychopathy in Adult Male Offenders: A Latent Profile Analysis. *Journal of Abnormal Psychology, 124*(2), 372.
Morel, B. A. (1839). *Traité des Dégénérescences Physiques, Intellectuelles et Morales de l'Espèce Humaine.* Paris: J.-B. Baillière.
Murphy, B., Lilienfeld, S., Skeem, J. & Edens, J. F. (2016). Are Fearless Dominance Traits Superfluous in Operationalizing Psychopathy? Incremental Validity and Sex Differences. *Psychological Assessment, 28*(12), 1597–1607.
Ogloff, J. R. P., Campbell, R. E. & Shepherd, S. M. (2016). Disentangling Psychopathy from Antisocial Personality Disorder: An Australian Analysis. *Journal of Forensic Psychology Practice, 16*(3), 198–215.
Pardini, D. & Byrd, A. L. (2012). Perceptions of Aggressive Conflicts and Others' Distress in Children with Callous-Unemotional Traits: "I'll Show You Who's Boss, Even If You Suffer and I Get in Trouble!". *Journal of Child Psychology and Psychiatry, 53*(3), 283–291.
Partridge, G. E. (1930). Current Conceptions of Psychopathic Personality. *American Journal of Psychiatry, 87*(1), 53–99. doi: 10.1176/ajp.87.1.53.
Paulhus, D. L., Neumann, C. S. & Hare, R. D. (2016). *Hare Self-Report Psychopathy Scale: Technical Manual* (4th ed.). Toronto: Multi-Health Systems.
Pinel, P. (1806). *A Treatise on Insanity.* London: W. Todd.
Poythress, N. G., Lilienfeld, S. O., Skeem, J. L., Douglas, K. S., Edens, J. F., Epstein, M. & Patrick, C. J. (2010). Using the PCL-R to Help Estimate the Validity of Two Self-Report Measures of Psychopathy with Offenders. *Assessment, 17*(2), 206–219.
Preszler, J., Marcus, D. K., Edens, J. F. & McDermott, B. E. (2018). Network Analysis of Psychopathy in Forensic Patients. *Journal of Abnormal Psychology, 127*(2), 171–182.
Prichard, J. (1835). *A Treatise on Insanity and Other Disorders Affecting the Mind.* London: Sherwood, Gilbert, and Piper.
Ray, J. V., Hall, J., Rivera-Hudson, N., Poythress, N. G., Lilienfeld, S. O. & Morano, M. (2013). The Relation between Self-Reported Psychopathic Traits and Distorted Response Styles: A Meta-analytic Review. *Personality Disorders: Theory, Research, and Treatment, 4*(1), 1–14.

Ruchensky, J. R., Edens, J. F., Donnellan, M. B. & Witt, E. A. (2017). Examining the Reliability and Validity of an Abbreviated Psychopathic Personality Inventory – Revised (PPI-R) in Four Samples. *Psychological Assessment, 29*(2), 238–244.

Rush, B. (1812). *Medical Inquiries and Observations upon the Diseases of the Mind.* London: Doubleday.

Schneider, K. (1923). *Die Psychopathische Persönlich-keiten.* Leipzig: F. Deuticke.

Sebastian, C. L., De Brito, S. A., McCrory, E. J., Hyde, Z. H., Lockwood, P. L., Cecil, C. A. M. & Viding, E. (2015). Grey Matter Volumes in Children with Conduct Problems and Varying Levels of Callous-Unemotional Traits. *Journal of Abnormal Child Psychology, 44*(4), 639–649.

Skeem, J. L. & Cooke, D. J. (2010a). Is Criminal Behavior a Central Component of Psychopathy? Conceptual Directions for Resolving the Debate. *Psychological Assessment, 22*(2), 433–445.

Skeem, J. L. & Cooke, D. J. (2010b). One Measure Does Not a Construct Make: Directions toward Reinvigorating Psychopathy Research – Reply to Hare and Neumann (2010). *Psychological Assessment, 22*(2), 455–459.

Sprague, J., Javdani, S., Sadeh, N., Newman, J. P. & Verona, E. (2012). Borderline Personality Disorder as a Female Phenotypic Expression of Psychopathy? *Personality Disorders, 3*(2), 127–139.

Theophrastus. (1714). *The Moral Characters of Theophrastus.* London: Montgomery

Vincent, G. M., Odgers, C. L., McCormick, A. V. & Corrado, R. R. (2008). The PCL: YV and Recidivism in Male and Female Juveniles: A Follow-Up into Young Adulthood. *International Journal of Law and Psychiatry, 31*(3), 287–296.

Vitacco, M. J., Neumann, C. S., Caldwell, M. F., Leistico, A.-M. & Van Rybroek, G. J. (2006). Testing Factor Models of the Psychopathy Checklist: Youth Version and Their Association With Instrumental Aggression. *Journal of Personality Assessment, 87*(1), 74–83.

Vitacco, M. J., Neumann, C. S. & Jackson, R. L. (2005). Testing a Four-Factor Model of Psychopathy and Its Association With Ethnicity, Gender, Intelligence, and Violence. *Journal of Consulting and Clinical Psychology, 73*(3), 466–476.

Werner, K. B., Few, L. R. & Bucholz, K. K. (2015). Epidemiology, Comorbidity, and Behavioral Genetics of Antisocial Personality Disorder and Psychopathy. *Psychiatric Annals, 45*(4), 195–199.

World Health Organization. (1992). *The ICD-10 Classification of Mental and Behavioural Disorders: Clinical Descriptions and Diagnostic Guidelines.* Geneva: World Health Organization.

Yildirim, B. O. & Derksen, J. J. L. (2013). Systematic Review, Structural Analysis, and New Theoretical Perspectives on the Role of Serotonin and Associated Genes in the Etiology of Psychopathy and Sociopathy. *Neuroscience & Biobehavioral Reviews, 37*(7), 1254–1296.

3

PSYCHOPATHY AND VIOLENT CRIME

It was the early hours of March 29, 2014, in Colchester, England, when 15-year-old James Fairweather, armed with a knife and wearing gloves, snuck out of his parents' home with the intention to attack and kill someone. A mile from his home, Fairweather came across James Attfield sleeping in a park. Recounting to police, Fairweather reported stabbing him first in the abdomen with all his strength, four or five times, and then in the head several times. There were a large number of comparatively superficial wounds consistent with just the tip of the knife penetrating, which in the pathologist's opinion indicated deliberation, with those injuries demonstrating an element of control inconsistent with the defendant's description of "going into a rage" (Spencer, 2016, pp. 3–4).

Three months later, Fairweather ruthlessly attacked again. This time the victim was Nahid Almanea, a 31-year-old student at the University of Essex. On her way to university in broad daylight, Fairweather stabbed Almanea from behind with a bayonet. Fairweather spun Almanea around, knocked off her sunglasses and stabbed her in the eye. Falling to the floor, Fairweather struck her again, this time stabbing her in the other eye. The pathologist's report found Almanea suffered from "eight superficial puncture wounds over the left side of the chest and upper abdomen, caused with the tip of the knife which, in the view of the pathologist, were likely to have been inflicted with a significant degree of control" (Spencer, 2016, p. 6). As with his first murder, Fairweather calmly covered his tracks; he wore gloves, cleaned the knife and threw it into a fast-flowing stream, and dumped the blood-stained clothes with other rubbish ready for collection. On May 26, 2015, Fairweather was looking for another victim. Fortunately, police were informed that there was an intimidating man lurking near the location of the death of Nahid Almanea, and Fairweather was subsequently arrested.

At the police station, Fairweather fully admitted to the murders, describing them with "chilling frankness" (Spencer, 2016, p. 8). Although Fairweather was too young to be formally diagnosed as a psychopath, the prosecution's psychiatric assessment stated that Fairweather displayed an emerging psychopathic personality. Justice Spencer stated, "there was a significant degree of planning or premeditation in respect of each of the killings . . . You knew exactly what you were intending to do, and you achieved it". The murders were sadistic; his first victim suffered from a drawn-out attack with over hundred superficial wounds, and his second victim stabbed in both eyes was a "horrific sadistic conduct" (ibid., p. 11). When discussing his second murder with a psychiatrist, Fairweather, in typical psychopathic form, blamed the victim for his actions, "she [Almanea] should not have been walking there alone as she should have known there was a murderer in town" (ibid., p. 10). Although Fairweather is a unique case, his conduct during and after the murders demonstrated prototypical psychopathic behavior. His violence was planned, yet opportunistic and horrifically sadistic. During his trial, Fairweather displayed no remorse or guilt and rejected full responsibility for his actions with an attempt to feign mental illness.

Psychopathy, as a construct and a disorder, is important for both forensic practitioners and researchers. Psychopaths pose a great risk of violence. But even more valuable is how the dimensional construct of psychopathy lends itself to identifying risk of specific forms of violence, and how these associations differ for males and females. Understanding the specific risks that psychopathic traits pose is pivotal to designing interventions and tailoring treatment plans, as well as identifying a person's vulnerability to recidivism prior to release from prison. Given the overwhelming empirical evidence, the study of violence and psychopathy should go hand in hand, which is why psychopathy has become recognized as the unified theory of crime (for a review, see DeLisi, 2016). This chapter will review the recent literature on the link between psychopathy and multiple forms and functions of violence.

Rates of violent crime

Since 2000, global rates of homicide have fallen by about 16% (World Health Organization, 2014). Yet, globally, over 475,000 homicides occur each year (ibid.). In 2015–2016, there were 571 homicides in the UK, an 11% increase from the prior year (Office for National Statistics, 2017a). During the same year, there were 1.3 million reported incidents of violence, with 106,098 sexual assaults. Fifty-five percent of violent crimes result in no injury, with the remaining 45% including wounding (24%) and assault with minor injury (21%; Office for National Statistics, 2017b). Although it is impossible to accurately compare countries on rates of violence, primarily because of different terminology and classification systems, methods of assessment and proportional rates of reported crimes versus unreported, rates of violence have been generally considered comparable. During the same period (2014–2015), England and Wales reported 14 violent crimes per 1,000 persons (Office for National Statistics, 2015), while the US reported about 18.6 per 1,000 persons (Truman & Morgan, 2016). Again, this statistic should be interpreted with caution because of inconsistencies in definitions and categorizations of violence and levels of police disclosure. However, allowing for disparate reporting methods, rates of violence can be considered somewhat comparable for most countries. The present chapter will review four forms of violent crime – homicide, sexual assault and rape, assault (including intimate partner violence) and robbery. In addition, relevant to the forensic practitioner and criminologist, this chapter will include a review of the link between psychopathy and institutional violence (e.g., prison, inpatient) and aggression subtypes.

Homicide

There is a limited amount of research exploring the link between psychopathy and homicide, and overall the research suggests adults who are convicted of homicides are not more likely to be psychopathic. However, homicides by psychopaths are more often premeditated and goal-directed (Woodworth & Porter, 2002). In youth, research has found homicide offenders ($n = 20$) scored higher than non-homicide offenders on total scores of psychopathy, and on all facets (Interpersonal, Affective, Lifestyle, and Antisocial; Cope et al., 2014). Of note, of the 20 homicide offenders, only four had been convicted of homicide, and the remaining 16 disclosed this information to a researcher even though they had not been convicted. While prior research has shown that psychopathic traits are linked to successfully avoiding prosecution for violent crimes (Aharoni & Kiehl, 2013), it is also possible that those who admitted to getting away with murder are lying. Psychopaths are notorious liars even when there seems that there is no reason for them to lie; often it can simply be to elevate themselves in the company of others, especially in the prison environment.

In adult prisoners, there is evidence to suggest murderers are not more likely to be psychopathic, and actually show lower levels of psychopathy. Sherretts, Boduszek, Debowska and Willmott (2017) found in a large ($n = 478$) sample of male prisoners that homicide offenders ($n = 94$) were *not* more psychopathic than prisoners who were recidivists or first-time offenders. Further, the results showed homicide offenders scored significantly lower than recidivists on Interpersonal and Lifestyle psychopathic traits. Thus, the results demonstrate recidivists display superficial charm, egocentricity and conning and manipulative behaviors, which may further their criminal career (ibid.). The authors note that the link between higher levels of Antisocial psychopathic traits and recidivism were unsurprising because of the strong overlap between the two. The authors go on to suggest that the Antisocial facet should "be treated as a consequence rather than an integral part of the psychopathy construct" (ibid., p. 91), as discussed in Chapter 2.

Psychopathic male prisoners from the Dangerous and Severe Personality Disordered (DSPD) unit in the United Kingdom were not found to be overly represented in the homicide offender population (Casey, Rogers, Burns & Yiend, 2013). Similarly, in a sample of 132 maximum security female offender, Warren and colleagues (2005) found homicide offenders scored significantly lower on total scores of psychopathy than those not convicted of homicide. Exploring the two-factor and three-facet models of the PCL-R, it was found that homicide offenders' lower psychopathy scores were largely due to lower scores on factor 2 (impulsive-antisocial), and the Lifestyle facet on the three-facet model. This finding is supported by research from Klein Tuente, de Vogel and Stam (2014) who, in a sample of 221 female offenders, found that homicide offending was predictive of not meeting a diagnosis of psychopathy (PCL-R > 25). Consistent with this result, it has been found that compared to women convicted of "other" crimes, women who murdered their child(ren) scored lower the on the PCL-R (de Vogel et al., 2014; Klein Tuente et al., 2014).

Violence perpetrated by psychopaths is typically non-discriminant and opportunistic, and their victim is more likely to be a stranger (Pajevic, Batinic & Stevanovic, 2017; Porter, Woodworth, Earle, Drugge & Boer, 2003). However, there are times when psychopaths commit domestic homicide. Domestic homicide typically occurs with a degree of high emotionality (e.g., anger). Unsurprisingly, then, when compared to non-domestic homicide offenders, domestic homicide offenders have been found to have lower scores on total psychopathy, factor 1 and factor 2 (Juodis, Starzomski, Porter & Woodworth, 2014). Nevertheless, domestic homicide crimes committed by psychopaths are more dispassionate, planned and gratuitously violent (ibid.). This supports prior work that has demonstrated that psychopathic homicide offenders are more likely to perpetrate instrumental homicides than reactive homicides (see Porter & Woodworth, 2007). After committing homicide, psychopaths attempt to minimize their crimes and shed the blame by describing their murders as more reactive when they were instrumental and often do not disclose incriminating information (ibid.).

In sum, there are several limitations to the research presented thus far, including small samples sizes, a lack of detail in how homicide offender groups were classified, broad age ranges without controlling for the effect of age, and in some cases, studies did not consider the influence of sex in mixed offender samples. Nevertheless, purely based on this research, there is moderate evidence that male psychopaths are not more likely to be convicted of homicides than non-psychopaths, while there is more substantial evidence that female psychopaths are not more likely to be convicted of homicide than non-psychopaths. However, most of the research determines history of homicide using official records of conviction. It is possible that those who commit homicide without prosecution may be more psychopathic, as has been found in youth (Cope et al., 2014). Indeed, more research is needed to explore this before conclusions can be drawn. The research is fairly clear that psychopaths who do kill perpetrate instrumental and dispassionate murders, committing more gratuitous violence, such as overkill and inflicting more non-fatal injuries prior to death. Yet, after being caught, psychopaths put to use their manipulative and pathological lying expertise, trying to minimize the instrumental nature of their crime. Thus, male and female psychopaths are just as likely to commit homicide as non-psychopaths, but those who do will wreak greater suffering to their victim for their own hedonistic gain.

Assault

In 2014–2015, there were 3,996,200 violent assaults in the US, and 829,720 "violence against the person" offenses in England and Wales. There are significant differences in the legal definitions and categorization of assault from country to country, and within a country there are multiple classifications. In the US, there are two main categories of assault: simple (without a weapon) and aggravated (with a weapon). Rape, attempted rape, sexual assault and robbery (including attempted robbery) are not included in this crime category (Bureau of Justice Statistics, 2017). In comparison, in England and Wales Parliament created three categories of assault based on the level of injury. Common assault is charged when there are no injuries, or the injuries are not serious. Actual bodily harm (ABH) is charged when serious injury is inflicted, and grievous bodily harm (GBH) is charged when there "is really serious injury" (Crown Prosecution Service, 2017). It is important to highlight that a limitation in current research exploring risk factors for assault is that there are only a handful of studies differentiating assault categories. As we have seen already, the most severe form of violence, homicide, is inconsistently associated with psychopathy. Yet, psychopaths perpetrate more gratuitous violence. This may mean that the link between psychopathy and all forms of violence is not linear but may be specific to certain forms of perpetration. Therefore, not accounting for the type of assault (e.g., simple or aggravated assault, or GBH or ABH) may produce different findings based on the prevalence of the crime within the sample being studied. In addition, assault crimes (as with any conviction data) represent only those individuals who have been caught by police and convicted, and not those who have escaped being caught and/or have no criminal history. Therefore, research in community populations tends to assess violent behavior using self-report measures of physical aggression. Overall, most of this research suggests there is a strong link between psychopathy and assault, both arrest history and self-report data. In addition, psychopathy has become a recognized risk factor for identifying a subgroup of individuals who will engage in chronic violent offending (McCuish, Corrado, Hart & DeLisi, 2015).

Drawing from a community sample of men without a criminal history, Reidy et al. (2016) found the Affective and Lifestyle facets were predictors of physical fights, but only the Affective facet predicted both simple and aggravated assault. The authors found the same results using the three-facet and four-facet model. In their second sample of men with a criminal history, the authors found different results for the three-facet and four-facet model. In the analysis including the three-facet model, the Affective facet predicted physical fights, and simple and aggravated assault, while the Lifestyle facet predicted simple assault. This finding was similar to the sample without a criminal history. However, when testing the four-facet model, which includes the Antisocial facet, the Antisocial facet was predictive of physical fights, simple assault and aggravated assault, and the Lifestyle facet predicted simple assault. Including the Antisocial facet into the statistical model resulted in the Affective facet no longer being predictive of assault.

This study demonstrates that men with and without a criminal history are more likely to commit both forms of assault if they have high affective psychopathic traits. However, when controlling for the Antisocial facet using the four-facet model, the link between affective traits and assault becomes nonsignificant for men with a criminal history. Given that antisocial psychopathic traits encompass past criminal, deviant and antisocial behavior (e.g., assault), what may be occurring is a statistical model that is asking the question "do antisocial psychopathic traits (e.g., past criminal and delinquent behavior) predict assault?" The answer is obviously going to be yes because antisocial psychopathic traits and violent behavior are similar constructs (past criminal behavior and past assaults). Another consideration demonstrated by this study is that affective psychopathic traits increase the risk of assault for men. Therefore, higher antisocial psychopathic traits, which include past criminality and childhood delinquency, may be a downstream product of having high affective psychopathic traits. Findings such as these emphasize the importance of studying both factor and facet models of psychopathy to properly discern causes of the psychopathy–violence link.

Exploring the role of psychopathic traits for differentiating violent and white collar crime, Boduszek, Debowska and Willmott (2017) found 7% of their male prisoner sample (n =1,126), who scored high across all facets of psychopathy, were more likely to fall into their "general violent offender" category. These individuals had an array of criminal offenses, including assault, battery and domestic violence. In contrast, those with higher interpersonal manipulative psychopathic traits were more likely to have a history of white collar and property crime. Thus, psychopathy as a construct seems to best predict violence across context, while at the dimensional level it is able to distinguish those who perpetrate unique types of crimes. Violence is a heterogeneous construct, and violence can occur because of different contexts (Thomson, 2018). Indeed, one of these contexts is the involvement of drugs. In a sample of 125 female prisoners, Thomson (2017) found self-report antisocial psychopathic traits were higher in women who had been convicted of a drug-related violent assault, while those convicted of a violent assault that was unrelated to drugs had higher affective psychopathic traits. Thus, Reidy et al. (2016) and Thomson (2017) demonstrate that psychopathic traits across context and sex are an important risk factor for assault, but also show that the dimensional construct is advantageous for understanding context-dependent violence.

Robbery

Robbery is defined as taking property from a person using physical force, coercion and/or intimidation (Bureau of Justice Statistics, 2017; UK Government, 1968), whereas theft is to dishonestly take property belonging from another person with the intention to permanently deprive the other person of it. Recent US cost estimates suggest each robbery amounts to $148,568 (DeLisi, Reidy,

Heirigs, Tostlebe & Vaughn, 2017). Given that in 2016 over 500,000 robberies occurred in the US, the total cost of robbery becomes astronomical (over $74 billion). Unfortunately, there is a lack of research looking at the association between psychopathy and robbery. However, based on a cost analysis study by DeLisi and colleagues (2017) it was found that affective psychopathic traits were related to greater costs of violent crime, including robbery. Assessing the link between psychopathy and robbery, Haapasalo (1994) found psychopaths were more often convicted for robbery (43.3%), when compared to offenders scoring low on psychopathy (24.1%). Before conclusions can be drawn on the link between psychopathy and robbery, much more research is needed. Nevertheless, the link is likely to be strong as psychopaths demonstrate criminal versatility.

Sexual offending

Based on the Crime Survey Data from England and Wales, about 2.5% of women and 0.4% of men will be a victim of a sexual offense in a 12-month period, representing 473,000 victims per year (Ministry of Justice, 2013). These statistics include both "serious sexual offenses" (e.g., rape and sexual assault) and "other sexual offenses" (e.g., exposure, voyeurism). About 92,000 people are victims of a serious sexual offense (ibid.). Based on the National Crime Victimization Survey, during 2015 in the United States 431,840 people were the victims of rape and sexual assault (see Truman & Morgan, 2016). Research exploring the association between psychopathy and sexual offending does not differentiate perpetrators of "serious sexual offenses", such as rape or sexual assault versus "other sexual offenses". As a result, this section of the chapter will discuss sexual offending as a single construct, unless stated otherwise.

There is considerable evidence to suggest adults and youth with psychopathic traits are at greater risk of sexual offending and sexual homicides committed by psychopaths are more sadistic (Cale, Lussier, McCuish & Corrado, 2015; Meloy, 2000; Porter et al., 2003). Because of this strong link, Texas requires all registered sex offenders to have a PCL-R to assess community supervision needs (Hawes, Boccaccini & Murrie, 2013; Texas Health and Safety Code, 2000, §841.023). Further, higher levels of psychopathic traits in nonclinical samples are linked to endorsing supportive beliefs about rape, and these individuals place greater blame on the victim rather than the perpetrator (Willis, Birthrong, King, Nelson-Gray & Latzman, 2017). At the factor level, blaming the victim is associated with Interpersonal-Affective psychopathic traits, whereas believing that rape is insignificant is associated with both Interpersonal-Affective and Impulsive-Antisocial psychopathic traits (Mouilso & Calhoun, 2013). Understanding the links between psychopathy and the factor/facet structure helps determine what treatments are more/less suitable for psychopathic sexual offenders.

In a sample of 958 male sexual offenders, Krstic and colleagues (2017) predicted profiles of sexual offending using the four-facet structure of psychopathy. The authors found the Affective and Antisocial facets best predicted sexually violent crimes, whereas the Interpersonal facet was uniquely associated with more paraphilic history. Using person-centered analysis to group sexual offenders by their scores on the PCL-R facets, Krstic et al. (ibid.) found those with the prototypical psychopathic profile (high on all four facets) had more sexual offenses.

Not only do psychopaths pose a high risk of sexual offending, but this risk remains even after being caught, imprisoned, treated and released (Reidy, Kearns & DeGue, 2013). Hawes, Boccaccini, and Murrie (2013) conducted a meta-analysis including 20 research studies ($n = 5,239$) to test how PCL-R scores were related to sexual recidivism. The authors found psychopathy as a total score was a good predictor of sexual recidivism but was most strongly related to mixed forms of violence, including nonsexual and sexual violence. This suggests psychopaths pose the greatest risk to violence in general – not just sexual violence. Exploring the construct of psychopathy, it was found that Impulsive-Antisocial traits on the two-factor model, and only the Antisocial facet of the four-facet model were the best predictors of sexual re-offending, whereas the interpersonal-affective features of psychopathy were not predictive. Based on this meta-analysis, total levels of psychopathic traits increase the risk of multiple-forms of violence, and not just sexual offending. This may indicate that psychopaths are non-discriminant in their perpetration of violence, and this association is generally driven by factor 2 psychopathic traits.

In support of this statement, Brown, Dargis, Mattern, Tsonis and Newman (2015) found psychopathy scores differentiated types of sexual offenders. Using the PCL-R, the authors found sex offenders who victimized both adults and children (mixed sex offenders) scored higher on psychopathy than sex offenders who victimized either only children or only adults, as well as non-sex offender prisoners. This finding is consistent with adolescent sex offenders. Parks and Bard (2006) found adolescent mixed sex offenders also scored highest on psychopathy when compared to child or adult sex offenders. Testing the factor and facet structure of psychopathy, the personality features of psychopathy were found to be most predictive of being in the mixed group for adolescents (Affective facet; Parks & Bard, 2006) and adults (Interpersonal-Affective factor; Brown et al., 2015). Furthermore, in a sample of 229 sex offenders Porter and colleagues (2000) found a larger proportion of psychopaths (PCL-R>30) were mixed sex offenders (64%) when compared to rapists (36%), incest offenders (6%), child molesters (9%) and non-sex offenders (36%). Collectively these studies establish that psychopathy is predictive with non-discriminant sexual offending and re-offending, as well as a proclivity for sexual behavior that is violent, both of which fall in line with the opportunistic and callous nature of the psychopath.

Intimate partner violence

Intimate partner violence (IPV) is a pervasive problem. In England and Wales, about 27% of women and 13% of men experience IPV in their lifetime (Office for National Statistics, 2016), which is similar to the lifetime prevalence of IPV in the US (27% female victims and 11% male victims; Centers for Disease Control and Prevention, 2017). While IPV is typically thought of as being physically hurt by a current or former partner, IPV actually includes psychological aggression, as well as physical violence, sexual violence and stalking (ibid.). Psychological aggression, such as coercion, towards a former or current partner has been consistently linked to higher levels of psychopathic traits (Centifanti, Thomson & Kwok, 2015; Hoffmann & Verona, 2018; Khan, Brewer, Kim & Centifanti, 2017), and there is strong evidence to suggest psychopathic traits are predictive of physical and sexual IPV.

Drawing from 703 clinical participants and 870 university students, Okano, Langille and Walsh (2016) found psychopathic traits predicted IPV even while controlling for sex and alcohol use. The authors also found psychopathic traits were a stronger predictor of IPV than alcohol use. In a sample of 152 male IPV perpetrators, Cunha, Braga and Abrunhosa Gonçalves (2018) found total scores on the PCL-R to be associated with a greater frequency of IPV, even after controlling for other important criminal history data (e.g., IPV history, other history of violence). Testing the facet structure, only the Affective facet emerged as a significant predictor of IPV frequency. This finding is similar to that of Mager, Bresin and Verona (2014), who found both factor 1 and factor 2 predicted frequency of IPV, but the link between factor 1 and IPV frequency was stronger for men than women. Thus, factor 2 seems to be a generalizable risk factor for male and female perpetrators of IPV, while higher factor 1 scores are unique to male IPV perpetrators. This stronger link between factor 1 and IPV in males is suggested to be because of the overlap between personality features of psychopathy and IPV perpetration with goal-directed aggression. That is, IPV may be used to achieve a goal, such as intimidation to gain dominance over a partner, and Interpersonal-Affective psychopathic features are strongly linked with goal-directed aggression and dominance. Thus, people who are callous and manipulative, and lack empathy, may use IPV to achieve dominance or control over their partner. Yet, this link may not be unique to IPV.

The Cambridge Study in Delinquent Development has followed more than 400 males in the UK from the ages of eight through to 48 years (Theobald, Farrington, Coid & Piquero, 2016). Theobald and colleagues (ibid.) grouped the men based on their life history of violence. These four groups included a (i) violent conviction only group, (ii) a generally violent group who committed intra- and extra-familial violence, (iii) a family-only violent group, and (iv) a non-violent group. Men in the generally violent group scored highest on total scores of the screening version of the psychopathy checklist (PCL:SV), and across all four facets. In contrast, the family-only IPV group and the non-violent group scored significantly lower than the generally violent and violent conviction groups. Because this study was able to compare groups of violent offenders, it is fairly clear that psychopathic traits are related to IPV. However, individuals high on psychopathic traits who perpetrate IPV will also perpetrate violence outside of the home. Again, total scores of psychopathic traits are related to violence across multiple contexts and without victim discrimination.

Prison and inpatient violence

Even while incarcerated where freedom of independence is limited, psychopaths are notorious for continuing to be violent (Thomson, 2018), and emerge as inmate leaders (Schrag, 1954). The link between prison violence and psychopathy has been confirmed for both men and women, however, there are significant distinctions (and similarities) at the dimensional level of psychopathy (Warren, Wellbeloved-Stone, Dietz & Millspaugh, 2017), which may warrant sex-specific violence interventions. The most consistent finding, which is somewhat unsurprising, is that antisocial psychopathic traits predict prison violence, and this is a gender-neutral risk factor (ibid.). In men, however, affective psychopathic traits have not been associated with prison violence (Chakhssi, Kersten, de Ruiter & Bernstein, 2014; Edens, Poythress, Lilienfeld, Patrick & Test, 2008; Walters & Heilbrun, 2010). This is somewhat unexpected as affective psychopathic traits in men are associated with criminal history of severe violence (Hall, Benning & Patrick, 2004), assault (Reidy et al., 2016) and IPV (Mager et al., 2014). In non-treatment-seeking female prisoners, affective psychopathic traits are a robust predictor of future prison violence even while controlling for past violent history (Thomson et al., 2016; Richards et al., 2003). However, recent evidence from Warren and colleagues (2017) has suggested that different measures of prison violence, such as official records of institutional violence versus self-report, may be differently related to psychopathy, which could explain some of the mixed findings. For instance, any report of violence (including self-report and institutional records) is associated with factor 1 and factor 2 for both male and female prisoners (Warren et al., 2017). However, using just institutional records of violence for men, only factor 2 predicted prison violence, whereas self-report violence was related to all facets and total score of psychopathy. In contrast, comparing self-report and institutional records of prison violence were more consistent for female offenders, with total scores and factor 2 predicting both self-report and institutional records. There are several possibilities for the different findings between Warren et al. (2017) and Thomson et al. (2016). Firstly, Thomson et al. (2016) used a self-report measure of psychopathy to prospectively predict institutional records of violence, whereas Warren et al. (2017) used the PCL-R to predict dichotomous prison violence (0 = no, 1 = yes). Therefore, it may be that those who engage in chronic prison violence, violence that continues over a period of time, are more callous than women who perpetrate less frequent prison violence (Thomson et al., 2016). Instead, those who engage in any level of violence are more likely to have higher levels of antisocial psychopathic traits. It is also important to note that Warren and colleagues tested the two-factor model, whereas Thomson et al. (2016) tested the three-facet model. Using the three-facet model,

Thomson et al. did not find interpersonal psychopathic traits to predict prison violence. Thus, combing interpersonal psychopathic traits with affective psychopathic traits may diminish any association between the personality features of psychopathy and prison violence in women.

Results from forensic inpatients using the PCL-R demonstrate a clear link between psychopathy scores and inpatient violence (de Vries Robbé, de Vogel, Wever, Douglas & Nijman, 2016; Heilbrun et al., 1998; Hildebrand, De Ruiter & Nijman, 2004). De Vogel and de Ruiter (2005) compared the PCL-R two-factor model for predicting violence in male and female Dutch forensic inpatients. The authors found psychopathy was not predictive for their female sample, but total PCL-R and factor 2 scores predicted inpatient violence for men. More recently, de Vogel and Lancel (2016) compared a larger sample of men and women from a Dutch inpatient setting and found female violence during treatment was predicted by total PCL-R scores, and the Lifestyle and Antisocial facets, but not the Interpersonal or Affective facets, whereas all facets predicted inpatient violence for men.

In contrast to this, in the UK, Langton and colleagues (2011) found factor 1 and the Interpersonal and Affective facets were predictors of interpersonal physical aggression for personality disordered male offenders. In a large sample of US inpatients, McDermott and colleagues (2008) reported that prospective incidents of predatory aggression were predicted by the Interpersonal and Lifestyle facets. Using the Psychopathic Personality Inventory – Revised (PPI-R), Smith, Edens and McDermott (2013) showed both factors, Fearless Dominance and Impulsive-Antisociality, predicted predatory inpatient aggression, but did not predict impulsive or psychotic aggression. The authors found the combination of the two PPI-R subscales drastically improved the prediction of predatory inpatient aggression. In sum, the link between psychopathy and inpatient violence is clearly strong, and the construct of psychopathy is an important risk assessment measure. However, there are a lot of mixed findings, with some studies showing the personality features of psychopathy as robust predictors of institutional violence, while others only find this association for the lifestyle and antisocial features.

Violent recidivism

Once released from prison, psychopathic traits in men and women continue to predict violent behavior in the community (Dhingra & Boduszek, 2013). Coid and colleagues (2009) assessed the predictive ability of psychopathy for violent reconviction rates among 1,353 male and 304 female released prisoners. The authors found psychopathy was a reliable predictor of violent reconviction. Factor 1 showed good predictive ability for violent re-offending for women, but it was not predictive for men. Factor 2 was predictive of violent re-offending for both men and women. Using a post-release sample of male and female former inpatients, Gray and Snowden (2016) found violent recidivism within a year of release was predicted by both factor 1 and and factor 2 for men and women.

Using the Comprehensive Assessment of Psychopathic Personality (CAPP) in a sample of male ex-offenders, Pedersen, Kunz, Rasmussen and Elsass (2010) found violent recidivism (within a 6-year period) was predicted by total CAPP scores as well as four of the six domains – Attachment, Behavioral, Dominance and Emotionality. The domains that did not predict violent recidivism were Cognitive and Self, whereas non-violent recidivism was predicted by all six domains. Thus, for former prisoners and inpatients, men and women with psychopathic traits are at a significant risk for violent re-offending.

Subtypes of aggression

Reactive aggression is characterized as an intense response to provocation or threat and may be perceived as being "hot headed" because there is a loss of emotional and behavioral control (Barratt, 1991; Berkowitz, 1993). Reactive aggression can best be understood by the frustration-anger theory of aggression (see Berkowitz, 1993; Dollard, Miller, Doob, Mowrer & Sears, 1939). Thus, if an individual perceives a threat, feels provoked or is frustrated, then she may respond with anger. This response induces autonomic reactivity, which prepares the body to deal with the situation, via fight, flight or freeze responses. Reactive aggression does not always manifest in violence; it could take the form of verbal abuse, intimidation or threats. It is important to recognize that reactive aggression may be advantageous in certain circumstances – from an evolutionary perspective reactive aggression may have offered an advantage when dealing with a legitimate and immediate threat. However, reactive aggression is most often studied as a function of maladaptive behavior, such that the response is above and beyond what is needed for the situation. Prior research has suggested that reactive aggression results from problems with social information processing (Crick & Dodge, 1996; Dodge et al., 2015). Crick and Dodge (1996) proposed that the social information processing model includes five stages: (i) encoding of cues, (ii) interpretation of cues, (iii) clarification of goals, (iv) access of responses and (v) response decision. Reactive aggression is thought to stem from problems in the first two stages of social information processing: encoding of cues and interpretation of cues (Crick & Dodge, 1996; Schwartz et al., 1998).

In contrast, proactive aggression is defined by aggression that is "cold-blooded", predatory and used for personal gain, such as physical (e.g., financial), social (e.g., dominance), or psychological goals (e.g., feeling superior). Deviant social decision-making, which is further down the social-information processing stream, is considered central to why individuals engage in proactive aggression (Crick & Dodge, 1994, 1996). In line with Bandura's (1973) social learning theory, proactive aggression may be learned through reinforcement of one's own behavior and by observing others (Huesmann, 1998). A child who intimidates others to achieve a reward (e.g., monetary gain, getting a toy) is reinforced by the positive outcome, which strengthens the negative behavior for many years to come.

Because proactive aggression resembles many characteristics within the construct of psychopathy, such as a willingness to hurt others for personal gain, the two constructs share many overlapping risk factors (e.g., hypoarousal to threat, low anxiety, positive appraisal of aggression). Thus, there is a strong link between psychopathic traits and proactive aggression. In a sample of 121 male offenders, Cima and Raine (2009) reported total scores of psychopathic traits on the PPI-R predicted proactive aggression but not reactive aggression. Assessing the two-factor structure of the PPI-R, Fearless-Dominance and Impulsive-Antisociality predicted proactive aggression, whereas only Impulsive-Antisociality was associated with reactive aggression. Using two samples of violent offenders (pretrial and sentenced inmates), Cornell and colleagues (1996) found offenders whose violent crime was proactive had higher psychopathy scores using the PCL-R than those whose violent crime was reactive. Declercq, Willemsen, Audenaert and Verhaeghe (2012) found in their male offender sample that the Interpersonal facet was the best predictor of predatory violence, while the Antisocial facet was related to less predatory violence and planning. Indeed, Woodworth and Porter (2002) found homicides committed by psychopaths were more often (93.3%) proactive than reactive.

Studies of child and adolescent samples have begun to use person-centered analysis to explore the link between aggression subtypes and psychopathic traits. These studies demonstrate that there are typically three types of aggressors – low aggressors, reactive-only aggressors, and a group who commit high levels of both reactive and proactive aggression (termed the mixed group). Person-centered methods have shown that purely proactive aggressors are rare (Vitaro & Brendgen, 2005, p. 190), and instead, individuals who display high levels of proactive aggression also show high levels of reactive aggression (Centifanti, Fanti, Thomson, Demetriou & Anastassiou-Hadjicharalambous, 2015; Marsee et al., 2014; Muñoz, Frick, Kimonis & Aucoin, 2008; Thomson & Centifanti, 2018). In these studies, the mixed group is typically found to have higher levels of psychopathic traits. Experimental studies have found when young adults with high psychopathic traits were physically provoked by a loud blast of white noise, they responded with high levels of reactive aggression, as well as high levels of aggression without provocation (Jones & Paulhus, 2010). Therefore, as with other forms of violent offending, individuals high on psychopathic traits are less discriminant in their use of aggression, engaging in multiple forms across contexts, including aggression used for their own personal gain and in response to provocation.

Summary

Psychopathic traits increase the risk of multiple forms of violence and aggression across many contexts. However, this association has its limits, as the association between psychopathic traits and homicide convictions is tenuous. However, that does not mean psychopaths do not commit homicide. Psychopaths who do kill commit their crimes more dispassionately and with instrumentality, and more often than not the instrumentality is for hedonistic pleasure. The construct of psychopathy includes criminal versatility, and indeed individuals with high levels psychopathic traits do demonstrate versatility in their violent behavior.

Psychopaths do not discriminate who they hurt, and they are more likely to fall into the "mixed" sexual offender group because they sexually assault both children and adults, and are more likely to physical harm both family members and strangers. Even under tight control, psychopaths continue to wreak havoc by perpetrating violence during incarceration and while receiving treatment in inpatient settings. After being "reformed" and completing their prison sentence, male and female psychopaths continue to pose high risk for violent reoffending while in the community. At the dimensional level of psychopathy, there are mixed findings depending on the population being assessed and the context. However, the most consistent findings between samples and context is that affective and antisocial psychopathic traits are important predictors of violence. Psychopaths are opportunistic in their violence, and given that people with high levels of psychopathic traits are better able to identify vulnerable people simply by the way they walk (Ritchie, Blais, Forth & Book, 2018), psychopathy can be considered the most dangerous disorder.

Acknowledgments

Thank you to Dr. Matt DeLisi and Dr. Dennis Reidy for their valuable contribution to this chapter. Dr. DeLisi is Professor and Coordinator of Criminal Justice Studies in the Department of Sociology and Faculty Affiliate for the Study of Violence at Iowa State University. Dr. DeLisi serves as the Editor-in-Chief for the *Journal of Criminal Justice*, and his research specialty includes psychopathy, crime, genetics of antisocial behavior, and offender/inmate behavior. Dr. Reidy is an Assistant Professor of Health Promotion & Behavior in the School of Public Health at Georgia State University. Formerly, Dr. Reidy worked as a scientist in the Division of Violence Prevention at the Centers for Disease Control and Prevention. His research focuses on informing, developing, and evaluating innovative interventions to prevent violence and associated delinquency outcomes, and promote health and well-being.

References

Aharoni, E. & Kiehl, K. A. (2013). Evading Justice. *Criminal Justice and Behavior*, 40(6), 629–645.
Bandura, A. (1973). *Aggression: A Social Learning Analysis*. Oxford: Prentice-Hall.
Barratt, E. S. (1991). Measuring and Predicting Aggression within the Context of a Personality Theory. *The Journal of Neuropsychiatry and Clinical Neurosciences*, 3(2), S35–S39.
Berkowitz, L. (1993). *Aggression: Its Causes, Consequences, and Control*. New York: McGraw-Hill.
Boduszek, D., Debowska, A. & Willmott, D. (2017). Latent Profile Analysis of Psychopathic Traits among Homicide, General Violent, Property, and White-Collar Offenders. *Journal of Criminal Justice*, 51, 17–23.
Brown, A. R., Dargis, M. A., Mattern, A. C., Tsonis, M. A. & Newman, J. P. (2015). Elevated Psychopathy Scores Among Mixed Sexual Offenders: Replication and Extension. *Criminal Justice and Behavior*, 42(10), 1032–1044.

Bureau of Justice Statistics. (2017). Violent Crime. Retrieved from www.bjs.gov/index.cfm?ty=tp&tid=31

Cale, J., Lussier, P., McCuish, E. & Corrado, R. (2015). The Prevalence of Psychopathic Personality Disturbances among Incarcerated Youth: Comparing Serious, Chronic, Violent and Sex Offenders. *Journal of Criminal Justice*, *43*(4), 337–344.

Casey, H., Rogers, R. D., Burns, T. & Yiend, J. (2013). Emotion Regulation in Psychopathy. *Biological Psychology*, *92*(3), 541–548.

Centers for Disease Control and Prevention. (2017). National Intimate Partner and Sexual Violence Survey. Retrieved from www.cdc.gov/violenceprevention/nisvs/summaryreports.html

Centifanti, L. C., Fanti, K. A., Thomson, N. D., Demetriou, V. & Anastassiou-Hadjicharalambous, X. (2015). Types of Relational Aggression in Girls Are Differentiated by Callous-Unemotional Traits, Peers and Parental Overcontrol. *Behavioral Sciences (Basel, Switzerland)*, *5*(4), 518–536.

Centifanti, L., Thomson, N. D. & Kwok, A. H. (2015). Identifying the Manipulative Mating Methods Associated with Psychopathic traits and BPD Features. *Journal of Personality Disorders*, *30*(6).

Chakhssi, F., Kersten, T., de Ruiter, C. & Bernstein, D. P. (2014). Treating the Untreatable: A Single Case Study of a Psychopathic Inpatient Treated with Schema Therapy. *Psychotherapy*, *51*(3), 447–461.

Cima, M. & Raine, A. (2009). Distinct Characteristics of Psychopathy Relate to Different Subtypes of Aggression. *Personality and Individual Differences*, *47*(8), 835–840.

Coid, J., Yang, M., Ullrich, S., Zhang, T., Sizmur, S., Roberts, C., . . . Rogers, R. D. (2009). Gender Differences in Structured Risk Assessment: Comparing the Accuracy of Five Instruments. *Journal of Consulting and Clinical Psychology*, *77*(2), 337–348.

Cope, L. M., Ermer, E., Gaudet, L. M., Steele, V. R., Eckhardt, A. L., Arbabshirani, M. R., . . . Kiehl, K. A. (2014). Abnormal Brain Structure in Youth Who Commit Homicide. *NeuroImage: Clinical*, *4*, 800–807.

Cornell, D. G., Warren, J., Hawk, G., Stafford, E., Oram, G. & Pine, D. (1996). Psychopathy in Instrumental and Reactive Violent Offenders. *Journal of Consulting and Clinical Psychology*, *64*(4), 783–790.

Crick, N. R. & Dodge, K. A. (1994). A Review and Reformulation of Social Information-Processing Mechanisms in Children's Social Adjustment. *Psychological Bulletin*, *115*(1), 74–101.

Crick, N. R. & Dodge, K. A. (1996). Social Information-Processing Mechanisms in Reactive and Proactive Aggression. *Child Development*, *67*(3), 993–1002.

Crown Prosecution Service. (2017). Offences against the Person, Incorporating the Charging Standard. Retrieved from www.cps.gov.uk/legal-guidance/offences-against-person-incorporating-charging-standard

Cunha, O., Braga, T. & Gonçalves, R. A. (2018). Psychopathy and Intimate Partner Violence. *Journal of Interpersonal Violence*, 088626051875487.

De Vogel, V. & de Ruiter, C. (2005). The HCR-20 in Personality Disordered Female Offenders: A Comparison with a Matched Sample of Males. *Clinical Psychology & Psychotherapy: An International Journal of Theory & Practice*, *12*(3), 226–240.

De Vogel, V. & Lancel, M. (2016). Gender Differences in the Assessment and Manifestation of Psychopathy: Results from a Multicenter Study in Forensic Psychiatric Patients. *International Journal of Forensic Mental Health*, *15*(1), 97–110.

De Vogel, V., Stam, J., Bouman, Y., Ter Horst, P. & Lancel, M. (2014). Violent Women: Results from a Dutch Multicentre Comparison Study into Characteristics of Female and Male Forensic Psychiatric Patients. Unpublished manuscript.

De Vries Robbé, M., de Vogel, V., Wever, E. C., Douglas, K. S. & Nijman, H. L. I. (2016). Risk and Protective Factors for Inpatient Aggression. *Criminal Justice and Behavior, 43*(10), 1364–1385.
Declercq, F., Willemsen, J., Audenaert, K. & Verhaeghe, P. (2012). Psychopathy and Predatory Violence in Homicide, Violent, and Sexual Offences: Factor and Facet Relations. *Legal and Criminological Psychology, 17*(1), 59–74.
DeLisi, M. (2016). *Psychopathy as Unified Theory of Crime*. New York: Palgrave Macmillan.
DeLisi, M., Reidy, D. E., Heirigs, M. H., Tostlebe, J. J. & Vaughn, M. G. (2017). Psychopathic Costs: A Monetization Study of the Fiscal Toll of Psychopathy Features among Institutionalized Delinquents. *Journal of Criminal Psychology, 8*(2), 112–124.
Dhingra, K. & Boduszek, D. (2013). Psychopathy and Criminal Behaviour: A Psychosocial Research Perspective. *Journal of Criminal Psychology, 3*(2), 83–107.
Dodge, K. A., Malone, P. S., Lansford, J. E., Sorbring, E., Skinner, A. T., Tapanya, S., . . . Pastorelli, C. (2015). Hostile Attributional Bias and Aggressive Behavior in Global Context. *Proceedings of the National Academy of Sciences of the United States of America, 112*(30), 9310–9315.
Dollard, J., Miller, N. E., Doob, L. W., Mowrer, O. H. & Sears, R. R. (1939). *Frustration and Aggression*. New Haven, CT: Yale University Press.
Edens, J. F., Poythress, N. G., Lilienfeld, S. O., Patrick, C. J. & Test, A. (2008). Further Evidence of the Divergent Correlates of the Psychopathic Personality Inventory Factors: Prediction of Institutional Misconduct among Male Prisoners. *Psychological Assessment, 20*(1), 86–91.
Gray, N. S. & Snowden, R. J. (2016). Psychopathy in Women: Prediction of Criminality and Violence in UK and USA Psychiatric Patients Resident in the Community. *Psychiatry Research, 237*, 339–343.
Haapasalo, J. (1994). Types of Offense among the Cleckley Psychopaths. *International Journal of Offender Therapy and Comparative Criminology, 38*(1), 59–67.
Hall, J. R., Benning, S. D. & Patrick, C. J. (2004). Criterion-Related Validity of the Three-Factor Model of Psychopathy. *Assessment, 11*(1), 4–16.
Hawes, S. W., Boccaccini, M. T. & Murrie, D. C. (2013). Psychopathy and the Combination of Psychopathy and Sexual Deviance as Predictors of Sexual Recidivism: Meta-analytic Findings Using the Psychopathy Checklist – Revised. *Psychological Assessment, 25*(1), 233–243.
Heilbrun, K., Hart, S. D., Hare, R. D., Gustafson, D., Nunez, C. & White, A. J. (1998). Inpatient and Postdischarge Aggression in Mentally Disordered Offenders. *Journal of Interpersonal Violence, 13*(4), 514–527.
Hildebrand, M., De Ruiter, C. & Nijman, H. (2004). PCL-R Psychopathy Predicts Disruptive Behavior Among Male Offenders in a Dutch Forensic Psychiatric Hospital. *Journal of Interpersonal Violence, 19*(1), 13–29.
Hoffmann, A. M. & Verona, E. (2018). Psychopathic Traits and Sexual Coercion Against Relationship Partners in Men and Women. *Journal of Interpersonal Violence*, 088626051875487.
Huesmann, L. R. (1998). The Role of Social Information Processing and Cognitive Schema in the Acquisition and Maintenance of Habitual Aggressive Behavior. In R. G. Geen & E. Donnerstein (Eds.), *Human Aggression: Theories, Research, and Implications for Social Policy* (pp. 73–109). San Diego, CA: Academic Press.
Jones, D. N. & Paulhus, D. L. (2010). Different Provocations Trigger Aggression in Narcissists and Psychopaths. *Social Psychological and Personality Science, 1*(1), 12–18.
Juodis, M., Starzomski, A., Porter, S. & Woodworth, M. (2014). A Comparison of Domestic and Non-Domestic Homicides: Further Evidence for Distinct Dynamics and Heterogeneity of Domestic Homicide Perpetrators. *Journal of Family Violence, 29*(3), 299–313.

Khan, R., Brewer, G., Kim, S. & Centifanti, L. (2017). Students, Sex, and Psychopathy: Borderline and Psychopathy Personality Traits Are Differently Related to Women and Men's Use of Sexual Coercion, Partner Poaching, and Promiscuity. *Personality and Individual Differences*, 107, 72–77.

Klein Tuente, S., de Vogel, V. & Stam, J. (2014). Exploring the Criminal Behavior of Women with Psychopathy: Results from a Multicenter Study into Psychopathy and Violent Offending in Female Forensic Psychiatric Patients. *International Journal of Forensic Mental Health*, 13(4), 311–322.

Krstic, S., Neumann, C. S., Roy, S., Robertson, C. A., Knight, R. A. & Hare, R. D. (2017). Using Latent Variable- and Person-Centered Approaches to Examine the Role of Psychopathic Traits in Sex Offenders. *Personality Disorders: Theory, Research, and Treatment*, 9(3), 207–216.

Langton, C. M., Hogue, T. E., Daffern, M., Mannion, A. & Howells, K. (2011). Personality Traits as Predictors of Inpatient Aggression in a High-Security Forensic Psychiatric Setting: Prospective Evaluation of the PCL-R and IPDE Dimension Ratings. *International Journal of Offender Therapy and Comparative Criminology*, 55(3), 392–415.

Mager, K. L., Bresin, K. & Verona, E. (2014). Gender, Psychopathy Factors, and Intimate Partner Violence. *Personality Disorders*, 5(3), 257–267.

Marsee, M. A., Frick, P. J., Barry, C. T., Kimonis, E. R., Muñoz Centifanti, L. C. & Aucoin, K. J. (2014). Profiles of the Forms and Functions of Self-Reported Aggression in Three Adolescent Samples. *Development and Psychopathology*, 26(3), 705–720.

McCuish, E. C., Corrado, R. R., Hart, S. D. & DeLisi, M. (2015). The Role of Symptoms of Psychopathy in Persistent Violence Over the Criminal Career into Full Adulthood. *Journal of Criminal Justice*, 43(4), 345–356.

McDermott, B. E., Quanbeck, C. D., Busse, D., Yastro, K. & Scott, C. L. (2008). The Accuracy of Risk Assessment Instruments in the Prediction of Impulsive versus Predatory Aggression. *Behavioral Sciences & the Law*, 26(6), 759–777.

Meloy, J. R. (2000). The Nature and Dynamics of Sexual Homicide: An Integrative Review. *Aggression and Violent Behavior*, 5(1), 1–22.

Ministry of Justice. (2013). *An Overview of Sexual Offending in England and Wales*.

Mouilso, E. R. & Calhoun, K. S. (2013). The Role of Rape Myth Acceptance and Psychopathy in Sexual Assault Perpetration. *Journal of Aggression, Maltreatment & Trauma*, 22(2), 159–174.

Muñoz, L. C., Frick, P. J., Kimonis, E. R. & Aucoin, K. J. (2008). Types of Aggression, Responsiveness to Provocation, and Callous-Unemotional Traits in Detained Adolescents. *Journal of Abnormal Child Psychology*, 36(1), 15–28.

Office for National Statistics. (2015). Crime in England and Wales: Year Ending June 2015. Retrieved from www.ons.gov.uk/peoplepopulationandcommunity/crimeandjustice/bulletins/crimeinenglandandwales/2015-10-15

Office for National Statistics. (2016). Intimate Personal Violence and Partner Abuse. Retrieved from www.ons.gov.uk/peoplepopulationandcommunity/crimeandjustice/compendium/focusonviolentcrimeandsexualoffences/yearendingmarch2015/chapter4intimatepersonalviolenceandpartnerabuse

Office for National Statistics. (2017a). Homicide. Retrieved from www.ons.gov.uk/peoplepopulationandcommunity/crimeandjustice/articles/homicideinenglandandwales/yearendingmarch2017

Office for National Statistics. (2017b). Overview of Violent Crime and Sexual Offences. Retrieved from www.ons.gov.uk/peoplepopulationandcommunity/crimeandjustice/compendium/focusonviolentcrimeandsexualoffences/yearendingmarch2016/overviewofviolentcrimeandsexualoffences

Okano, M., Langille, J. & Walsh, Z. (2016). Psychopathy, Alcohol Use, and Intimate Partner Violence: Evidence from Two Samples. *Law and Human Behavior*, *40*(5), 517–523.

Pajevic, M., Batinic, B. & Stevanovic, N. (2017). Subtypes of Homicide Offenders Based on Psychopathic Traits. *International Journal of Law and Psychiatry*, *55*, 45–53.

Parks, G. A. & Bard, D. E. (2006). Risk Factors for Adolescent Sex Offender Recidivism: Evaluation of Predictive Factors and Comparison of Three Groups Based Upon Victim Type. *Sexual Abuse: A Journal of Research and Treatment*, *18*(4), 319–342.

Pedersen, L., Kunz, C., Rasmussen, K. & Elsass, P. (2010). Psychopathy as a Risk Factor for Violent Recidivism: Investigating the Psychopathy Checklist Screening Version (PCL:SV) and the Comprehensive Assessment of Psychopathic Personality (CAPP) in a Forensic Psychiatric Setting. *International Journal of Forensic Mental Health*, *9*(4), 308–315.

Porter, S., Fairweather, D., Drugge, J., Herve, H., Birt, A. & Boer, D. P. (2000). Profiles of Psychopathy in Incarcerated Sexual Offenders. *Criminal Justice and Behavior*, *27*(2), 216–233.

Porter, S. & Woodworth, M. (2007). "I'm Sorry I Did it . . . but He Started it": A Comparison of the Official and Self-Reported Homicide Descriptions of Psychopaths and Non-psychopaths. *Law and Human Behavior*, *31*(1), 91–107.

Porter, S., Woodworth, M., Earle, J., Drugge, J. & Boer, D. (2003). Characteristics of Sexual Homicides Committed by Psychopathic and Nonpsychopathic Offenders. *Law and Human Behavior*, *27*(5), 459–470.

Reidy, D. E., Kearns, M. C. & DeGue, S. (2013). Reducing Psychopathic Violence: A Review of the Treatment Literature. *Aggression and Violent Behavior*, *18*(5), 527–538.

Reidy, D. E., Lilienfeld, S. O., Berke, D. S., Gentile, B. & Zeichner, A. (2016). Psychopathy Traits and Violent Assault among Men With and Without History of Arrest. *Journal of Interpersonal Violence*, 088626051666097.

Richards, H. J., Casey, J. O. & Lucente, S. W. (2003). Psychopathy and Treatment Response in Incarcerated Female Substance Abusers. *Criminal Justice and Behavior*, *30*(2), 251–276.

Ritchie, M. B., Blais, J., Forth, A. E. & Book, A. S. (2018). Identifying Vulnerability to Violence: The Role of Psychopathy and Gender. *Journal of Criminal Psychology*, *8*(2), 125–137.

Schrag, C. (1954). Leadership among Prison Inmates. *American Sociological Review*, *19*(1), 37.

Schwartz, D., Dodge, K. A., Coie, J. D., Hubbard, J. A., Cillessen, A. H., Lemerise, E. A. & Bateman, H. (1998). Social-Cognitive and Behavioral Correlates of Aggression and Victimization in Boys' Play Groups. *Journal of Abnormal Child Psychology*, *26*(6), 431–440.

Sherretts, N., Boduszek, D., Debowska, A. & Willmott, D. (2017). Comparison of Murderers with Recidivists and First Time Incarcerated Offenders from US Prisons on Psychopathy and Identity as a Criminal: An Exploratory Analysis. *Journal of Criminal Justice*, *51*, 89–92.

Smith, S. T., Edens, J. F. & McDermott, B. E. (2013). Fearless Dominance and Self-Centered Impulsivity Interact to Predict Predatory Aggression among Forensic Psychiatric Inpatients. *International Journal of Forensic Mental Health*, *12*(1), 33–41.

Spencer, J. (2016). Sentencing Remarks of Mr Justice Spencer. *The Queen v. James Fairweather*, Central Criminal Court, Judiciary of England and Wales.

Texas Health and Safety Code, §841.023 (2000). Texas Health and Safety Code, §841.*023*. Retrieved from www.statutes.legis.state.tx.us/Docs/HS/htm/HS.841.htm

Theobald, D., Farrington, D. P., Coid, J. W. & Piquero, A. R. (2016). Are Male Perpetrators of Intimate Partner Violence Different From Convicted Violent Offenders? Examination of Psychopathic Traits and Life Success in Males From a Community Survey. *Journal of Interpersonal Violence*, *31*(9), 1687–1718.

Thomson, N. D. (2017). An Exploratory Study of Female Psychopathy and Drug-Related Violent Crime. *Journal of Interpersonal Violence*, 088626051769087.

Thomson, N. D. (2018). Psychopathy and Violent Crime. In M. DeLisi (Ed.), *Routledge International Handbook of Psychopathy and Crime* (pp. 508–525). London: Routledge.

Thomson, N. D. & Centifanti, L. C. M. (2018). Proactive and Reactive Aggression Subgroups in Typically Developing Children: The Role of Executive Functioning, Psychophysiology, and Psychopathy. *Child Psychiatry & Human Development*, *49*(2), 197–208.

Thomson, N. D., Towl, G. J. & Centifanti, L. C. M. (2016). The Habitual Female Offender Inside: How Psychopathic Traits Predict Chronic Prison Violence. *Law and Human Behavior*, *40*(3).

Truman, J. L. & Morgan, R. E. (2016). Criminal Victimization, 2015. *Bureau of Justice Statistics*. Retrieved from www.bjs.gov/content/pub/pdf/cv15.pdf

UK Government. (1968). Theft Act 1968. Retrieved from www.legislation.gov.uk/ukpga/1968/60/crossheading/theft-robbery-burglary-etc

Vitaro, F. & Brendgen, M. (2005). Proactive and Reactive Aggression: A Developmental Perspective. In R. E. Tremblay, W. W. Hartup & J. Archer (Eds.), *Developmental Origins of Aggression* (pp. 178–201). New York: Guilford Press.

Walters, G. D. & Heilbrun, K. (2010). Violence Risk Assessment and Facet 4 of the Psychopathy Checklist: Predicting Institutional and Community Aggression in Two Forensic Samples. *Assessment*, *17*(2), 259–268.

Warren, J., South, S. C., Burnette, M. L., Rogers, A., Friend, R., Bale, R. & Van Patten, I. (2005). Understanding the Risk Factors for Violence and Criminality in Women: The Concurrent Validity of the PCL-R and HCR-20. *International Journal of Law and Psychiatry*, *28*(3), 269–289.

Warren, J., Wellbeloved-Stone, J. M., Dietz, P. E. & Millspaugh, S. B. (2017). Gender and Violence Risk Assessment in Prisons. *Psychological Services*, *15*(4), 543–552.

Willis, M., Birthrong, A., King, J. S., Nelson-Gray, R. O. & Latzman, R. D. (2017). Are Infidelity Tolerance and Rape Myth Acceptance Related Constructs? An Association Moderated by Psychopathy and Narcissism. *Personality and Individual Differences*, *117*, 230–235.

Woodworth, M. & Porter, S. (2002). In Cold Blood: Characteristics of Criminal Homicides as a Function of Psychopathy. *Journal of Abnormal Psychology*, *111*(3), 436–445.

World Health Organization. (2014). *Global Status Report on Violence Prevention, 2014*. Retrieved from www.who.int/violence_injury_prevention/violence/status_report/2014/en

4
GENETICS AND THE ENVIRONMENT

In 2007, Abdelmalek Bayout confessed to stabbing and killing Walter Felipe Novoa Perez because he had mocked Bayout for wearing eye makeup, which Bayout wore for religious reasons. After considering three psychiatric reports, the judge determined mental illness was a mitigating factor in the murder. Bayout was convicted and sentenced to just over nine years in prison, three years less than typical because of mental illness. However, in an Italian appeals court, Bayout underwent a further evaluation, which included brain scans and genetic testing. Both the scans and the genetic testing revealed abnormalities. Bayout was found to have a variant of the MAOA gene that encodes the neurotransmitter-metabolizing enzyme monoamine oxidase A (MAOA), which was suggested to place him at risk for violent behavior. In response to this evidence, Bayout's sentence was reduced further by one year. This court case sparked a great deal of debate about the ethical considerations of genetic research being used in court, including if, and to what extent, biological measures should be considered as a mitigating factor in the defense in court cases, and likewise for use by prosecutors. World-leading geneticist Professor Steve Jones of the University College of London stated, "90% of all murders are committed by people with a Y chromosome – males. Should we always give males a shorter sentence?" (Feresin, 2009). In actual fact, according to Professor Nita Farahany, a specialist in legal and ethical issues pertaining to behavioral genetics and neuroscience, geneticists are only able to characterize general population trends, and cannot use genetics data to explain an individual's behavior (ibid.).

The evidence presented in this chapter does not suggest an individual with a biological marker of psychopathy will be psychopathic; instead based on large population statistics we can draw inferences about the link between genetics and psychopathy. In general, research has provided compelling evidence that psychopathy is a disorder with a significant genetic basis, but as vital, this research also provides consistent support that environmental factors are as important in the development of psychopathy. Thus, starting the discussion on the role of the biopsychosocial approach to understand psychopathy is best illustrated by the evidence from genetics.

Behavioral genetics

The Human Genome Project estimates that humans have 20,000–25,000 genes. These genes are transmitted from parents to progeny; each individual inherits two copies of each gene, one from each parent. Most of the genome (~99%) is the same in all people, with less than 1% of the total being different. This 1% of our genetic makeup explains the individual differences between people. In order to understand the role of genetics in psychopathy, there are two fields of study – behavioral genetics and molecular genetics. Molecular genetics will be discussed later in this chapter. Most of what we know about the role of genes in psychopathy has come from behavioral genetics research. Behavioral geneticists seek to understand the relative contributions of genetic versus environmental factors to psychopathy by using twin, adoption and other genetically informative research designs. Differences and similarities between twins allow geneticists to estimate the extent to which genes and environmental influences contribute to the development of psychopathy. The basic premise of twin studies is that monozygotic (identical) twins share 100% of their genetic makeup. Thus, the 1% that differs from one individual to another in the general population is presumed to be the same in identical twins. This is because monozygotic twins develop from a single fertilized egg (zygote), which splits into two. By contrast, dizygotic (fraternal) twins share about 50% of the genes that explain individual differences, which is the same percentage as regular siblings. Dizygotic twins develop from two separate eggs, each fertilized by a different sperm cell. Twin studies operate under the presumption that monozygotic and dizygotic twins share largely the same environment during development; for example, both sets of twins share the same prenatal environment, are exposed to the same germs, eat the same food, and are raised by the same parent(s) or guardian(s) at the same time. Therefore, behavioral geneticists assume that both monozygotic and dizygotic twins share the same environment, as much as two people could.

Comparing the degree of similarity between twins of these two types can help to elucidate the role of genetics as compared to environmental influences in the development of psychopathic traits. If psychopathy were entirely due to genetics, we would expect two main patterns to emerge. First, identical twins should be mostly concordant for psychopathy. On the other hand, fraternal twins should be about 50% concordant for psychopathy. Thus, identical twins should have somewhat similar psychopathy levels, while fraternal should have different levels of psychopathy. If environmental factors were the sole determining factor in psychopathy, we would expect similar concordance for psychopathy in twins of both types, because they share the same environment. For example, if poor parenting practices contributed importantly to the development of psychopathy, both monozygotic and dizygotic twin pairs exposed to poor parenting practices would show similar levels of psychopathy.

There are two types of environmental influences, termed "shared" and "non-shared". Shared environmental influences comprise features of the environment that different children within a family experience (e.g., beliefs of the parents, socioeconomic status, general parenting style and parent personality), whereas non-shared environmental influences consist of features that are experienced uniquely by each child within a household (e.g., peers, immune system, birth order). However, it is important to recognize that different characteristics of children within a household may affect shared environmental influences, making them non-shared environmental influences. For example, a defiant twin may experience more conflict with parents, resulting in a combative parenting style, whereas a less dominant and shy twin in the same family may avoid confrontation which results in a different parenting approach. Therefore, while parenting may be considered a shared environmental influence, depending on the child's characteristics parenting style may be unique to a child and therefore non-shared.

Another methodology that behavioral geneticists use to assess the contributions of genetic and environmental influences to psychopathy is the adoption study approach. If an adopted child resembles their biological parents on psychopathy more than their adoptive parents, a strong heritable component of psychopathy can be inferred. In contrast, if the adopted child resembles their adoptive parents more than their biological parents on psychopathy, it can be inferred that environmental factors are crucial to the development of psychopathy. Another adoption study method is to compare adopted and non-adopted children within the same household. Similar levels of psychopathy between non-biological siblings would suggest a strong environmental influence. An even more refined methodology is to use a combined twin and adoption approach. This approach assesses identical twin pairs where one twin is adopted and the other remains in the biological parents' home. This provides for comparison of identical twins who are raised separately. If these twins exhibit similar levels of psychopathic behavior, genetics can be presumed to play an important role in the development of psychopathy. If the twins do not show similar levels of psychopathic behavior, then one can conclude that environmental effects have a significant role in the development of psychopathy. However, there are noteworthy limitations even with this sophisticated methodology. Adoptive parents are typically not assigned at random, and are often more wealthy, healthy and committed to raising a child. Further, adoption agencies will often seek to match children with parents who share similarities with the biological parents. Unfortunately, there are no adoption studies at this time in the field of psychopathy, and therefore the current review focuses exclusively on findings from twin and molecular genetic studies. The next section provides an overview of published twin studies grouped according to participant age levels, as there are notable differences in findings for toddlers as compared to older children and adolescents.

Twin studies and psychopathic traits in children

One of the youngest twin samples is from a study in Boston, which included 314 two-year-old twin pairs (Flom & Saudino, 2017). The aim of the study was to assess genetic and environmental contributions to the stability of Callous-Unemotional (CU) traits from aged 2–3 years. The study showed that CU traits were largely explained by genetic influences (72%) at the age of two years, continuing up to age 3 (65%). The remaining variance was explained by non-shared environmental influences at age 2 (28%) and 3 years (35%). The stability of CU traits from ages two to three was moderately due to genetics, and change in Callous-Unemotional traits was due to both genetics and non-shared environmental influences. However, statistical estimates indicated that about 50% of the genetic contribution to CU traits at aged two remained at age three, whereas 100% of the non-shared environmental influences were different from ages two to three. Thus, while genes appeared to account for a significant proportion of the stability in CU traits from infancy to early childhood, the genes associated with CU traits changed over time. This implication is that risk factors for psychopathic traits change during the early developmental period.

Although this study provides evidence for a moderate contribution of genetic influences to CU traits, environmental factors also played a significant role in alteration of these traits across time. This is a promising finding, in that it suggests interventions at this early age may help curb the development of psychopathic traits and antisocial behavior in later childhood, adolescence, and even adulthood. Importantly, the authors of this report highlighted a need for research examining within-family differences for individual children to clarify the nature of non-shared risk factors contributing to CU traits. Interestingly, because this cohort of twins was young, many of the expected risk factors – such as different peers and teachers – did not apply, particularly at the earlier age (i.e., 2 years).

This raises the question of what child-specific environmental risk factors might be occurring at such a young age? A likely candidate is child-specific parenting styles. For instance, children higher on CU traits are likely to experience more negativity from parents (Fontaine, McCrory, Boivin, Moffitt & Viding, 2011). This may be the case for several reasons. Children with psychopathic traits may be more challenging to parents, given that they display a lack of emotional connection, act with less concern for others' feelings and engage in externalizing behaviors (e.g., defiant and rule-breaking acts). This may directly affect how parents manage a specific child. Interestingly, research has shown lower parental warmth in early childhood to be associated with high levels of CU traits at a later age. Moreover, the link between parental warmth and CU traits appears to be bidirectional: low parental warmth contributes to the development of CU traits, and high levels of CU traits decreases parental warmth (Waller et al., 2014, 2015).

As discussed in Chapter 2 of this volume, CU traits encompass the affective features of psychopathy in youth but do include other characteristic features. A recent study from Sweden assessed psychopathic traits using the Child Problematic

Traits Inventory (CPTI), which assesses psychopathy in terms of three symptom domains – Grandiose-Deceitfulness, Callous-Unemotionality and Impulsivity-Need for Stimulation (Tuvblad, Fanti, Andershed, Colins & Larsson, 2017). The sample for this study consisted of 1261 twin pairs, both boys and girls, assessed at age 5. Tuvblad and colleagues (ibid.) sought to understand how genetics and environmental factors contributed to the development of each of these symptom domains. The authors found no sex differences in the association between psychopathic traits and genetics and environmental influences, and thus their report focused on findings for the sample as a whole. The results indicated that genetics accounted for only a modest portion of variance in Callous-Unemotionality (25%), a moderate portion of variance in Grandiose-Deceitfulness (57%) traits, and a large portion of variance in Impulsivity-Need for Stimulation (74%). Along with genetic influences, shared environmental influences also contributed notably to Callous-Unemotionality (48%) and Grandiose-Deceitfulness (17%) traits, but only weakly to Impulsivity-Need for Stimulation (9%). Finally, non-shared environmental influences explained 27% of Callous-Unemotionality, 26% of Grandiose-Deceitfulness and 17% of Impulsivity-Need for Stimulation. In contrast with the Bostonian 2–3-year-old twin study, the affective-interpersonal features of psychopathy (Callous-Unemotionality and Grandiose-Deceitfulness) were explained by a fairly equal combination of genetic, shared and non-shared environmental factors, whereas the behavioral features (Impulsivity-Need for Stimulation) were largely explained by genetic and non-shared environmental factors.

These two twin studies, which focused on toddlers and young children, provide clear evidence for a genetic susceptibility to psychopathic traits; however, in both studies environmental factors also played a significant role. This highlights that psychopathy is not a purely biologically-based disorder. That is, the development of psychopathic traits, at least early in childhood, may be contingent on genetic and environmental factors, and the interactive effects of these. This supports the idea that a multidisciplinary approach is needed to fully understand the development of psychopathy, which can be achieved using the biopsychosocial model.

Turning to studies of older children, Viding, Blair, Moffitt and Plomin (2005) utilized data from the Twins Early Development Study (TEDS) in the UK to evaluate the contribution of genetic influences to CU traits with and without high levels of antisocial behavior, and high levels of antisocial behavior without CU traits in a representative sample of 7-year-old children. CU traits were measured using a combination of items from teacher-report versions of the Antisocial Process Screening Device (APSD) and the Strengths and Difficulties Questionnaire (SDQ). The authors found evidence for a strong contribution of genetic influences for children with high levels of CU traits. However, further differences emerged when considering antisocial behavior. That is, genetics evidenced an extremely high influence among children with high levels of both antisocial behavior and CU traits, with no contribution of shared environment. In contrast, evidence of moderate-level contributions of both genetic and shared environmental influences was found among children with high levels of antisocial behavior and low levels of

CU traits. Results from this study indicate a strong contribution of genetic influences to antisocial behavior when accompanied by high levels of CU traits and antisocial behavior.

Using a different measure of psychopathy, the Child Psychopathy Scale (CPS), Bezdjian, Raine, Baker and Lynam (2011) found comparable results in a community sample of 9- to 10-year-old twins and triplets ($n = 1,219$). That is, the Callous/Disinhibited factor of psychopathy showed an estimated heritability of ~60%, with non-shared environmental factors explaining the remaining variance.

Twin studies and psychopathic traits in adolescents

Drawing from a large child and adolescent sample (5–18 years), Fick, Dong and Waldman (2014) assessed the genetic and environmental contribution to psychopathic traits using the APSD, which includes three dimensions of psychopathy – Callous-Unemotional, Narcissism and Impulsivity. The authors found genetics and non-shared environmental influences moderately contributed to Callous-Unemotional and Narcissism, whereas shared environmental influences were modest for Callous-Unemotional and low for Narcissism. Impulsivity was largely explained by genetic influences, which is consistent with research in toddlers (see Tuvblad et al., 2017).

Many of the studies thus far have used various parent, teacher, or self-report measures of psychopathy. However, a study including adolescents (14–15 years), conducted by Tuvblad, Bezdjian, Raine and Baker (2014), used a multi-rater and multi-measure approach to assess psychopathic traits. The authors included child- and parent-report on the CPS and the APSD, as well as the Psychopathy Checklist: Youth Version (PCL:YV). Overall, the authors found less genetic influence for youth report of the CPS and ASPD (total and dimensional), when compared to parent report. Even so, the genetic and non-shared environmental influence each explained about half of the total scores of the CPS and ASPD. This is similar for each of the dimensions/facets on the CPS and ASPD, except genetics explained less than a third of the variance on the Narcissism dimension of the APSD child report. Shared environmental factors did not have any influence on self or teacher reports. In contrast, less genetic and greater non-shared environmental influence was found for the PCL:YV than for either parent or youth reports. The total PCL:YV score was explained by ~30% genetic and ~70% non-shared environmental factors. Each of the four facets was also largely explained by non-shared environmental factors: interpersonal (~82%), affective (~79%), behavioral (~68%) and antisocial (~19%). Shared environmental factors only contributed to the Interpersonal facet of the PCL:YV (~10%). This is interesting, given that the PCL is considered by some to be the "gold standard" for measuring psychopathic traits, and many parent–teacher reports are modeled after the PCL (i.e., APSD). Importantly, this research highlights two considerations: (1) the measure of psychopathy may impact the estimates of genetic and environmental influence, and (2) regardless of measurement or reporter, both genetics and environment play a significant role in total scores as well as the dimensional construct of psychopathy, albeit to different degrees.

Larsson, Andershed and Lichtenstein (2006) analyzed data for a self-report measure of psychopathy, the Youth Psychopathic Traits Inventory (YPI), in a sample consisting of 1090 twin adolescent pairs, aged 16–17 years. These authors found similar genetic influence for each of the dimensions, Callous-Unemotional (43%), Grandiose-Manipulative (51%) and Impulsive/Irresponsible (56%) with the remaining variance in each largely accounted for by non-shared environmental factors (44–57%). Thus, consistent with other informant reports (e.g., parent and teacher), environmental and genetics account for roughly equal variance in psychopathic traits.

Twin studies of psychopathic traits in adults

At this point in time, there are relatively few adult twin studies in the field of psychopathy. Much of the existing research extrapolates from criminality research or research testing the genetic contribution of Antisocial Personality Disorder (ASPD). Twin studies suggest genetics account for roughly 40–50% of the variance in ASPD. However, the existing twin research on psychopathy indicates that there is a stronger genetic influence on psychopathy than there is on ASPD, although environmental influences do make a substantial contribution to psychopathy in adulthood.

Blonigen, Carlson, Krueger and Patrick (2003) examined the genetic and environmental influences on psychopathic traits using the psychopathic personality inventory (PPI) in male adult twins. The PPI assesses psychopathy in terms of eight subscales. Genetics accounted for 47% of the explained variance on total PPI psychopathy scores, with the remaining 53% attributable to non-shared environmental influence. Genetics explained 29% in Machiavellian Egocentricity subscale of the PPI, 51% in the Fearlessness subscale, 38% in Coldheartedness, 50% in Impulsive Nonconformity, 38% in Carefree Nonplanfulness, 42% in Stress Immunity, 54% in Social Potency and 56% in Blame Externalizing. The remaining percentage of variance in each case was explained by non-shared environmental influences. In sum, the authors found that both genetics (29–56%) and non-shared environmental factors contributed to psychopathy scores. Consistent with older children and adolescents, the shared environment did not show a significant contribution.

Using the Multidimensional Personality Questionnaire (MPQ) to estimate dimensional scores on the PPI, Brook and colleagues (2010) found that genetic and environmental influences best explained both Fearless-Dominance and Impulsive-Antisociality dimensions of psychopathy. Specifically, Fearless-Dominance was equally influenced by both genetics and environmental factors, while Impulsive-Antisociality was influenced more by environmental factors than genetic. In two community samples, Finnish (Johansson et al., 2008) and North American (aged 17–92 years; Vernon, Villani, Vickers & Harris, 2008), total scores on the Self-Report Psychopathy Scale (SRP-III) were found to be explained predominantly by genetics (54% and 64%, respectively). In the North American sample, shared environmental factors explained only 4% of the variance in psychopathy, and did not contribute in the Finnish sample. Non-shared environmental factors explained the remaining variance (46% and 32%, respectively). Thus, cross-culturally, both genetics and non-shared environmental factors contribute to the etiology of psychopathy.

Sex differences in the genetic cause of psychopathy

There are several studies that have explored etiological differences for males and females in psychopathic traits. However, the research that is available from twin studies provides both support and disagreement that males and females share similar genetic and environmental contributions to psychopathy. Fontaine, Rijsdijk, McCrory and Viding (2010) assessed the stability of CU traits (a combination scale of the Callousness facet of the APSD and four items from the SDQ) over a 5-year period (ages 7–12 years). The authors found, compared to girls, boys whose CU traits remained stably high over the 5-year period were explained mostly by genetics (78%). In contrast, for girls, shared (75%) and non-shared (25%) environmental factors contributed to stably high CU traits. This is similar to the findings of Viding, Frick and Plomin (2007), who reported that shared environmental influences modestly contributed to CU traits in 7-year-old girls. Testing the two-factor model using the CPS in 9- and 10-year-olds, Bezdjian et al. (2011) found that boys and girls differed in the magnitude of genetic and non-shared environmental contribution to psychopathy. Genetics accounted for 64% of the explained variance in the Callous-Disinhibited factor for boys and 49% for girls, and 46% for boys and 58% for girls when explaining the Manipulative-Deceitful factor. The remaining variance was explained by non-shared environmental influences. Thus, in this sample, genetics mostly explained the Callous-Disinhibited factor for boys, whereas environmental factors and genetics were roughly equally important for explaining the Callous-Disinhibited factor for girls. In contrast, the opposite was found for the Manipulative-Deceitful factor: For girls, genetics explained most of the variance in the Manipulative-Deceitful factor, whereas these traits for boys was mostly explained by environmental factors.

In contrast, several other studies assessing the dimensional structure of psychopathy have demonstrated boys and girls, from toddler to late adolescence, show little to no difference in the genetic and environmental contribution to psychopathic traits (Forsman, Lichtenstein, Andershed & Larsson, 2008; Larsson et al., 2006; Tuvblad et al., 2017). One study by Ficks, Dong and Waldman (2014) found that non-shared environmental factors (e.g., peers) contributed to impulsive psychopathic traits in boys, but not for girls; otherwise they found no other sex differences were present for CU traits or narcissistic psychopathic traits. These authors concluded that the etiology of psychopathic traits is very similar for boys and girls. This statement has been corroborated using parent and child report psychopathy measures, as well as by research using the PCL:YV (Tuvblad et al., 2014).

In sum, although there is compelling evidence that males and females generally differ in levels and manifestation of psychopathic traits, the majority of research indicates that environmental and genetic etiological contribute similarly to psychopathic traits in males and females. However, sex differences are evident in the stability of CU traits from childhood to early adolescence. That is, for a child to remain high on CU traits into early adolescence, this is contingent on genetic factors for boys and environmental factors for girls.

Behavioral genetics: summary

This section of the chapter has reviewed twin studies that have evaluated the comparative contributions of hereditary and environment to psychopathic traits. As a whole, this research has yielded strong evidence that psychopathic traits, as a whole and at the level of subdimensions, are hereditary. The percentage of genetic contribution ranges from study to study (25–72%), likely due to methodological variation – such as the type of psychopathy scale used, the reporter of psychopathy (e.g., self-report, clinical assessment), participant age, and the inclusion of the dimensional construct of psychopathy. Nevertheless, there is a general consensus that genetics account for about half of the variance in psychopathy, with the remaining half of the variance attributable to environmental factors. Of these environmental factors, it appears that compared to shared environmental factors (e.g., SES), non-shared environmental factors (e.g., peers, child-specific parenting styles) explained the most variance in psychopathy, from study to study; however, some studies have reported evidence for a contribution of shared environmental factors (e.g., SES) to the development of psychopathy.

Further, individuals who exhibit more severe levels of psychopathic traits may be more genetically predisposed, resulting in greater stability of these traits during childhood and early adolescence. Even though there is corroboration that genes and environmental factors contribute in similar degrees to psychopathic traits in males and females, when considering those children who present more severe symptoms, sex differences do emerge. In particular, high levels of psychopathic traits that remain stable over time in girls seems to be more influenced by environmental factors, while for boys' this stability is largely influenced by genetics.

Overall, while the estimated level of genetic contribution to the development of psychopathic traits varies, across a range of 25–72%, depending on the dimension of psychopathy being examined, there is a general consensus that approximately 40–60% of the explained variance in psychopathy is accounted for by genetics. However, there has been some suggestion from the field of molecular genetics that twin studies may be overestimating the heritability of psychopathic traits (Viding et al., 2013, p. 2). Even so, it is clear that both genetic and environmental factors, as well as the interaction of the two, are pivotal in the development and stability of psychopathy. Indeed, then, research from behavioral geneticist provide a compelling endorsement of the biopsychosocial approach to understanding the etiology of psychopathy.

Molecular genetic studies

As described in the preceding section, genetics play a significant role in the development of psychopathy. However, the research presented so far does not provide information about which specific genes contribute to the development of psychopathy. It is important to note at the outset of this section that finding a single gene that causes psychopathy is unrealistic (Viding & McCrory, 2012). Instead, it is more likely that many genes affect specific characteristics and biological function, which may increase the risk of developing psychopathic traits. Historically, mapping genes to traits has used either linkage or association-based approaches. While linkage studies are well-suited to single gene (Mendelian) disorders, association-based methods are better suited for mapping genes for complex traits, such as psychopathy, that are influenced by multiple genes of small effect.

Association studies explore if there are differences in the frequencies of DNA polymorphisms (elements of DNA sequence that vary between individuals) for different groups on the outcome (e.g., psychopathic versus non-psychopathic). Association-based gene mapping of human complex traits began with a method known as the candidate gene approach. This method tests for effects of specific genes based on theoretical associations. For instance, a gene may be studied in relation to psychopathy because the gene has been linked to sensation-seeking, and sensation-seeking is a behavior observed in psychopathy. Another example may be that the gene may be involved in neurotransmitter pathways thought to be involved in mediating psychopathic behaviors. The advantage of the candidate gene approach is that results may be easier to interpret because the gene function is already known. However, this research is limited to exploring relations for known genes. In contrast, genome-wide association (GWA) studies scan hundreds of thousands or millions of markers across the entire genome and identify genes with nontrivial effects. Scanning such a large number of markers comes with a very substantial likelihood of Type I errors. Therefore, genome-wide significance for a marker is typically considered to be p-value $< 5 \times 10^{-8}$. This exploratory method means a priori expectation is not required, but the regions associated with the outcome may not have been well-studied previously and may require more work to fully interpret the findings.

Molecular genetics: genome-wide association

To date, there have been four GWA studies conducted in the field of psychopathy, all of which have come from the Twins Early Development Study (TEDS) in the UK. The first of these screened 642,432 autosomal single-nucleotide polymorphisms (SNPs) for allele frequency differences in two groups of youth who scored either high or low on both CU traits and antisocial behavior. The authors found no genome-wide significant results but identified 30 top-ranking SNPs that were nominally associated with psychopathic traits (Viding et al., 2010). Of these 30 SNPs, one located in the *ROBO2* gene has received particular attention. *ROBO2* is a neurodevelopmental gene, which, as the authors note, is interesting given considerable evidence indicating that youth and adults with psychopathic traits differ in their brain structure and function from youth and adults without psychopathic traits (Hare, 2017; Poeppl et al., 2017; Pu et al., 2017). Thus, the *ROBO2* gene may be a risk factor for the neurodevelopmental differences between those with psychopathic traits and those without – but this finding will require replication in an independent sample.

As well as conducting a GWA analysis, a second study by Viding et al. (2013) implemented a newer method called genome-wide complex trait analysis (GWCTA). The authors also used a twin study approach to assess the heritability of CU traits, making it possible to compare results between methods of behavioral and molecular genetics. Similar to prior research, the heritability estimate for CU traits was 64%, but the counterpart GWCTA estimate of heritability was much lower (7%). There are three plausible explanations for the large differences in heritability between twin studies and this GWCTA study. The first is that twin studies may over-estimate the heritability of psychopathic traits. The second is that GWCTA is limited to only additive effects of DNA, such that the explained missing hereditary effects could be explained by non-additive effects. However, Viding et al. (2013) concluded that this explanation was not supported because the results from the twins disproved it. Instead, the authors state that another possible explanation is that less common DNA variants explain the heritability gap. That is, rare variants not captured by GWA arrays may have a large effect on CU traits. However, at this stage, this remains speculative, and the authors go on to say that the challenges that lie ahead in identifying such DNA variants are much greater than that of most complex traits (ibid., p. 7). Further, rare variants require sequencing-based approaches to fully elucidate and there are challenges in how these should be analyzed.

The third study, conducted by Trzaskowski, Dale and Plomin (2013), also compared DNA and twin heritability estimates for childhood behavior problems, while not the primary aim of the study it did include total scores of psychopathic traits on the APSD. Findings related to teacher-reported psychopathic traits showed the heritability estimates from twins to be ~60%, compared to ~15% for GWCTA. Parent report evidenced even lower heritability estimates for twins (50%) and GWCTA (0%). The fourth study by Cheesman and colleagues (2017), conducted as a follow-up to the study by Trzaskowski et al. (2013) but with double the sample size (4,653 unrelated individuals and 4,724 twin pairs), found inconsistencies in the heritability estimates for psychopathic traits in twins (~45% to ~60%) and for GWCTA (<20%). In contrast to Viding et al. (2013), Trzaskowski et al., (2013) and Cheesman et al. (2017) interpreted their results as indicating that non-additive effects are most likely to explain the missing heritability between twin studies and GWCTA. For instance, twin studies capture rare alleles, gene-gene interactions, and gene-by-shared-environment interactions (Cheesman et al., 2017, p. 7), whereas GWCTA and GWA only account for additive effects. Again, these assumptions are speculative at present. In conclusion, Cheesman et al. (2017) noted that GWA studies will struggle to find gene variants relevant to behavior problems (including psychopathic traits) because GWA and SNP heritability are restricted to assessing additive effects of common variants (ibid., p. 7).

Molecular genetics: candidate genes

As stated above, candidate genes are selected by researchers because of prior expectations. Because a candidate gene has already been shown to relate to a trait or behavior (e.g., aggression), it is then hypothesized to be related to psychopathy. Therefore, research in this area has tended to focus on candidate genes associated with neurological function and antisocial behavior, characteristics known to be associated with psychopathy.

Of particular interest to researchers has been the examination of genes related to serotonergic and dopaminergic activity. The neurotransmission of dopamine through D2 receptors (DRD2) has been implicated in emotional, reward and stress processing. The *DRD2* gene is located on chromosome 11 (q22–q23) and is expressed in the prefrontal cortex and striatum (Peciña et al., 2013). Because of the link that DRD2 shows with reward and other emotional processing, and its association with aggressive behavior and psychopathology, it has become a popular candidate gene to study in psychopathy.

Drawing from the National Longitudinal Study of Adolescent Health, Wu and Barnes (2013) assessed the association between psychopathic traits and two dopamine receptor genes (*DRD1* and *DRD2*) and the dopamine transporter gene *DAT1*. Psychopathic traits were measured using the Five Factor Model (FFM), and the sample included both males ($n = 1,135$) and females ($n = 1,245$). Both dopamine receptor genes, *DRD1* and *DRD2*, emerged as significant predictors of total psychopathy scores, while the dopamine transporter gene was not significant. These significant associations remained after controlling for sex and ethnicity. In the same predictive model, the authors did not find sex predicted psychopathy. This is unusual as males typically score higher than females on psychopathic traits. It is unclear why sex was not a significant predictor of psychopathy in the study by Wu and Barnes. While it was not tested in the study, the order of analyses may suggest that when including dopamine receptor and transporter genes (*DRD1, DRD2* and *DAT1*) sex does not predict psychopathy. But this is speculative because of the limited information provided in the article. It should also be noted that none of these genes are on the sex chromosomes, therefore men and women should not differ in their allele frequencies on these markers, so it would be unclear why these would explain sex differences in psychopathy.

Hoenicka (2007) assessed the association between the TaqIA SNP and PCL-R scores in 137 alcoholic men. TaqIA is located near to the *DRD2* gene and has been extensively researched in addictive and antisocial behavior studies. TaqIA may serve as a vulnerability to impulsive and reward-induced behaviors, which is why it may be important for explaining psychopathy. In addition to TaqIA SNP, the study also included the genotyping of C385A FAAH SNP, the 10-repeat allele of a variable number tandem repeat (VNTR) of *SLC6A3* gene, and the 3′-UTR microsatellite of the cannabinoid receptor 1 *CNR1* gene (ibid., p. 53). There were no significant predictors for factor 2. However, factor 1 scores were predicted TaqI-A1+, FAAH A− and CNR1 S+. While each of these markers predicted factor 1 independently, collectively, they accounted for about 11% of the variance. Comparing the additive effect of the risk genotypes, the authors found people with a greater number of risk genotypes had incrementally higher factor 1 scores (e.g., no risk genotypes = 0.7; 1 risk genotypes = 0.7; 2 risk genotypes = 2.6; 3 risk genotypes = 3.8; 4 risk genotypes = 6.5). Interestingly, both TaqI-A1+ and FAAH A− predicted ASPD. Given the close association between factor 2 and ASPD, these null findings for factor 2 are surprising but suggest the two may be linked to different neural functioning.

Ponce et al. (2008) furthered the above study, by assessing the link between TaqI-A and C957T polymorphisms and psychopathic traits in 176 alcohol-dependent males and 150 controls. The authors found significant associations for CC genotype of the C957T *DRD2* SNP and psychopathy (PCL-R total and factor 1 and 2 scores). Similar to the study by Hoenicka (2007), TaqI-A1+ predicted higher factor 1 scores only. The authors further found TaqI-A of the *ANKK1* gene and the C957T of the *DRD2* gene are epistatically associated with psychopathic traits. Further, the two factors of psychopathy are able to be disentangled at the genetic level, with TaqI-A+ only being associated with factor 1. Further, additive (and interactive) genetic effects seem to be more strongly linked with the personality features of psychopathy (factor 1). It is important to note that the majority of these results have come from studies including treatment-seeking alcohol-dependent male samples. Therefore, the generalizability of these results may not extend to women, children and/or non-alcohol dependent males. Nevertheless, these studies have been pivotal in our early understanding of potential candidate genes in psychopathy.

Another gene, which has been widely studied in aggression research, is the MAOA gene. MAOA gene provides instructions for making monoamine oxidase A. This enzyme breaks down monoamine neurotransmitters, including serotonin, epinephrine, norepinephrine and dopamine. Researchers have categorized MAOA polymorphisms as low-activity (MAOA-L) or high-activity (MAOA-H) variants. Another neurotransmitter degradation enzyme is catechol-O-methyltransferase (COMT). In contrast, 5-HTT encodes the serotonin transporter, a membrane protein that transports serotonin from synaptic spaces to presynaptic neurons. Thus, 5-HTT terminates the action of serotonin, which means 5-HTT has an integral role in determining the duration and intensity of serotonin signaling in the brain. 5-HTT has been researched based on two variations, with a short and a long allele.

In a sample of 237 forensic males with a history of psychosocial adversity (e.g., childhood abuse, life stress), Sadeh, Javdani and Verona (2013) found MAOA-L was associated with Impulsive-Antisocial psychopathic traits on the PCL-SV two-factor model. Using the three-facet model, MAOA-L remained significantly associated with only the Lifestyle facet. In contrast, men with 5-HTT long allele demonstrated higher Interpersonal-Affective psychopathic traits on the two-factor model. Exploring the three-facet model, 5-HTT long allele was associated with high scores on the Affective facet. However, when the authors controlled for the non-significant factors of psychopathy, both of these associations disappeared. The authors suggest this may be due to a substantial overlap between the psychopathy factors and facets in how they relate to 5-HTT.

In a sample of adolescents aged 12–19 years diagnosed with Attention Deficit Disorder (ADHD), variants in genes encoding 5-HTT, as well as *MAOA* and *COMT* have been linked to affective features of psychopathy, as measured by the PCL:YV. These gene variants were selected because of prior research linking them to antisocial and aggressive behavior (Craig, 2007; Fowler et al., 2009; Retz, Retz-Junginger, Supprian, Thome & Rösler, 2004; Volavka, Bilder & Nolan, 2006). Fowler and colleagues (2009) found COMT was associated with both affective psychopathic traits and conduct disorder symptoms, whereas MAOA-L and 5-HTT long allele was only associated with affective psychopathic traits. As demonstrated in prior molecular studies, exploring the factor structure of psychopathy demonstrated personality features of psychopathy to be more often uniquely associated with genetic risk factors.

Similarly, a recent study by Brammer, Jezior and Lee (2016) found 5-HTT long allele was associated with psychopathic traits in children aged 5–9 years. This was specific to Callous-Unemotional and Narcissism dimensions on APSD. The authors found the Narcissism dimension mediated the association between 5-HTT and antisocial behavior. Further, the Narcissism dimension was found to mediate the association between 5-HTT and Oppositional Defiant Disorder (ODD) symptoms, but only for girls.

Somewhat different to these studies, Sadeh et al. (2010) found youth with homozygous 5-HTT short allele displayed higher levels of impulsive psychopathic traits, whereas youth who had homozygous long alleles and were raised in low socioeconomic environment displayed the highest levels of Callous-Unemotional traits and Narcissistic traits. This latter finding illustrates the importance of considering the gene–environment interaction to understand the development of psychopathic traits.

A final study involving two samples of children and adolescents (4–16 years) found variations of oxytocin (OXT) gene to be associated with the development of CU traits (Dadds et al., 2014a). OXT plays an integral role in prosocial behavior, including empathy, social cognition, group serving behaviors, theory of mind and trust (Bartz et al., 2010; DeLisi et al., 2016; Domes, Heinrichs, Michel, Berger & Herpertz, 2007; Gordon & Berson, 2018; Keech, Crowe & Hocking, 2018; Kosfeld, Heinrichs, Zak, Fischbacher & Fehr, 2005). Variations in the OXT receptor gene (OXTR) have been linked to high levels of CU traits in youth (Beitchman et al., 2012; Dadds et al., 2014b; Malik, Zai, Abu, Nowrouzi & Beitchman, 2012). Dadds and colleagues (2014a) found greater methylation of OXTR was linked to high levels of CU traits and conduct problems in adolescent males. Greater methylation is linked with lower circulating OXT, which may in turn functionally impair interpersonal empathy. It is important to note, methylation of genes can occur as a result of environmental stressors (Meaney & Szyf, 2005).

A chimpanzee perspective

Recently, studies have begun to examine the etiology of psychopathic traits in chimpanzees. Unlike other species, chimpanzees share many emotional processes with humans (Phillips et al., 2014), as well as sharing a large proportion of the same genes. As with humans, chimpanzees live in complex social environments that require important social cognition and behaviors (Latzman et al., 2016). Therefore, chimpanzees provide an exceptional animal model for understanding human emotion (ibid.). Latzman and colleagues (ibid.) developed and validated a chimpanzee version of a newer psychopathy inventory, the Triarchic Psychopathy Measure (TriPM), with the abbreviated name CHMP-Tri. As with the human TriPM inventory, the CHMP-Tri measures psychopathic traits in terms of three dimensions – Boldness, Meanness and Disinhibition. These dimensions are represented to varying degrees in all conceptualizations and measures of psychopathy (Patrick, Fowles & Krueger, 2009). The CHMP-Tri Boldness scale includes items such as "Daring, not restrained or tentative. Not timid, shy, or coy". The Meanness scale includes items such as "Overbearing and intimidating toward younger or lower ranking chimpanzees". The Disinhibition scale includes items like "Often displays spontaneous or sudden behavior" and "Acts inappropriately in a social setting". These traits were rated by chimp-colony staff members who had worked with chimpanzees for a substantial amount of time.

Using this CHMP-Tri measure, Latzman, Patrick and colleagues (2017) assessed the etiology of psychopathic traits in 178 socially housed chimpanzees through use of a genealogical analysis. As with humans, the authors found additive genetic and non-shared environmental factors contributed to individual differences in psychopathic traits (ibid.). Utilizing DNA samples collected from 164 of these chimpanzees, Latzman, Schapiro and Hopkins (2017) investigated how psychopathic traits were related to the influence of gene–environment associations, and (i) early social rearing experiences and (ii) genetic variation in the vasopressin Receptor 1A gene (*AVPR1A*). Vasopressin is a neuropeptide that is known to be associated with the development of socio-emotional behaviors. Interestingly, no association was found between AVPR1A and psychopathic traits for chimpanzees raised in a nursery. However, for chimpanzees raised by their biological mothers, there was a significant association between AVPR1A and Disinhibition, and sex-specific ways for Boldness and Meanness. These results suggest, in chimpanzees, that V1A receptor genotype variation plays a role in the development of psychopathy, but that this genetic disposition is dependent on early rearing conditions.

Molecular genetics: summary

While molecular genetic studies of psychopathy are in their infancy and face many challenges, the findings thus far have been promising in furthering our understanding of specific genes that contribute to the development of psychopathy. Several key findings have emerged, with some replication between studies that include different aged participants. Compared to twin studies, GWA studies have demonstrated much lower estimates of heritability, which suggests either twin studies have overestimated the heritability of psychopathic traits, or that psychopathic traits are best explained by the combination of additive effects, rare alleles, gene-gene interactions, and gene-by-shared-environment interactions. Research from candidate gene studies have found factor 1 to be most consistently related to the genes associated with neurological function, and this association appears stronger when assessing the additive effects of risky genes. The most consistent finding across samples has been for the homozygous 5-HTT long allele, which has been found to relate to personality features of psychopathy in children, adolescents (with ADHD) and adults. Interestingly, the association with CU traits in youth was also found to be contingent on a gene-environment interaction, whereby individuals with the 5-HTT long allele from low SES backgrounds displayed the highest levels of CU traits. The importance of the gene-environment interaction was also illustrated in nonhuman primates, whereby early upbringing interacted with AVPR1A in predicting psychopathic traits.

In sum, there is growing evidence that specific genes contribute to the development of psychopathic traits, but there is unlikely to be a distinct "psychopathic" gene. Instead, psychopathy is expected to develop because of a combination of genetic and environmental factors, which, individually and interactively, contribute to traits that collectively fit the model of psychopathy.

The biopsychosocial model: psychopathy, genetics and social influences

Genetics are considered the first stage in biology that determines individual differences in psychopathic traits (Glenn & Raine, 2014). It is also the first stage in human development that demonstrates that the biomedical approach is insufficient for fully understanding the development of psychopathy. Breaking psychopathy down to its most primitive form, genetic etiology, demonstrates genetics explain 40–60% of the disorder according to twin studies, but only 20% (at most) according to molecular genetic studies. Notably, twin studies have evidenced variation in this percentage depending on the age of participants, level of psychopathic symptomatology being measured (e.g., facet, factor, or total scores), modality of assessment (e.g., parent, self, teacher), and specific measurement instrument used (e.g., PPI, SPR, APSD, MMPI, FFM, YPI, CPI, CPS, ICU, PCL:SV). On one hand, the differences in explained variance between measures of psychopathy suggest we need to get more specific about unifying the constructs of psychopathy. But on the other hand, the fact that the majority of twin studies tend to gravitate towards 40–60% of the explained variance in psychopathy suggests there is a uniformity in the core construct, even from child to adult samples. Although it is commonplace to read disputes about constructs and measures of psychopathy, there are more similarities than differences between them, at least as they relate to the genetic and environmental origins of psychopathy.

Summary

As demonstrated by the research findings reviewed in this chapter, adopting a purely biological approach to understanding psychopathy will result in explaining only half the picture, or more specifically 40–60% of it. Thus, acknowledging the evidence, and integrating multidisciplinary research and practice, we can begin to formulate a more complete and nuanced model of the origins of psychopathy. The need for a biopsychosocial approach to the study of psychopathy is well illustrated by genetic research. We now appreciate that, at the very least, about half the variance in psychopathic traits can be explained by shared and non-shared environmental influences. Indeed, the majority of available research suggests non-shared environmental influences explain most of the environmental influences in the development of psychopathy (Waldman & Rhee, 2017). Non-shared influences may be driven by individual differences in the environment, such as different teachers, peers, parenting strategies, but they may also reflect biological and psychological differences too. Even so, we must recognize the existence of some evidence for shared factors as playing a role, particularly in early childhood. In addition, we must be open to the possibility of gene-environment interactive effects.

From these standpoints, use of the biopsychosocial approach to understanding psychopathy can allow researchers to explore, without boundaries, the influence of social and psychological factors, in conjunction with biological. Obviously, there is substantial overlap between the bio-, psycho- and sociological factors, which in itself highlights the suitability of the biopsychosocial model when studying disorders. Therefore, subsequent chapters of this volume provide coverage for each of these factors separately, but with the understanding that they overlap and interact with one another in important ways.

Acknowledgments

Thank you to Dr. Christopher Patrick and Dr. Joseph McClay for providing a valuable review of this chapter. Dr. Patrick is Professor of Clinical Psychology at Florida State University, and he is the Editor of the *Handbook of Psychopathy* (Guilford Press, 2018). Dr. Patrick is a Past President of both the Society for Scientific Study of Psychopathy and Society for Psychophysiological Research. Dr. Patrick's research expertise includes psychopathy, antisocial behavior, substance abuse, personality, fear and fearlessness, psychophysiology, and affective and cognitive neuroscience. Dr. McClay is Assistant Professor in the Department of Pharmacotherapy and Outcomes Science at Virginia Commonwealth University School of Pharmacy. His research focuses on translational genomic approaches to better understand and treat psychiatric disorders.

References

Bartz, J. A., Zaki, J., Bolger, N., Hollander, E., Ludwig, N. N., Kolevzon, A. & Ochsner, K. N. (2010). Oxytocin Selectively Improves Empathic Accuracy. *Psychological Science*, 21(10), 1426–1428.

Beitchman, J. H., Zai, C. C., Muir, K., Berall, L., Nowrouzi, B., Choi, E. & Kennedy, J. L. (2012). Childhood Aggression, Callous-Unemotional Traits and Oxytocin Genes. *European Child & Adolescent Psychiatry*, 21(3), 125–132.

Bezdjian, S., Raine, A., Baker, L. A. & Lynam, D. R. (2011). Psychopathic Personality in Children: Genetic and Environmental Contributions. *Psychological Medicine*, *41*(3), 589–600.

Blonigen, D. M., Carlson, S. R., Krueger, R. F. & Patrick, C. J. (2003). A Twin Study of Self-Reported Psychopathic Personality Traits. *Personality and Individual Differences*, *35*(1), 179–197.

Brammer, W. A., Jezior, K. L. & Lee, S. S. (2016). Psychopathic Traits Mediate the Association of Serotonin Transporter Genotype and Child Externalizing Behavior. *Aggressive Behavior*, *42*(5), 455–470.

Brook, M., Panizzon, M. S., Kosson, D. S., Sullivan, E. A., Lyons, M. J., Franz, C. E., . . . Kremen, W. S. (2010). Psychopathic Personality Traits in Middle-Aged Male Twins: A Behavior Genetic Investigation. *Journal of Personality Disorders*, *24*(4), 473–486.

Cheesman, R., Selzam, S., Ronald, A., Dale, P. S., McAdams, T. A., Eley, T. C. & Plomin, R. (2017). Childhood Behaviour Problems Show the Greatest Gap between DNA-Based and Twin Heritability. *Translational Psychiatry*, *7*(12), 1284.

Craig, I. W. (2007). The Importance of Stress and Genetic Variation in Human Aggression. *BioEssays*, *29*(3), 227–236.

Dadds, M. R., Moul, C., Cauchi, A., Dobson-Stone, C., Hawes, D. J., Brennan, J. & Ebstein, R. E. (2014a). Methylation of the Oxytocin Receptor Gene and Oxytocin Blood Levels in the Development of Psychopathy. *Development and Psychopathology*, *26*(1), 33–40.

Dadds, M. R., Moul, C., Cauchi, A., Dobson-Stone, C., Hawes, D. J., Brennan, J., . . . Ebstein, R. E. (2014b). Polymorphisms in the Oxytocin Receptor Gene are Associated with the Development of Psychopathy. *Development and Psychopathology*, *26*(1), 21–31.

DeLisi, M., Caropreso, D. E., Drury, A. J., Elbert, M. J., Evans, J. L., Heinrichs, T. & Tahja, K. M. (2016). The Dark Figure of Sexual Offending: New Evidence from Federal Sex Offenders. *Journal of Criminal Psychology*, *6*(1), 3–15.

Domes, G., Heinrichs, M., Michel, A., Berger, C. & Herpertz, S. C. (2007). Oxytocin Improves "Mind-Reading" in Humans. *Biological Psychiatry*, *61*(6), 731–733. Retrieved from www.sciencedirect.com/science/article/pii/S0006322306009395

Feresin, E. (2009). Lighter Sentence for Murderer with "Bad Genes". Retrieved from www.scientificamerican.com/article/lighter-sentence-for-murderer-

Ficks, C. A., Dong, L. & Waldman, I. D. (2014). Sex Differences in the Etiology of Psychopathic Traits in Youth. *Journal of Abnormal Psychology*, *123*(2), 406–411.

Flom, M. & Saudino, K. J. (2017). Callous–Unemotional Behaviors in Early Childhood: Genetic and Environmental Contributions to Stability and Change. *Development and Psychopathology*, *29*(04), 1227–1234.

Fontaine, N. M. G. G., McCrory, E. J. P., Boivin, M., Moffitt, T. E. & Viding, E. (2011). Predictors and Outcomes of Joint Trajectories of Callous–Unemotional Traits and Conduct Problems in Childhood. *Journal of Abnormal Psychology*, *120*(3), 730–742.

Fontaine, N. M. G., Rijsdijk, F. V., McCrory, E. J. P. & Viding, E. (2010). Etiology of Different Developmental Trajectories of Callous-Unemotional Traits. *Journal of the American Academy of Child & Adolescent Psychiatry*, *49*(7), 656–664.

Forsman, M., Lichtenstein, P., Andershed, H. & Larsson, H. (2008). Genetic Effects Explain the Stability of Psychopathic Personality from Mid- to Late Adolescence. *Journal of Abnormal Psychology*, *117*(3), 606–617.

Fowler, T., Langley, K., Rice, F., van den Bree, M. B. M., Ross, K., Wilkinson, L. S., . . . Thapar, A. (2009). Psychopathy Trait Scores in Adolescents with Childhood ADHD: The Contribution of Genotypes Affecting MAOA, 5HTT and COMT Activity. *Psychiatric Genetics*, *19*(6), 312–319.

Glenn, A. L. & Raine, A. (2014). *Psychopathy: An Introduction to Biological Findings and Their Implications*. New York: New York University Press.

Gordon, I. & Berson, Y. (2018). Oxytocin Modulates Charismatic Influence in Groups. *Journal of Experimental Psychology: General*, 147(1), 132–138.

Hare, R. D. (2017). A Person-Centered Approach to Research on the Nature and Meaning of Psychopathy–Brain Relations. *Biological Psychiatry: Cognitive Neuroscience and Neuroimaging*, 2(2), 111–112.

Hoenicka, J., Ponce, G., JiméNez-Arriero, M. A., Ampuero, I., RodríGuez-Jiménez, R., Rubio, G., . . . Palomo, T. (2007). Association in Alcoholic Patients between Psychopathic Traits and the Additive Effect Of Allelic Forms of theCNR1 and FAAH Endocannabinoid Genes, and the 3′ Region of the DRD2 Gene. *Neurotoxicity Research*, 11(1), 51–59.

Johansson, A., Santtila, P., Harlaar, N., von der Pahlen, B., Witting, K., Ålgars, M., . . . Sandnabba, N. K. (2008). Genetic Effects on Male Sexual Coercion. *Aggressive Behavior*, 34(2), 190–202.

Keech, B., Crowe, S. & Hocking, D. R. (2018). Intranasal Oxytocin, Social Cognition and Neurodevelopmental Disorders: A Meta-analysis. *Psychoneuroendocrinology*, 87, 9–19.

Kosfeld, M., Heinrichs, M., Zak, P. J., Fischbacher, U. & Fehr, E. (2005). Oxytocin Increases Trust in Humans. *Nature*, 435(7042), 673–676.

Larsson, H., Andershed, H. & Lichtenstein, P. (2006). A Genetic Factor Explains Most of the Variation in the Psychopathic Personality. *Journal of Abnormal Psychology*, 115(2), 221–230.

Latzman, R. D., Drislane, L. E., Hecht, L. K., Brislin, S. J., Patrick, C. J., Lilienfeld, S. O., . . . Hopkins, W. D. (2016). A Chimpanzee (*Pan Troglodytes*) Model of Triarchic Psychopathy Constructs. *Clinical Psychological Science*, 4(1), 50–66.

Latzman, R. D., Patrick, C. J., Freeman, H. D., Schapiro, S. J. & Hopkins, W. D. (2017). Etiology of Triarchic Psychopathy Dimensions in Chimpanzees (*Pan Troglodytes*). *Clinical Psychological Science*, 5(2), 341–354.

Latzman, R. D., Schapiro, S. J. & Hopkins, W. D. (2017). Triarchic Psychopathy Dimensions in Chimpanzees (*Pan Troglodytes*): Investigating Associations with Genetic Variation in the Vasopressin Receptor 1A Gene. *Frontiers in Neuroscience*, 11, 407.

Malik, A. I., Zai, C. C., Abu, Z., Nowrouzi, B. & Beitchman, J. H. (2012). The Role of Oxytocin and Oxytocin Receptor Gene Variants in Childhood-Onset Aggression. *Genes, Brain and Behavior*, 11(5), 545–551.

Meaney, M. J. & Szyf, M. (2005). Environmental Programming of Stress Responses through DNA Methylation: Life at the Interface between a Dynamic Environment and a Fixed Genome. *Dialogues in Clinical Neuroscience*, 7(2), 103–123.

Patrick, C. J., Fowles, D. C. & Krueger, R. F. (2009). Triarchic Conceptualization of Psychopathy: Developmental Origins of Disinhibition, Boldness, and Meanness. *Development and Psychopathology*, 21(3), 913.

Peciña, M., Mickey, B. J., Love, T., Wang, H., Langenecker, S. A., Hodgkinson, C., . . . Zubieta, J.-K. (2013). DRD2 Polymorphisms Modulate Reward and Emotion Processing, Dopamine Neurotransmission and Openness to Experience. *Cortex*, 49(3), 877–890.

Phillips, K. A., Bales, K. L., Capitanio, J. P., Conley, A., Czoty, P. W., 't Hart, B. A., . . . Voytko, M. Lou. (2014). Why Primate Models Matter. *American Journal of Primatology*, 76(9), 801–827.

Poeppl, T., Donges, M., Rupprecht, R., Fox, P., Laird, A., Bzdok, D., . . . Eickhoff, S. (2017). Meta-analysis of Aberrant Brain Activity in Psychopathy. *European Psychiatry*, 41, S349.

Ponce, G., Hoenicka, J., Jiménez-Arriero, M. A., Rodríguez-Jiménez, R., Aragüés, M., Martín-Suñé, N., . . . Palomo, T. (2008). DRD2 and ANKK1 Genotype in Alcohol-Dependent Patients with Psychopathic Traits: Association and Interaction Study. *British Journal of Psychiatry*, *193*(02), 121–125.

Pu, W., Luo, Q., Jiang, Y., Gao, Y., Ming, Q. & Yao, S. (2017). Alterations of Brain Functional Architecture Associated with Psychopathic Traits in Male Adolescents with Conduct Disorder. *Scientific Reports*, *7*(1), 11349.

Retz, W., Retz-Junginger, P., Supprian, T., Thome, J. & Rösler, M. (2004). Association of Serotonin Transporter Promoter Gene Polymorphism with Violence: Relation with Personality Disorders, Impulsivity, and Childhood ADHD Psychopathology. *Behavioral Sciences & the Law*, *22*(3), 415–425.

Sadeh, N., Javdani, S., Jackson, J. J., Reynolds, E. K., Potenza, M. N., Gelernter, J., Lejuez, C. W. & Verona, E. (2010). Serotonin Transporter Gene Associations with Psychopathic Traits in Youth Vary as a Function of Socioeconomic Resources. *Journal of Abnormal Psychology*, *119*(3), 604–609.

Sadeh, N., Javdani, S. & Verona, E. (2013). Analysis of Monoaminergic Genes, Childhood Abuse, and Dimensions of Psychopathy. *Journal of Abnormal Psychology*, *122*(1), 167–179.

Trzaskowski, M., Dale, P. S. & Plomin, R. (2013). No Genetic Influence for Childhood Behavior Problems from DNA Analysis. *Journal of the American Academy of Child and Adolescent Psychiatry*, *52*(10), 1048–1056.

Tuvblad, C., Bezdjian, S., Raine, A. & Baker, L. A. (2014). The Heritability of Psychopathic Personality in 14- to 15-Year-Old Twins: A Multirater, Multimeasure Approach. *Psychological Assessment*, *26*(3), 704–716.

Tuvblad, C., Fanti, K. A., Andershed, H., Colins, O. F. & Larsson, H. (2017). Psychopathic Personality Traits in 5-Year-Old Twins: The Importance of Genetic and Shared Environmental Influences. *European Child & Adolescent Psychiatry*, *26*(4), 469–479.

Vernon, P. A., Villani, V. C., Vickers, L. C. & Harris, J. A. (2008). A Behavioral Genetic Investigation of the Dark Triad and the Big 5. *Personality and Individual Differences*, *44*(2), 445–452.

Viding, E., Blair, R. J. R., Moffitt, T. E. & Plomin, R. (2005). Evidence for Substantial Genetic Risk for Psychopathy in 7-Year-Olds. *Journal of Child Psychology and Psychiatry, and Allied Disciplines*, *46*(6), 592–597.

Viding, E., Frick, P. J. & Plomin, R. (2007). Aetiology of the Relationship between Callous-Unemotional Traits and Conduct Problems in Childhood. *British Journal of Psychiatry*, *190*(S49), s33–s38.

Viding, E., Hanscombe, K. B., Curtis, C. J. C., Davis, O. S. P., Meaburn, E. L. & Plomin, R. (2010). In Search of Genes Associated with Risk for Psychopathic Tendencies in Children: A Two-Stage Genome-Wide Association Study of Pooled DNA. *Journal of Child Psychology and Psychiatry*, *51*(7), 780–788.

Viding, E. & McCrory, E. J. (2012). Genetic and Neurocognitive Contributions to the Development of Psychopathy. *Development and Psychopathology*, *24*(3), 969–983.

Viding, E., Price, T. S., Jaffee, S. R., Trzaskowski, M., Davis, O. S. P., Meaburn, E. L., . . . Plomin, R. (2013). Genetics of Callous-Unemotional Behavior in Children. *PloS One*, *8*(7), e65789.

Volavka, J., Bilder, R. & Nolan, K. (2006). Catecholamines and Aggression: The Role of COMT and MAO Polymorphisms. *Annals of the New York Academy of Sciences*, *1036*(1), 393–398.

Waldman, I. D. & Rhee, S. H. (2017). Genetic and Environmental Influences on Psychopathy and Antisocial Behavior. In C. J. Patrick (Ed.), *Handbook of psychopathy* (2nd ed., pp. 335–353). New York: Guilford Press.

Waller, R., Gardner, F., Shaw, D. S., Dishion, T. J., Wilson, M. N. & Hyde, L. W. (2015). Callous-Unemotional Behavior and Early-Childhood Onset of Behavior Problems: The Role of Parental Harshness and Warmth. *Journal of Clinical Child and Adolescent Psychology: The Official Journal for the Society of Clinical Child and Adolescent Psychology, American Psychological Association, Division 53, 44*(4), 655–667.

Waller, R., Gardner, F., Viding, E., Shaw, D. S., Dishion, T. J., Wilson, M. N. & Hyde, L. W. (2014). Bidirectional Associations between Parental Warmth, Callous Unemotional Behavior, and Behavior Problems in High-Risk Preschoolers. *Journal of Abnormal Child Psychology, 42*(8), 1275–1285.

Wu, T. & Barnes, J. C. (2013). Two Dopamine Receptor Genes (DRD2 and DRD4) Predict Psychopathic Personality Traits in a Sample of American Adults. *Journal of Criminal Justice, 41*(3), 188–195.

5
BIOLOGICAL FACTORS

The aim of this chapter is to provide an understanding of the biological characteristics of psychopathy. It is important to note early on in this chapter that there is no single biological cause of psychopathy, just like there is no single psychopathy gene. Instead, evidence from neuroscientists and biological psychologists show that psychopathy is related to a variety of biological vulnerabilities. This should not come as a surprise as the construct of psychopathy is made up of many similar and different symptoms, which is why psychopathy has become best understood by studying the dimensional construct to help delineate what specific psychopathic traits are related to. For instance, the Interpersonal-Affective (factor 1) features of psychopathy are typically related to low arousal and hypoactivity in the brain, yet Impulsive-Antisocial features (factor 2) are more often related to heightened physiological arousal and hyperactivity in the brain. Again, this should not come unexpectedly because the symptoms of factor 1 and factor 2 are different.

Because the field of psychopathy has moved towards studying the disorder as a dimensional construct we are able to identify overlapping biological factors with other disorders too. This suggests psychopathy, much like other disorders, are linked to multiple biological vulnerabilities based on the specific set of symptoms. For instance, aberrant resting activity of the parasympathetic nervous system (PNS) is linked to psychopathic traits in youth (Thomson & Centifanti, 2018) and adults (Thomson, Kiehl, & Bjork, 2019), as well as anxiety disorders (e.g., Thayer, Friedman & Borkovec, 1996), depression (e.g., Kemp, Quintana, Felmingham, Matthews & Jelinek, 2012), borderline personality (e.g., Koenig, Kemp, Feeling, Thayer & Kaess, 2016; Thomson & Beauchaine, 2018) and suicidality (e.g., Rottenberg, Wilhelm, Gross & Gotlib, 2002). Therefore, atypical PNS function is likely to be a biological vulnerability of common symptoms between these disorders, such as emotion regulation problems, rather than a biomarker for a specific disorder. Studying psychiatric disorders and psychological constructs using multiple forms of measures and a dimensional construct is consistent with the National Institute of Mental Health's (NIMH) Research Domain Criteria (RDoC) initiative, whereby multiple neurobiological systems interact to affect behavior. By studying these interactions across biopsychosocial indices, we are more likely to refine our understanding of psychopathy. In the same way that psychopathy is made up of a cluster of personality and behavioral traits, it is only reasonable to expect that psychopathy is made up by a host of biological factors, as well as social and psychological. This chapter will provide an overview of biological correlates of the unitary and dimensional construct of psychopathy in adults and youth, drawing from neuroimaging, endocrinology and psychophysiology research. The chapter will first discuss the neuroimaging research on brain structures and functions found to be implicated in people with psychopathic traits. Next, the link between psychophysiology and psychopathy research will be reviewed, and lastly an overview of hormones and psychopathy will be assessed.

Neuroimaging

Blair (2006, 2013) and Kiehl (2006) have paved the way in neuroimaging research, developing two neurobiological models of psychopathy. Both of these models suggest psychopathy is associated with dysfunction in the limbic system, which is a connecting network of brain structures that are involved in affect, emotions, motivation, long-term memory and olfaction. The limbic system plays an integral role in influencing the autonomic nervous system, which is discussed later in this chapter. Blair's (2013) integrated emotion system (IES) model places dysfunction of the amygdala at the center of psychopathy, which falls in line with Lykken's (1957) proposal that psychopaths are fearless. Amygdala dysfunction leads to impaired stimulus-reinforcement learning, as well as deficits in emotional and physiological responsiveness to the distress of other people. Blair proposes other brain regions are implicated too (e.g., ventromedial prefrontal cortex) but it is the amygdala that is central to the affective deficits of psychopathy. In contrast, Kiehl's (2006) paralimbic dysfunction model suggests psychopathy is related to a wider distribution of abnormalities and hypo-functioning in the brain (e.g., amygdala, insula, orbital frontal cortex, ventral striatum, anterior and posterior cingulate, superior temporal cortex and the hippocampus). Hypo-functioning in these brain regions have been found in psychopaths during attention and orienting as well as during affective processing (ibid.).

Prefrontal cortex

The prefrontal cortex (PFC) is a cortical area of the brain located in the anterior frontal lobe. The PFC plays an integral role in executive functions, such as planning, attention, problem-solving, cognitive flexibility, working memory and error-monitoring, as well as decision-making and social cognition. One of neuroscience's most famous cases is that of Phineas Gage. Working as a railroad foreman in 1848, Gage's tamping iron ignited the explosive powder, driving the 43 inch iron rod straight into his left cheek and through his skull landing 80 feet feet away, taking with it a significant proportion of Gage's medial PFC (Damasio, Grabowski, Frank, Galaburda & Damasio, 1994). Gage miraculously survived the accident. However, friends and family noted that Gage's personality had dramatically changed from a reliable, responsible and well-liked man to disrespectful and unpredictable. After the accident, Gage offended those around him with his profanity, and because he had no sense of responsibility following his accident he lost the trust of his employer and was sacked. In the words of his friends, "Gage was no longer Gage" (Harlow, 1868). Although it is not definitive that Gage became a psychopath, it is clear that Gage developed psychopathic behavioral tendencies. The term "pseudopsychopathy" was introduced to describe personality changes in patients following PFC damage, and falls in line with the changes seen in Gage (Blumer & Benson, 1975; Eslinger & Damasio, 1985; Koenigs, 2012). In the last 50 years, neuroscience has been conclusive that psychopathic traits are linked to abnormalities in the PFC, both functioning and structural. Structurally, psychopathy has been related to low grey matter volume (Contreras-Rodríguez et al., 2015; Müller et al., 2008; Yang et al., 2005), which may explain why psychopaths suffer from "poor behavioral controls" (Hare, 2003). A recent meta-analysis, which included 28 imaging studies, found psychopathy was repeatedly related to decreased activity in the PFC (i.e., dorsomedial prefrontal cortex, and bilateral and bilaterally in the lateral prefrontal cortex) and the amygdala. The key PFC regions discussed here are the ventromedial prefrontal cortex, the orbitofrontal cortex and the anterior cingulate cortex. Following on from the PFC, a review of the literature linking psychopathy to amygdala dysfunction will be conducted.

The ventromedial prefrontal cortex/orbitofrontal cortex

The vmPFC and orbitofrontal cortex (OFC) are often used interchangeably in research because the vmPFC overlaps with the OFC. The vmPFC is responsible for decision-making, moral reasoning, and is associated with fear extinction (Phelps et al., 2004). Using functional magnetic resonance imaging (fMRI), increased activation of the OFC (Ochsner et al., 2004)/vmPFC (Urry et al., 2006) is linked with decreased amygdala activity during emotion regulation (Morawetz, Bode, Baudewig & Heekeren, 2017). Thus, the OFC/vmPFC has an integral role in down-regulating neural responses in the amygdala, in response to emotional stimuli (ibid.). Research conducted by Damasio and colleagues have found damage to the vmPFC is linked to deficits of guilt, shame, empathy, and greater irritability and irresponsibility, including a failure to learn from punishment – all characteristics similar to those seen in psychopaths (Bechara, Tranel, Damasio & Damasio, 1996; Eslinger & Damasio, 1985; Koenigs, 2012).

Interestingly, patients with vmPFC damage demonstrate similar utilitarian moral and economic decision-making behaviors as prototypical low-anxious psychopaths (Koenigs, Kruepke & Newman, 2010; Koenigs, Kruepke, Zeier & Newman, 2012).

Based on these lesion studies, it seems that psychopathy is related to impairments in the vmPFC. In support of this view, fMRI research has found psychopathy to be related to reduced activity in the vmPFC during fear conditioning (Birbaumer et al., 2005), moral decision-making (Harenski, Harenski, Shane & Kiehl, 2010), and emotional processing (Kiehl et al., 2001). Assessing the interconnectivity between the vmPFC and other brain regions, psychopathic criminals show abnormal connective functioning between the vmPFC and the amygdala (Decety, Skelly, Yoder & Kiehl, 2014; Motzkin, Newman, Kiehl & Koenigs, 2011). This may suggest aberrant functional connectivity between the vmPFC and the amygdala could be a neurobiological mechanism behind psychopathic decision-making and socioemotional processing (Motzkin et al., 2011). Because the amygdala plays an integral role in signaling affective information from the environment, a deficient relay of information from the amygdala to the vmPFC may justify why psychopaths are unresponsive to punishment and unperturbed by other's distress (Decety, Skelly & Kiehl, 2013). However, many of the studies conducted to date do not show directionality between brain regions.

Anterior cingulate cortex

The anterior cingulate cortex (ACC) has been subdivided by functionality into ventral (affective) and dorsal (cognitive) regions (Cersosimo & Benarroch, 2013). These regions have different cytoarchitecture, connectivity and functions (Vogt, Vogt, Farber & Bush, 2005). Overall, the ACC is involved in emotion formation and processing, learning and memory. Compared to healthy controls, psychopathic criminals demonstrate reduced activity in the ACC (as well as the left amygdala, insula and OFC) during an aversive condition task (Birbaumer et al., 2005). Psychopaths also demonstrate less affect-related activity in the ACC (Kiehl et al., 2001). When choosing to defect and go against a confederate while playing the Prisoner's Dilemma game, people typically demonstrate increased activation of the rostral ACC (and dorsolateral PFC). These areas of the brain are involved in making tough personal moral decisions, especially if those decisions require violating the rights of others (Greene, Nystrom, Engell, Darley & Cohen, 2004). Interestingly, in a small sample of students, self-report psychopathic traits were linked to weaker activation in the ACC when choosing to go against a confederate in the Prisoner's Dilemma game (Rilling et al., 2007), suggesting people with psychopathic traits are unencumbered by the difficult decision to violate the rights of others.

Neuroimaging research on psychopathy is not all about deficits. A novel study by Bjork, Chen and Hommer (2012) recruited healthy participants from the community to test how psychopathic traits, measured by the Psychopathic Personality Inventory – Revised (PPI-R), were related to the neurocircuitry of incentivized behavior. The authors found higher levels of psychopathic traits were related to a faster reaction time to incentivized (money) targets, but not in reaction to non-incentivized targets. Also, psychopathy scores were positively correlated with recruitment of ventral striatum and ACC during reward instrumental anticipation. This research shows that psychopathic traits are related, neurobiologically, to reward sensitivity (ibid.). This coincides with research in youth with Callous-Unemotional (CU) traits, who are found to be less responsive to punishment and highly motivated by reward (Frick, Lilienfeld, Ellis, Loney & Silverthorn, 1999). Recent evidence by Ewbank and colleagues (2018) assessed the association between psychopathic traits and amygdala activity and effective connectivity when processing emotional faces. In their sample of 16–21-year-old males, the authors found reduced connectivity between the amygdala and ventral ACC when viewing angry faces compared to neutral faces. Passamonti et al. (2008) state the ACC sends proportionally more projections to the amygdala than it receives, and this direction of effect coincides with the role that the ventral ACC plays in the extinction of negative emotions (ibid., p. 568). Further, this neurobiological pathway is linked to emotional conflict resolution, suggesting a top-down regulation/inhibition (Etkin, Egner, Peraza, Kandel & Hirsch, 2006; Passamonti et al., 2008). Collectively, this may suggest psychopathy is related to a lack of communication between brain structures that facilitate top-down inhibition and emotional regulation. This indicates that while the amygdala is a key player in the affective dysfunction seen in psychopaths, it may not be the center of the dysfunction.

Amygdala

A deficient relay of information between the amygdala and the vmPFC and ACC may explain why psychopaths are less responsive to emotional stimuli. But researchers exploring amygdala activity have argued that the amygdala itself may be central to the emotional deficits seen in psychopaths. The amygdala is part of the limbic system and receives input from all senses. It plays an important role in the processing of emotions and emotional learning and is linked to fear and pleasure responses. A famous female patient, referred to as S.M., suffered from complete amygdala destruction as a result of a rare genetic disorder called Urbach-Wiethe disease. S.M. displayed very little fear during fear-inducing experiments and actual life-threatening events (e.g., held up at gunpoint, a victim of numerous violent and traumatic crimes). Similarly, psychopaths have been proposed as being fearless, and some evidence suggests this may be due, in part, to amygdala dysfunction and abnormal structure (Schultz, Balderston, Baskin-Sommers, Larson & Helmstetter, 2016). A case study evaluation of S.M. and her levels of psychopathic traits has recently been conducted by Lilienfeld and colleagues (2018). The authors assessed S.M.'s psychopathic traits using self-report measures – the Triarchic Psychopathy Measure (TriPM), Levenson Self-Report of Psychopathy Scale (LSRP) and the PPI-R. Overall, relative to a normative sample, S.M had significantly elevated scores but only on the PPI-R fearlessness scale, and none of the other dimensions of the three measures. This finding suggest that people who are fearless, by virtue of amygdala dysfunction, are not evidently psychopathic in the clinical sense, and are still highly capable of empathy, guilt and compassion for others (Lilienfeld et al., 2018). Instead, a more likely explanation is that lower fear (e.g., managing social situations) is a characteristic of psychopathy, but all those who are "fearless" are not psychopathic. Even though the discussion on fear and psychopathy has been longstanding and contentious, much more research is needed to determine if fearlessness and the amygdala underlie the psychopathic personality.

Nevertheless, research is fairly conclusive that psychopathy is related to atypical amygdala function and structure. A great deal of the research to date on functional connectivity and psychopathy comes from Professor Kiehl's lab, which has the world's largest neuroimaging database on prisoners. Early findings from Kiehl and colleagues (2011) finds psychopathy is linked to functional abnormalities in the amygdala when processing affective stimuli (Kiehl et al., 2001). More recently from Kiehl's lab, Espinoza and colleagues (2018) tested the functional network connectivity in a sample of 985 incarcerated males. The authors found resting state networks from the paralimbic system (the insula, anterior and posterior cingulate cortex, amygdala, orbital frontal cortex and superior temporal gyrus) were related to Psychopathy Checklist – Revised (PCL-R) factor 1 scores, but not factor 2 or total PCL-R scores. This study suggests the core personality features of psychopathy are linked to atypical functioning of brain regions beyond the amygdala, and instead these traits are linked to an overall paralimbic dysfunction.

In addition to functional deficits in the amygdala, structural research indicates reduced amygdala volume is related to psychopathy (Ermer, Cope, Nyalakanti, Calhoun & Kiehl, 2012). That is, psychopaths display reduced amygdala activity in response to affective stimuli. Although not synonymous with psychopathy, youth with CU traits have also been found to exhibit the same reduced amygdala response when imagining other people experiencing pain (Marsh et al., 2013) and viewing fearful facial expressions (Jones, Laurens, Herba, Barker & Viding, 2009). Further, Lozier and colleagues (2014) found the link between CU traits and goal-directed aggression (proactive aggression) was due, in part, to reduced amygdala reactivity to emotional distress cues in others. Therefore, while an average person experiences emotional/physiological discomfort when witnessing someone in distress, youth with CU traits do not get disturbed by the distress of others, possibly because of the hypo-reactivity of the amygdala.

The relationship between psychopathy and the amygdala has been found in longitudinal studies too. Pardini and colleagues (2014) assessed functional brain activity in a cohort of men at 26 years old to post-dict psychopathic traits during childhood. This sample of men was part of the Pittsburgh Youth Study, a longitudinal study that followed children from 7 years old into adulthood. The authors found lower amygdala volume at age 26 was related to higher levels of psychopathic traits (and aggression and violence) throughout childhood and into adulthood. This study suggests there is a developmental relationship between amygdala dysfunction and psychopathy; however, before this conclusion can be drawn prospective research is needed.

In sum, the neuroimaging research to date indicates that the amygdala plays an integral role in psychopathy, and so do several regions of the PFC. Yet, when considering the larger body of research, it seems the role of the amygdala and specific brain regions have a contributive role and one brain region (e.g., the amygdala) is not *the* underlying mechanism. Instead, and somewhat expectedly with complex personality disorders, which are shaped by a host of bio-behavioral and -interpersonal factors, psychopathy is likely to be explained by a collective system of integrated brain regions that are implicated in the job of emotion regulation, social cognition, threat perception/recognition, attention, decision-making and affective processing.

Autonomic nervous system

The autonomic nervous system (ANS) is part of the peripheral nervous system and regulates the functions of internal organs, including the heart, lungs and secretion glands. The ANS consists of three parts, the sympathetic nervous system (SNS), the parasympathetic nervous system (PNS) and enteric nervous system (ENS). The ENS is a system of neurons that controls the gastrointestinal tract and can act independently from the SNS and PNS. This section will focus entirely on the SNS and PNS, as they are popularly studied in conjunction with psychopathy and CU traits.

The primary aim of the SNS is to engage the fight-or-flight response to manage a situation by increasing the blood supply to the brain, heart and muscles. Although the SNS function is to manage emergency situations, the SNS will also engage because of social situations (e.g., giving a business presentation), and in situations where we know we are not in immediate danger (e.g., watching a horror movie). The SNS is popularly referred to as the bodily function that manages the fight or flight (and freeze) response. Although the SNS is imperative to how we deal with emergency situations, the SNS is always active even when we are not facing challenging situations. The SNS works in synchrony with the PNS to maintain a physiological balance in accordance to the person's environment. The PNS is responsible for the "rest-and-digest" stage. The most frequent measures of SNS activity are skin conductance and pre-ejection period. Skin conductance is also known as electrodermal response and galvanic skin response. When there is an increase in SNS, the body becomes prepared to deal with the arousing situation by increasing sweat production for sensory discrimination and thermoregulation. Increase in SNS is assessed by the increase in electrical conductance between two points. The hands and feet are considered the most sensitive places on the body to measure skin conductance. Thus, skin conductance is a measure of SNS activity from the skin. In contrast, pre-ejection period (PEP) is a cardiac measure of SNS. PEP is measured using the combination of electrocardiography and impedance cardiography. PEP is the time period from when the left ventricle of the heart generates force (or the interval from the onset of ventricular depolarization) through to the beginning of ejection (Fox, Schmidt, Henderson & Marshall, 2007). Shorter PEP indicates greater SNS activity. It is important to note that SNS measures from the skin (e.g., skin conductance) and the heart (e.g., PEP) may reflect different aspects of sympathetic activity, as they are two different organs being measured (de Geus, Gerssen-Goedhart & Willemsen, 2014).

Two frequent measures of parasympathetic activity are heart rate variability (HRV; the variation of time between heartbeats) and respiratory sinus arrhythmia (RSA; the variation of time between heartbeats occurring during the respiration cycle). For the most part autonomic activity is measured during two scenarios, ANS reactivity reflects physiological change because of situational context (e.g., stress induction, conditioning tasks), whereas resting states (also called baseline) marks a person's biological disposition to respond to the environment, internally and externally, prior to the occurrence of an event such as attention, emotion regulation and social communication.

There are several prominent theoretical explanations of the link between ANS activity and antisocial behavior, which may extend to psychopathic traits. The first theory is that physiological under-arousal may be an unpleasant state (Quay, 1965; Raine, 2002). Therefore, an under-aroused person may pursue risky behaviors to seek out stimulation to increase their physiological state to "normal" or "optimum" levels (Schechter, Brennan, Cunningham, Foster & Whitmore, 2012). Indeed, psychopathy is strongly linked to risk-taking and stimulation-seeking behaviors and physiological under-arousal, so this theory may extend to psychopathic traits. Next, according to Raine's (2013) fearlessness theory, being fearless increases the likelihood of engaging in violent and antisocial behavior because fearless people are less concerned with consequences and risks linked with antisocial behavior (e.g., being caught, physical injury). Fearlessness can be measured by low arousal of the ANS (Raine, 2005). Because fearlessness has been proposed to be a central feature of psychopathy, this theory may extend to predicting psychopathic traits. Indeed, the low fear hypothesis of psychopathy was first introduced by Lykken (1957), who suggested the underlying characteristic of psychopathy is a deficient emotional response to aversive stimuli (Fowles, 1983; Hare, 1965; Lykken, 1957). This theory is suggested to be supported by neuroimaging research showing psychopaths have low amygdala reactivity to aversive stimuli, and thus, indicating fearlessness. However, this theory conflicts with the dimensional construct of psychopathy. In fact, evidence suggests that factor 1, and not factor 2, is associated with abnormal response pattern associated with fearlessness (Patrick, 1994; Vaidyanathan, Hall, Patrick & Bernat, 2011). According to the dual pathway models of psychopathy (Fowles & Dindo, 2006), factor 1 is linked to fearlessness and associated with a pattern of hypo-reactivity to aversive-punitive stimuli. In contrast, factor 2 is associated with emotion dysregulation and externalizing proneness and hyper-reactivity (Fanti, 2018). Therefore, ANS fear reactivity seems to be differently related to factor 1 and factor 2 traits.

Another likely explanation of the ANS-psychopathy link is that dysfunctional ANS activity seen in psychopaths could be due to neurobiological dysfunction. For instance, the ACC (which is implicated in psychopaths; Kiehl et al., 2001) is interconnected with the insula, PFC, amygdala, hypothalamus and the brainstem, and via these interconnections the ACC manages the functions of SNS and PNS activity (see Cersosimo & Benarroch, 2013; Hurley, Herbert, Moga & Saper, 1991; Ter Horst, Hautvast, Jongste & Korf, 1996; Terreberry & Neafsey, 1987; Verberne

& Owens, 1998). Therefore, ANS activity and reactivity may serve as a peripheral biomarker for neurobiological function and dysfunction.

Heart rate

Heart rate is affected by three neural influences: the intrinsic pacemaker cells in the sinoatrial node, PNS fibers and SNS fibers (Levenson, 2014). Therefore, heart rate could be influenced by either parasympathetic or sympathetic arousal at any given time. This may be why the findings have been mixed, with some research finding a link between psychopathic traits and low resting heart rate (Kavish, Vaughn, et al., 2017) and others not (see Kavish, Fu, Vaughn, Qian & Boutwell, 2017; Lorber, 2004). However, it seems that low resting heart is most related to psychopathic-like behaviors, such as goal-directed aggression (Raine, Fung, Portnoy, Choy & Spring, 2014). Instead, specific measures of the SNS and PNS may be better suited for understanding ANS correlates of psychopathic personality.

Sympathetic nervous system

A meta-analysis conducted by Lorber (2004) found psychopathy was related to lower skin conductance level, suggesting individuals high on psychopathy tend to be fearless and less aroused to aversive stimuli. Blair, Jones, Clark and Smith (1997) found that compared to a control group, psychopaths (PCL-R > 30) had lower skin conductance response to distress cues, but did not differ when presented with threatening or neutral stimuli. At the factor level, differences do emerge. For instance, factor 1 is most related to diminished skin conductance response to aversive stimuli and fear induction (Benning, Patrick & Iacono, 2005; Dindo & Fowles, 2011; Kyranides, Fanti, Sikki & Patrick, 2017; López, Poy, Patrick & Moltó, 2013), which suggests the personality features of psychopathy are specifically related to low SNS reactivity to negative affect, threat and fear. In contrast, the link between skin conductance and factor 2 is less clear, with some research not finding the association, while others find greater skin conductance reactivity to aversive stimuli (Dindo & Fowles, 2011; Fanti et al., 2017; Kyranides et al., 2017; López et al., 2013). To complicate matters further, additional work has linked factor 2 with lower skin conductance response across a variety of stimuli (i.e., pleasant, neutral and aversive; Benning, Patrick, Blonigen, Hicks & Iacono, 2005; Patrick, Cuthbert & Lang, 1994; Verschuere, Crombez, De Clercq & Koster, 2005). Therefore, evidence linking skin conductance with factor 2 is much less clear compared to evidence associating this physiological response to factor 1. Nevertheless, taking all the research into account the findings suggest a specific hypoarousal threat profile for those people with high interpersonal-affective psychopathic traits, as indicated by low skin conductance response during aversive conditions. In youth, there is also a strong link between CU traits and low SNS reactivity in response to provocation (Kimonis et al., 2008) and while experiencing pain (Northover, Thapar, Langley

& van Goozen, 2015). Thus, the personality features of psychopathy are more consistently related to low SNS activity and arousal, and this can be seen in children, adolescents and adults.

Parasympathetic nervous system

The link between PNS activity and psychopathy is less clear, largely because there is not a great deal of research in adults. Based on research from other disciplines, optimal PNS levels (higher at rest, lower during stress induction) are related to positive outcomes, such as school performance, and better cognitive ability (Marcovitch et al., 2010). In contrast, atypical PNS functioning (e.g., low PNS at rest, high PNS during stress induction) is related to externalizing behaviors and disorders related to problems with emotion regulation (Beauchaine, 2015). Thus, in recent years RSA and HRV have become widely used as biological markers of vulnerability to emotion dysregulation. In theory, it would be expected that Interpersonal-Affective traits should be unrelated or positively related to PNS activity, as factor 1 traits are not characteristically "hot-headed" or suffer from the loss of emotional control, as seen in people with impulsive-antisocial traits. Therefore, the expected link would be between factor 2 and aberrant PNS functioning. However, these expectations have only been partly supported. In sample of adult prisoners, higher scores on the Interpersonal, Affective and the Antisocial facets of the PCL-R were positively related to higher levels of baseline HRV (Hansen, Johnsen, Thornton, Waage & Thayer, 2007). This suggests that those who had had higher PNS activity (thus, physiologically relaxed) had higher scores on the personality and antisocial features of psychopathy, yet the facet we would expect to be related to lower PNS activity, the Lifestyle facet, was unrelated. Similar to prisoners, Thomson, Kiehl and Bjork (2019) found young women with greater PNS activity at rest scored higher on the Affective facet on the Self-Report Psychopathy Scale (SRP). Collectively then, these two studies suggest affective psychopathic traits in forensic and non-clinical populations are associated with greater PNS activity while at rest, which suggests they are calmer and more relaxed.

These findings are somewhat consistent in youths. Gao, Huang and Li (2017) found CU traits in children was associated with higher PNS activity at rest. Relatedly, 2-year-old toddlers with higher CU traits and higher PNS at rest were found to develop greater externalizing problems at age 4 years (Wagner, Hastings & Rubin, 2017). These studies suggest psychopathic traits, particularly the personality features, are related to higher PNS activity while at rest, suggesting a more relaxed physiological profile. However, it should be noted that some research in children has shown CU traits is linked to lower PNS activity, and thus a vulnerability to emotion dysregulation (Thomson & Centifanti, 2018; Wagner et al., 2015).

However, without measuring both branches of the autonomic nervous system it is difficult to understand what is actually going on. For instance, we may perceive a person as being physiologically calm by having high PNS at rest, but they may also be exhibiting proportionally higher SNS activity, which collectively indicates the person is highly aroused. Unfortunately, studies including both branches of the ANS are very limited. To address this, a recent study integrated both PNS and SNS measures while testing the low-fear hypothesis of psychopathy using a virtual reality (VR) horror game (Thomson, Aboutanos et al., 2019). Increase in PNS activity (RSA augmentation) during fear induction predicted factor 2 psychopathic traits, but there was no link between factor 2 and SNS reactivity. This indicates people with greater antisocial behavior, impulsivity, and poor behavioral controls respond the fear by increasing PNS activity. This physiological profile indicates a neurobiological vulnerability to emotion dysregulation. In contrast, low fear reactivity in both branches of the ANS predicted factor 1. This physiological response is called coinhibition and is an atypical response to fear. In addition to physiological measures, the authors asked participants how they felt during the VR horror game. Participants higher on factor 1 reported feeling happier and more in control after the fear induction, whereas those higher on factor 2 reported feeling out of control and less dominant. Although this is the first study of its kind to integrate VR technology to assess the link between fear reactivity and psychopathic traits, it adds to the growing body of literature that there are different biological associations within the construct of psychopathy. That is, factor 2 is related to poor emotion regulation in challenging situations, which may explain the greater risk to emotionally charged violence, whereas factor 1 is related to a physiological hypoarousal to fear stimuli. This is consistent with neuroimaging research, which shows factor 1 traits are related to a poorly modulated neural circuitry for threat detection, as well as prior psychophysiological work using startle potentiation.

Startle potentiation

Reduced fear-potentiated startle has supported the theoretical perspective that psychopathic traits, during childhood and adulthood, are related to fearlessness. Startle potentiation is a physiological reflexive reaction to an unexpected noise. We are all familiar with the startle response, such as walking along a main road and being startled by a car horn. If we modify the scenario above we can expect the startle response also to change. For instance, the same person is walking down a main road but this time it is at night while listening to a podcast on serial killers, at which point the person is startled by the car horn. This time the startle response would typically be much greater because the individual is already in a heightened emotional state. This is called fear-potentiated startle response. Startle response is measured by placing an electrode under the eye (on the orbicularis oculi muscle) to measure blink response (Fridlund & Cacioppo, 1986). Overall, high levels of psychopathic traits are robustly related to low startle reflex when viewing emotionally provocative stimuli (Anderson, Stanford, Wan & Young, 2011; Baskin-Sommers, Curtin & Newman, 2013; Carmen Pastor, Moltó, Vila & Lang, 2003; Ellis, Schroder, Patrick & Moser, 2017; Esteller, Poy & Moltó, 2016; Levenston, Patrick, Bradley & Lang, 2000; Patrick, Bradley & Lang, 1993). Female psychopaths with low anxiety also demonstrate low startle potentiation, and female psychopaths higher in anxiety demonstrate higher reactivity (Sutton, Vitale & Newman, 2002). Low startle response is most consistently found for the Interpersonal-Affective features of psychopathy for men (Ellis et al., 2017) and women (Verona, Bresin & Patrick, 2013). Startle potentiation research has also become widely used to disentangle subgroups of youths with conduct problems. In adolescents, low startle potentiation has been found for youth with CU traits and conduct problems, whereas youths with low CU traits and high conduct problem show elevated levels of startle potentiation (Dackis, Rogosch & Cicchetti, 2015; Fanti, 2018; Fanti, Panayiotou, Kyranides & Avraamides, 2015; Fanti, Panayiotou, Lazarou, Michael & Georgiou, 2016; Kyranides, Fanti & Panayiotou, 2016). In line with the work by Thomson and colleagues (2018), this suggests that the core personality traits of psychopathy are associated with diminished fear reactivity, while the lifestyle and antisocial features are associated with greater reactivity.

Hormones: cortisol and testosterone

The hypothalamus–pituitary–adrenal (HPA) axis primary function is to regulate the body's stress response. Similar to the autonomic nervous system, the HPA axis is influenced by the limbic and paralimbic neurocircuitry (Johnson, Mikolajewski, Shirtcliff, Eckel & Taylor, 2015; Shirtcliff et al., 2009). As discussed above, when experiencing stress, the SNS engages and the PNS withdraws. Seconds later the HPA axis is triggered, and the hypothalamus releases corticotropin-releasing factor (CRF) into the bloodstream. Because of the increase in CRF, adrenocorticotropic hormone (ACTH) is released from the pituitary gland and into the bloodstream. Once ACTH reaches the outer layer of the adrenal glands (adrenal cortex) it binds to receptors resulting in the secretion of glucocorticoids (including cortisol, aldosterone and epinephrine) from the adrenal glands. An increase in cortisol gives the body extra energy to manage the stressful event. This is why cortisol has been termed the "stress hormone". Based on the ANS research it is expected that psychopathic traits, particularly factor 1, would be related to lower levels of cortisol, because these traits are related to blunted physiological response; however, the findings so far are limited and mixed.

Expectedly, adult psychopathic criminals and violent adolescent offenders scoring high on the PCL:YV have been found to have lower cortisol levels (Cima, Smeets & Jelicic, 2008; Holi, Auvinen-Lintunen, Lindberg, Tani & Virkkunen, 2006). Assessing the two-factor model in violent adolescent offenders, Holi et al. (2006) found factor 1 scores were negatively related to cortisol and no significant association was found with factor 2. These findings are consistent with the neuroimaging and psychophysiological research showing a greater hypoactivity during rest is associated with the personality features of psychopathy. However, research in adult non-forensic samples is mixed, with some finding psychopathic traits to be negatively related to baseline cortisol levels (O'Leary, Loney & Eckel, 2007), others finding positive associations (Dane, Jonason & McCaffrey, 2018), and some finding no significant associations (Pfattheicher, 2016). There seems to be more consistency between forensic and non-forensic samples when assessing the change in cortisol levels in response to a stressor. O'Leary and colleagues (2007) found factor 1 psychopathic traits in a non-clinical sample were associated with reduced cortisol reactivity to stress induction. Similarly, results from a male prison sample found total psychopathy scores, as well as factor 1 and the Affective facet, were related to low cortisol reactivity (Johnson et al., 2015). These associations were only found in males and not for females (O'Leary et al., 2007).

A second hormone that has become increasingly studied is testosterone, which has a longstanding empirical association with antisocial behavior (Chen, Dariotis & Granger, 2018), dominance (Lobbestael, Arntz, Voncken & Potegal, 2017) and aggression (Probst, Golle, Lory & Lobmaier, 2018), and there is some evidence that testosterone is related to psychopathic traits (Yildirim & Derksen, 2012). Testosterone is a male sex hormone (androgen) almost entirely produced in Leydig cells of testes in males, and in ovaries in females (Celec, Ostatníková & Hodosy, 2015). A recent community-based study including men showed higher testosterone after stress induction was positively related to factor 2 on the PPI-R (Lobbestael et al., 2017). Similar results were found in a forensic psychiatric sample, whereby factor 2 on the PCL-R was associated with higher testosterone levels (Stålenheim, Eriksson, von Knorring & Wide, 1998). However, in two large community samples, Glenn and colleagues (2011) did not find any significant associations between the PCL-R and testosterone in adults, and Grotzinger and colleagues (2018) found no significant association with CU traits and testosterone in adolescents. This may suggest that higher testosterone is only related to factor 2 psychopathy in those individuals with more extensive criminal behaviors. This may be a common sense extrapolation because research has found higher levels of testosterone are related to symptoms and correlates of factor 2 – antisocial behavior, impulsivity, poor behavioral controls and reactive aggression (Carré, Campbell, Lozoya, Goetz & Welker, 2013; Montoya, Terburg, Bos & van Honk, 2012; van Wingen, Ossewaarde, Bäckström, Hermans & Fernández, 2011; Volman et al., 2016). Psychopaths with high levels of testosterone have less activity in the anterior PFC, as well as communication between the anterior PFC and the amygdala (Volman et al., 2016), which may explain why some psychopaths (i.e., high-anxious psychopaths, aka secondary psychopaths) have difficulties in emotion regulation and may engage in reactive aggression (ibid.).

To date there have been two studies exploring the combined influence of cortisol and testosterone in understanding psychopathy, and both are from non-forensic samples. The first by Welker and colleagues (2014) found psychopathic traits were only associated with high testosterone when accompanied with high cortisol levels, and this association was found for men and not women. Glenn and colleagues (2011) did not find a significant interaction between baseline cortisol and testosterone but found the ratio of baseline testosterone to cortisol reactivity (the testosterone/cortisol ratio) predicted higher levels of factor 2 on the PCL-R when testosterone levels were high. Given the lack of consistency of these results, these studies need replication before firm conclusions can be drawn. Nevertheless, collectively the research shows both hormones are important for understanding the construct of psychopathy, particularly higher testosterone is related to factor 2, which may explain the emotional reactivity and hostile behavior linked to these traits, while low cortisol is relevant to factor 1, which may explain why these traits are associated with low stress responsivity. Of note, the research so far has typically focused on male populations, and few studies have included women. Of these studies that have included women, no significant associations were found between psychopathy and hormones. Much more research is needed before drawing conclusions between hormones and psychopathy in women.

Summary

A common theme has emerged: psychopathy is a disorder marked by atypical biological function. The Lifestyle and Antisocial facets of psychopathy and secondary variants of psychopathy in youth (low CU traits and high conduct problems) are associated with greater reactivity to aversive stimuli and biological profiles that suggest a vulnerability to emotion dysregulation. This is somewhat unsurprising, as these traits encompass impulsivity and poor behavioral controls, and are related to emotionally driven reactive forms of violence. In contrast, neuroimaging data shows factor 1 psychopathy is associated with diminished response to aversive stimuli and abnormalities in multiple brain regions involved in affective processing and decision-making. Further, this research highlights the importance of considering the interconnectedness of brain regions when understanding psychopathy. Clearly, the amygdala is important to understanding the symptoms of psychopathy but based on the evidence to date the amygdala is a cog in a larger machine. In line with the neuroimaging research, psychophysiological research finds factor 1 traits are linked to a blunted response to stress induction, and findings from endocrinology show factor 1 is linked to lower cortisol reactivity. This highlights the interconnectedness between biological measures, showing that neurological deficits have an impact on the way in which psychopaths are physiologically responsive to stress induction. Thus, across most biological measures, factor 1 is associated with hypoactive and hyporeactive biological states to aversive situations, which may explain why the prototypical psychopath is able to remain calm and in control during stressful and threatening situations. A calm and collective state may benefit the psychopath. For any practitioner who has worked extensively in the clinical and forensic setting with psychopaths, it is clear that successful conning and manipulation has less to do with what is being sold, and more to do with who is selling it. Research from economics and occupational psychology has shown a charming personality *and* stable emotionality are positively related to sales performance (Hurtz & Donovan, 2000; Kazén, Kuhl, Boermans & Koole, 2013). And in the case of the psychopath, who is selling the con, she is well-equipped with a personality and biological structure that is suited to manipulating even the most sagacious and cautious victim.

Acknowledgments

Thank you to Dr. Arielle Baskin-Sommers and Dr. Kostas Fanti for providing a valuable review of this chapter. Dr. Baskin-Sommers is a licensed clinical psychologist and an Assistant Professor of Psychology and Psychiatry at Yale University. Dr. Baskin-Sommers' research concentration is to understand individual differences in cognitive and affective processes as they relate to vulnerability for antisocial behavior. Dr. Fanti is the Director of the Developmental Psychopathology Lab and Associate Professor of Developmental Psychology at the Department of Psychology, University of Cyprus. His research investigates how individual, environmental, and biological factors influence maladaptive behavior and especially antisocial behavior from preschool to adolescence.

References

Anderson, N. E., Stanford, M. S., Wan, L. & Young, K. A. (2011). High Psychopathic Trait Females Exhibit Reduced Startle Potentiation and Increased P3 Amplitude. *Behavioral Sciences & the Law*, 29(5), 649–666.

Baskin-Sommers, A. R., Curtin, J. J. & Newman, J. P. (2013). Emotion-Modulated Startle in Psychopathy: Clarifying Familiar Effects. *Journal of Abnormal Psychology*, 122(2), 458–468.

Beauchaine, T. P. (2015). Respiratory Sinus Arrhythmia: A Transdiagnostic Biomarker of Emotion Dysregulation and Psychopathology. *Current Opinion in Psychology*, 3, 43–47.

Bechara, A., Tranel, D., Damasio, H. & Damasio, A. R. (1996). Failure to Respond Autonomically to Anticipated Future Outcomes Following Damage to Prefrontal Cortex. *Cerebral Cortex (New York, N.Y. : 1991)*, 6(2), 215–225.

Benning, S. D., Patrick, C. J., Blonigen, D. M., Hicks, B. M. & Iacono, W. G. (2005). Estimating Facets of Psychopathy From Normal Personality Traits. *Assessment*, 12(1), 3–18.

Benning, S. D., Patrick, C. J. & Iacono, W. G. (2005). Psychopathy, Startle Blink Modulation, and Electrodermal Reactivity in Twin Men. *Psychophysiology*, 42(6), 753–762.

Birbaumer, N., Veit, R., Lotze, M., Erb, M., Hermann, C., Grodd, W. & Flor, H. (2005). Deficient Fear Conditioning in Psychopathy. *Archives of General Psychiatry*, 62(7), 799.

Bjork, J. M., Chen, G. & Hommer, D. W. (2012). Psychopathic Tendencies and Mesolimbic Recruitment by Cues for Instrumental and Passively Obtained rewards. *Biological Psychology*, 89(2), 408–415.

Blair, R. J. R. (2006). The Emergence of Psychopathy: Implications for the Neuropsychological Approach to Developmental Disorders. *Cognition*, 101(2), 414–442.

Blair, R. J. R. (2013). Psychopathy: Cognitive and Neural Dysfunction. *Dialogues in Clinical Neuroscience*, 15(2), 181–190.

Blair, R. J. R., Jones, L., Clark, F. & Smith, M. (1997). The Psychopathic Individual: A Lack of Responsiveness to Distress Cues? *Psychophysiology*, 34(2), 192–198.

Blumer, D. & Benson, D. (1975). Personality Changes with Frontal and Temporal Lesions. In D. Blumer & D. Benson (Eds.), *Psychiatric Aspects of Neurological Disease* (pp. 151–170). New York: Stratton.

Carmen Pastor, M., Moltó, J., Vila, J. & Lang, P. J. (2003). Startle Reflex Modulation, Affective Ratings and Autonomic Reactivity in Incarcerated Spanish psychopaths. *Psychophysiology*, 40(6), 934–938.

Carré, J. M., Campbell, J. A., Lozoya, E., Goetz, S. M. M. & Welker, K. M. (2013). Changes in Testosterone Mediate the Effect of Winning on Subsequent Aggressive Behaviour. *Psychoneuroendocrinology, 38*(10), 2034–2041.

Celec, P., Ostatníková, D. & Hodosy, J. (2015). On the Effects of Testosterone on Brain Behavioral Functions. *Frontiers in Neuroscience, 9*, 12.

Cersosimo, M. G. & Benarroch, E. E. (2013). Central Control of Autonomic Function and Involvement in Neurodegenerative Disorders. *Handbook of Clinical Neurology, 117*, 45–57.

Chen, F. R., Dariotis, J. K. & Granger, D. A. (2018). Linking Testosterone and Antisocial Behavior in at-Risk Transitional Aged Youth: Contextual Effects of Parentification. *Psychoneuroendocrinology, 91*, 1–10. https://doi.org/10.1016/J.PSYNEUEN.2018.02.023

Cima, M., Smeets, T. & Jelicic, M. (2008). Self-Reported Trauma, Cortisol Levels, and Aggression in Psychopathic and Non-psychopathic Prison Inmates. *Biological Psychology, 78*(1), 75–86.

Contreras-Rodríguez, O., Pujol, J., Batalla, I., Harrison, B. J., Soriano-Mas, C., Deus, J., . . . Cardoner, N. (2015). Functional Connectivity Bias in the Prefrontal Cortex of Psychopaths. *Biological Psychiatry, 78*(9), 647–655.

Dackis, M. N., Rogosch, F. A. & Cicchetti, D. (2015). Child Maltreatment, Callous-Unemotional Traits, and Defensive Responding in High-Risk Children: An Investigation of Emotion-Modulated Startle Response. *Development and Psychopathology, 27*(4 Pt 2), 1527–1545.

Damasio, H., Grabowski, T., Frank, R., Galaburda, A. M. & Damasio, A. R. (1994). The Return of Phineas Gage: Clues about the Brain from the Skull of a Famous Patient. *Science (New York, N.Y.), 264*(5162), 1102–1105.

Dane, L. K., Jonason, P. K. & McCaffrey, M. (2018). Physiological Tests of the Cheater Hypothesis for the Dark Triad Traits: Testosterone, Cortisol, and a Social Stressor. *Personality and Individual Differences, 121*, 227–231.

De Geus, E. C. J., Gerssen-Goedhart, A. & Willemsen, G. (2014). Comparing Cardiac and Skin Sympathetic Nervous System Activity. In A. Spink, L. Loijens, M. Woloszynowska-Fraser & L. Noldus (Eds.), *Measuring Behavior 2014* (pp. 137–141). Wageningen, The Netherlands.

Decety, J., Skelly, L. R. & Kiehl, K. A. (2013). Brain Response to Empathy-Eliciting Scenarios Involving Pain in Incarcerated Individuals with Psychopathy. *JAMA Psychiatry, 70*(6), 638.

Decety, J., Skelly, L., Yoder, K. J. & Kiehl, K. A. (2014). Neural Processing of Dynamic Emotional Facial Expressions in Psychopaths. *Social Neuroscience, 9*(1), 36–49.

Dindo, L. & Fowles, D. (2011). Dual Temperamental Risk Factors for Psychopathic Personality: Evidence from Self-Report and Skin Conductance. *Journal of Personality and Social Psychology, 100*(3), 557–566.

Ellis, J. D., Schroder, H. S., Patrick, C. J. & Moser, J. S. (2017). Emotional Reactivity and Regulation in Individuals with Psychopathic Traits: Evidence for a Disconnect between Neurophysiology and Self-Report. *Psychophysiology, 54*(10), 1574–1585.

Ermer, E., Cope, L. M., Nyalakanti, P. K., Calhoun, V. D. & Kiehl, K. A. (2012). Aberrant Paralimbic Gray Matter in Criminal Psychopathy. *Journal of Abnormal Psychology, 121*(3), 649–658.

Eslinger, P. J. & Damasio, A. R. (1985). Severe Disturbance of Higher Cognition after Bilateral Frontal Lobe Ablation: Patient EVR. *Neurology, 35*(12), 1731–1731.

Espinoza, F. A., Vergara, V. M., Reyes, D., Anderson, N. E., Harenski, C. L., Decety, J., . . . Calhoun, V. D. (2018). Aberrant Functional Network Connectivity in Psychopathy from a Large (N = 985) Forensic Sample. *Human Brain Mapping*.

Esteller, À., Poy, R. & Moltó, J. (2016). Deficient Aversive-Potentiated Startle and the Triarchic Model of Psychopathy: The Role of Boldness. *Biological Psychology*, *117*, 131–140.

Etkin, A., Egner, T., Peraza, D. M., Kandel, E. R. & Hirsch, J. (2006). Resolving Emotional Conflict: A Role for the Rostral Anterior Cingulate Cortex in Modulating Activity in the Amygdala. *Neuron*, *51*(6), 871–882.

Ewbank, M. P., Passamonti, L., Hagan, C. C., Goodyer, I. M., Calder, A. J. & Fairchild, G. (2018). Psychopathic Traits Influence Amygdala–Anterior Cingulate Cortex Connectivity during Facial Emotion Processing. *Social Cognitive and Affective Neuroscience*, *13*(5), 525–534.

Fanti, K. A. (2018). Understanding Heterogeneity in Conduct Disorder: A Review of Psychophysiological Studies. *Neuroscience & Biobehavioral Reviews*, *91*, 4–20.

Fanti, K. A., Panayiotou, G., Kyranides, M. N. & Avraamides, M. N. (2015). Startle Modulation during Violent Films: Association with Callous–Unemotional Traits and Aggressive Behavior. *Motivation and Emotion*, *40*(2), 321–333.

Fanti, K. A., Panayiotou, G., Lazarou, C., Michael, R. & Georgiou, G. (2016). The Better of Two Evils? Evidence that Children Exhibiting Continuous Conduct Problems High or Low on Callous-Unemotional Traits Score on Opposite Directions on Physiological and Behavioral Measures of Fear. *Development and Psychopathology*, *28*(1), 185–198.

Fanti, K. A., Kyranides, M. N., Georgiou, G., Petridou, M., Colins, O. F., Tuvblad, C. & Andershed, H. (2017). Callous-Unemotional, Impulsive-Irresponsible, and Grandiose-Manipulative Traits: Distinct Associations with Heart Rate, Skin Conductance, and Startle Responses to Violent and Erotic Scenes. *Psychophysiology*, *54*(5), 663–672.

Fowles, D. C. (1983). Motivational Effects on Heart Rate and Electrodermal Activity: Implications for Research on Personality and Psychopathology. *Journal of Research in Personality*, *17*(1), 48–71.

Fowles, D. C. & Dindo, L. (2006). A Dual-Deficit Model of Psychopathy. In C. J. Patrick (Ed.), *Handbook of Psychopathy* (pp. 14–34). New York: Guilford Press.

Fox, N. A., Schmidt, L. A., Henderson, H. A. & Marshall, P. J. (2007). Developmental Psychophysiology: Conceptual and Methodological Issues. In J. T. Cacioppo, L. G. Tassinary & G. G. Bernston (Eds.), *Handbook of Psychophysiology* (3rd ed., pp. 453–481). New York: Cambridge University Press.

Frick, P. J., Lilienfeld, S. O., Ellis, M., Loney, B. & Silverthorn, P. (1999). The Association between Anxiety and Psychopathy Dimensions in Children. *Journal of Abnormal Child Psychology*, *27*(5), 383–392.

Fridlund, A. J. & Cacioppo, J. T. (1986). Guidelines for Human Electromyographic Research. *Psychophysiology*, *23*(5), 567–589.

Gao, Y., Huang, Y. & Li, X. (2017). Interaction between Prenatal Maternal Stress and Autonomic Arousal in Predicting Conduct Problems and Psychopathic Traits in Children. *Journal of Psychopathology and Behavioral Assessment*, *39*(1), 1–14.

Glenn, A. L., Raine, A., Schug, R. A., Gao, Y. & Granger, D. A. (2011). Increased Testosterone-to-Cortisol Ratio in Psychopathy. *Journal of Abnormal Psychology*, *120*(2), 389–399.

Greene, J. D., Nystrom, L. E., Engell, A. D., Darley, J. M. & Cohen, J. D. (2004). The Neural Bases of Cognitive Conflict and Control in Moral Judgment. *Neuron*, *44*(2), 389–400.

Grotzinger, A. D., Mann, F. D., Patterson, M. W., Tackett, J. L., Tucker-Drob, E. M. & Harden, K. P. (2018). Hair and Salivary Testosterone, Hair Cortisol, and Externalizing Behaviors in Adolescents. *Psychological Science*, *29*(5), 688–699.

Hansen, A. L., Johnsen, B. H., Thornton, D., Waage, L. & Thayer, J. F. (2007). Facets of Psychopathy, Heart Rate Variability and Cognitive Function. *Journal of Personality Disorders, 21*(5), 568–582.

Hare, R. D. (1965). Temporal Gradient of Fear Arousal in Psychopaths. *Journal of Abnormal Psychology, 70*(6), 442–445.

Hare, R. D. (2003). *The Hare Psychopathy Checklist – Revised* (2nd ed.). Toronto, Canada: Multi-Health Systems.

Harenski, C. L., Harenski, K. A., Shane, M. S. & Kiehl, K. A. (2010). Aberrant Neural Processing of Moral Violations in Criminal Psychopaths. *Journal of Abnormal Psychology, 119*(4), 863–874.

Harlow, J. M. (1868). Recovery from the Passage of an Publications of the Massachusetts Medical Society Iron Bar through the Head. *Publications of the Massachusetts Medical Society, 2*, 327–347.

Holi, M., Auvinen-Lintunen, L., Lindberg, N., Tani, P. & Virkkunen, M. (2006). Inverse Correlation between Severity of Psychopathic Traits and Serum Cortisol Levels in Young Adult Violent Male Offenders. *Psychopathology, 39*(2), 102–104.

Hurley, K. M., Herbert, H., Moga, M. M. & Saper, C. B. (1991). Efferent Projections of the Infralimbic Cortex of the Rat. *The Journal of Comparative Neurology, 308*(2), 249–276.

Hurtz, G. M. & Donovan, J. J. (2000). Personality and Job Performance: The Big Five Revisited. *The Journal of Applied Psychology, 85*(6), 869–879.

Johnson, M. M., Mikolajewski, A., Shirtcliff, E. A., Eckel, L. A. & Taylor, J. (2015). The Association between Affective Psychopathic Traits, Time Incarcerated, and Cortisol Response to Psychosocial Stress. *Hormones and Behavior, 72*, 20–27.

Jones, A. P., Laurens, K. R., Herba, C. M., Barker, G. J. & Viding, E. (2009). Amygdala Hypoactivity to Fearful Faces in Boys with Conduct Problems and Callous-Unemotional Traits. *The American Journal of Psychiatry, 166*(1), 95–102.

Kavish, N., Fu, Q., Vaughn, M., Qian, Z. & Boutwell, B. (2017). Resting Heart Rate and Psychopathy: Findings from the Add Health Survey – Add Health. *BioRxiv*. Retrieved from www.biorxiv.org/content/early/2018/06/13/205005

Kavish, N., Vaughn, M. G., Cho, E., Barth, A., Boutwell, B., Vaughn, S., . . . Martinez, L. (2017). Physiological Arousal and Juvenile Psychopathy: Is Low Resting Heart Rate Associated with Affective Dimensions? *Psychiatric Quarterly, 88*(1), 103–114.

Kazén, M., Kuhl, J., Boermans, S. & Koole, S. L. (2013). Excelling at Selling: The Charming Personality Style Predicts Occupational Activities, Sales Performance, and Persuasive Competence. *PsyCh Journal, 2*(2), 86–100.

Kemp, A. H., Quintana, D. S., Felmingham, K. L., Matthews, S. & Jelinek, H. F. (2012). Depression, Comorbid Anxiety Disorders, and Heart Rate Variability in Physically Healthy, Unmedicated Patients: Implications for Cardiovascular Risk. *PloS ONE, 7*(2), e30777.

Kiehl, K. A. (2006). A Cognitive Neuroscience Perspective on Psychopathy: Evidence for Paralimbic System Dysfunction. *Psychiatry Research, 142*(2–3), 107–28.

Kiehl, K. A., Smith, A. M., Hare, R. D., Mendrek, A., Forster, B. B., Brink, J. & Liddle, P. F. (2001). Limbic Abnormalities in Affective Processing by Criminal Psychopaths as Revealed by Functional Magnetic Resonance Imaging. *Biological Psychiatry, 50*(9), 677–684.

Kimonis, E. R., Frick, P. J., Skeem, J. L., Marsee, M. A., Cruise, K., Munoz, L. C., . . . Morris, A. S. (2008). Assessing Callous-Unemotional Traits in Adolescent Offenders: Validation of the Inventory of Callous-Unemotional Traits. *International Journal of Law and Psychiatry, 31*(3), 241–252.

Koenig, J., Kemp, A. H., Feeling, N. R., Thayer, J. F. & Kaess, M. (2016). Resting State Vagal Tone in Borderline Personality Disorder: A Meta-analysis. *Progress in Neuro-Psychopharmacology and Biological Psychiatry*, 64, 18–26.

Koenigs, M. (2012). The Role of Prefrontal Cortex in Psychopathy. *Reviews in the Neurosciences*, 23(3), 253–262.

Koenigs, M., Kruepke, M. & Newman, J. P. (2010). Economic Decision-Making in Psychopathy: A Comparison with Ventromedial Prefrontal Lesion Patients. *Neuropsychologia*, 48(7), 2198–2204.

Koenigs, M., Kruepke, M., Zeier, J. & Newman, J. P. (2012). Utilitarian Moral Judgment in Psychopathy. *Social Cognitive and Affective Neuroscience*, 7(6), 708–714.

Kyranides, M. N., Fanti, K. A. & Panayiotou, G. (2016). The Disruptive Adolescent as a Grown-Up: Predicting Adult Startle Responses to Violent and Erotic Films from Adolescent Conduct Problems and Callous-Unemotional Traits. *Journal of Psychopathology and Behavioral Assessment*, 38(2), 183–194.

Kyranides, M. N., Fanti, K. A., Sikki, M. & Patrick, C. J. (2017). Triarchic Dimensions of Psychopathy in Young Adulthood: Associations with Clinical and Physiological Measures after Accounting for Adolescent Psychopathic Traits. *Personality Disorders: Theory, Research, and Treatment*, 8(2), 140–149.

Levenson, R. W. (2014). The Autonomic Nervous System and Emotion. *Emotion Review*, 6(2), 100–112.

Levenston, G. K., Patrick, C. J., Bradley, M. M. & Lang, P. J. (2000). The Psychopath as Observer: Emotion and Attention in Picture Processing. *Journal of Abnormal Psychology*, 109(3), 373–385.

Lilienfeld, S. O., Sauvigné, K. C., Reber, J., Watts, A. L., Hamann, S., Smith, S. F., . . . Tranel, D. (2018). Potential Effects of Severe Bilateral Amygdala Damage on Psychopathic Personality Features: A Case Report. *Personality Disorders*, 9(2), 112–121.

Lobbestael, J., Arntz, A., Voncken, M. & Potegal, M. (2017). Responses to Dominance Challenge Are a Function of Psychopathy Level: A Multimethod Study. *Personality Disorders: Theory, Research, and Treatment*, 9(4), 305–314.

López, R., Poy, R., Patrick, C. J. & Moltó, J. (2013). Deficient Fear Conditioning and Self-reported Psychopathy: The Role of Fearless Dominance. *Psychophysiology*, 50(2), 210–218.

Lorber, M. F. (2004). Psychophysiology of Aggression, Psychopathy, and Conduct Problems: A Meta-analysis. *Psychological Bulletin*, 130(4), 531–552.

Lozier, L. M., Cardinale, E. M., VanMeter, J. W. & Marsh, A. A. (2014). Mediation of the Relationship between Callous-Unemotional Traits and Proactive Aggression by Amygdala Response to Fear among Children with Conduct Problems. *JAMA Psychiatry*, 71(6), 627–636.

Lykken, D. T. (1957). A Study of Anxiety in the Sociopathic Personality. *The Journal of Abnormal and Social Psychology*, 55(1), 6–10.

Marcovitch, S., Leigh, J., Calkins, S. D., Leerks, E. M., O'Brien, M. & Blankson, A. N. (2010). Moderate Vagal Withdrawal in 3.5-Year-Old Children is Associated with Optimal Performance on Executive Function Tasks. *Developmental Psychobiology*, 52(6), 603–608.

Marsh, A. A., Finger, E. C., Fowler, K. A., Adalio, C. J., Jurkowitz, I. T. N., Schechter, J. C., . . . Blair, R. J. R. (2013). Empathic Responsiveness in Amygdala and Anterior Cingulate Cortex in Youths with Psychopathic Traits. *Journal of Child Psychology and Psychiatry*, 54(8), 900–910.

Montoya, E. R., Terburg, D., Bos, P. A. & van Honk, J. (2012). Testosterone, Cortisol, and Serotonin as Key Regulators of Social Aggression: A Review and Theoretical Perspective. *Motivation and Emotion*, 36(1), 65–73.

Morawetz, C., Bode, S., Baudewig, J. & Heekeren, H. R. (2017). Effective Amygdala-Prefrontal Connectivity Predicts Individual Differences in Successful Emotion Regulation. *Social Cognitive and Affective Neuroscience, 12*(4), 569–585.

Motzkin, J. C., Newman, J. P., Kiehl, K. A. & Koenigs, M. (2011). Reduced Prefrontal Connectivity in Psychopathy. *The Journal of Neuroscience: The Official Journal of the Society for Neuroscience, 31*(48), 17348–17357.

Müller, J. L., Gänssbauer, S., Sommer, M., Döhnel, K., Weber, T., Schmidt-Wilcke, T. & Hajak, G. (2008). Gray Matter Changes in Right Superior Temporal Gyrus in Criminal Psychopaths: Evidence from Voxel-Based Morphometry. *Psychiatry Research, 163*(3), 213–222.

Northover, C., Thapar, A., Langley, K. & van Goozen, S. H. M. (2015). Pain Sensitivity in Adolescent Males with Attention-Deficit/Hyperactivity Disorder: Testing for Associations with Conduct Disorder and Callous and Unemotional Traits. *PloS One, 10*(7), e0134417.

Ochsner, K. N., Ray, R. D., Cooper, J. C., Robertson, E. R., Chopra, S., Gabrieli, J. D. & Gross, J. J. (2004). For Better or for Worse: Neural Systems Supporting the Cognitive Down- and Up-regulation of Negative Emotion. *Neuroimage, 23*(2), 483–499.

O'Leary, M. M., Loney, B. R. & Eckel, L. A. (2007). Gender Differences in the Association between Psychopathic Personality Traits and Cortisol Response to Induced Stress. *Psychoneuroendocrinology, 32*(2), 183–191.

Pardini, D. A. DA, Raine, A., Erickson, K. & Loeber, R. (2014). Lower Amygdala Volume in Men is Associated with Childhood Aggression, Early Psychopathic Traits, and Future Violence. *Biological Psychiatry, 75*(1), 73–80.

Passamonti, L., Rowe, J. B., Ewbank, M., Hampshire, A., Keane, J. & Calder, A. J. (2008). Connectivity from the Ventral Anterior Cingulate to the Amygdala is Modulated by Appetitive Motivation in Response to Facial Signals of Aggression. *NeuroImage, 43*(3), 562–570.

Patrick, C. J. (1994). Emotion and Psychopathy: Startling New Insights. *Psychophysiology, 31*(4), 319–330.

Patrick, C. J., Bradley, M. M. & Lang, P. J. (1993). Emotion in the Criminal Psychopath: Startle Reflex Modulation. *Journal of Abnormal Psychology, 102*(1), 82–92.

Patrick, C. J., Cuthbert, B. N. & Lang, P. J. (1994). Emotion in the Criminal Psychopath: Fear Image Processing. *Journal of Abnormal Psychology, 103*(3), 523–534.

Pfattheicher, S. (2016). Testosterone, Cortisol and the Dark Triad: Narcissism (but Not Machiavellianism or Psychopathy) is Positively Related to Basal Testosterone and Cortisol. *Personality and Individual Differences, 97*, 115–119.

Phelps, E. A., Delgado, M. R., Nearing, K. I. & LeDoux, J. E. (2004). Extinction Learning in Humans: Role of the Amygdala and vmPFC. *Neuron, 43*(6), 897–905.

Probst, F., Golle, J., Lory, V. & Lobmaier, J. S. (2018). Reactive Aggression Tracks Within-Participant Changes in Women's Salivary Testosterone. *Aggressive Behavior, 44*(4), 362–371.

Quay, H. C. (1965). Psychopathic Personality as Pathological Stimulation-Seeking. *American Journal of Psychiatry, 122*(2), 180–183.

Raine, A. (2002). Biosocial Studies of Antisocial and Violent Behavior in Children and Adults: A Review. *Journal of Abnormal Child Psychology, 30*(4), 311–326.

Raine, A. (2005). The Interaction of Biological and Social Measures in the Explanation of Antisocial and Violent Behaviour. In D. Stoff & E. J. Susman (Eds.), *Developmental Psychobiology Aggression* (pp. 13–42). New York: Cambridge University Press.

Raine, A. (2013). *The Psychopathology of Crime: Criminal Behavior as a Clinical Disorder*. San Diego, CA: Academic Press.

Raine, A., Fung, A. L. C., Portnoy, J., Choy, O. & Spring, V. L. (2014). Low Heart Rate as a Risk Factor for Child and Adolescent Proactive Aggressive and Impulsive Psychopathic Behavior. *Aggressive Behavior, 40*(4), 290–299.

Rilling, J. K., Glenn, A. L., Jairam, M. R., Pagnoni, G., Goldsmith, D. R., Elfenbein, H. A. & Lilienfeld, S. O. (2007). Neural Correlates of Social Cooperation and Non-Cooperation as a Function of Psychopathy. *Biological Psychiatry, 61*(11), 1260–1271.

Rottenberg, J., Wilhelm, F. H., Gross, J. J. & Gotlib, I. H. (2002). Respiratory Sinus Arrhythmia as a Predictor of Outcome in Major Depressive Disorder. *Journal of Affective Disorders, 71*(1–3), 265–272.

Schechter, J. C., Brennan, P. A., Cunningham, P. B., Foster, S. L. & Whitmore, E. (2012). Stress, Cortisol, and Externalizing Behavior in Adolescent Males: An Examination in the Context of Multisystemic Therapy. *Journal of Abnormal Child Psychology, 40*(6), 913–922.

Schultz, D. H., Balderston, N. L., Baskin-Sommers, A. R., Larson, C. L. & Helmstetter, F. J. (2016). Psychopaths Show Enhanced Amygdala Activation during Fear Conditioning. *Frontiers in Psychology, 7*, 348.

Shirtcliff, E. A., Vitacco, M. J., Graf, A. R., Gostisha, A. J., Merz, J. L. & Zahn-Waxler, C. (2009). Neurobiology of Empathy and Callousness: Implications for the Development of Antisocial Behavior. *Behavioral Sciences & the Law, 27*(2), 137–171.

Stålenheim, E. G., Eriksson, E., von Knorring, L. & Wide, L. (1998). Testosterone as a Biological Marker in Psychopathy and Alcoholism. *Psychiatry Research, 77*(2), 79–88.

Sutton, S. K., Vitale, J. E. & Newman, J. P. (2002). Emotion among Women with Psychopathy during Picture Perception. *Journal of Abnormal Psychology, 111*(4), 610–619.

Ter Horst, G. J., Hautvast, R. W. M., Jongste, M. J. L. & Korf, J. (1996). Neuroanatomy of Cardiac Activity-regulating Circuitry: A Transneuronal Retrograde Viral Labelling Study in the Rat. *European Journal of Neuroscience, 8*(10), 2029–2041.

Terreberry, R. R. & Neafsey, E. J. (1987). The Rat Medial Frontal Cortex Projects Directly to Autonomic Regions of the Brainstem. *Brain Research Bulletin, 19*(6), 639–649.

Thayer, J. F., Friedman, B. H. & Borkovec, T. D. (1996). Autonomic Characteristics of Generalized Anxiety Disorder and Worry. *Biological Psychiatry, 39*(4), 255–266.

Thomson, N. D., Aboutanos, M. B., Kiehl, K. A., Neumann, C. S., Galusha, C. & Fanti, K. A. (2019). Physiological Reactivity in Response to a Fear Induced Virtual Reality Experience: Associations with Psychopathic Traits. *Psychophysiology, 56*(1), e13276.

Thomson, N. D. & Beauchaine, T. P. (2018). Respiratory Sinus Arrhythmia Mediates Links Between Borderline Personality Disorder Symptoms and both Aggressive and Violent Behavior. *Journal of Personality Disorders, 32*, 1–16.

Thomson, N. D. & Centifanti, L. C. M. (2018). Proactive and Reactive Aggression Subgroups in Typically Developing Children: The Role of Executive Functioning, Psychophysiology, and Psychopathy. *Child Psychiatry & Human Development, 49*(2), 197–208.

Thomson, N. D., Kiehl, K. A. & Bjork, J. M. (2019). Violence and Aggression in Young Women: The Importance of Psychopathy and Neurobiological Function. *Physiology and Behavior, 201*, 130–138.

Urry, H. L., Van Reekum, C. M., Johnstone, T., Kalin, N. H., Thurow, M. E., Schaefer, H. S. . . . & Davidson, R. J. (2006). Amygdala and Ventromedial Prefrontal Cortex are Inversely Coupled during Regulation of Negative Affect and Predict the Diurnal Pattern of Cortisol Secretion among Older Adults. *Journal of Neuroscience, 26*(16), 4415–4425.

Vaidyanathan, U., Hall, J. R., Patrick, C. J. & Bernat, E. M. (2011). Clarifying the Role of Defensive Reactivity Deficits in Psychopathy and Antisocial Personality Using Startle Reflex Methodology. *Journal of Abnormal Psychology, 120*(1), 253–258.

Van Wingen, G. A., Ossewaarde, L., Bäckström, T., Hermans, E. J. & Fernández, G. (2011). Gonadal Hormone Regulation of the Emotion Circuitry in Humans. *Neuroscience*, *191*, 38–45.

Verberne, A. J. & Owens, N. C. (1998). Cortical Modulation of the Cardiovascular System. *Progress in Neurobiology*, *54*(2), 149–168.

Verona, E., Bresin, K. & Patrick, C. J. (2013). Revisiting Psychopathy in Women: Cleckley/Hare Conceptions and Affective Response. *Journal of Abnormal Psychology*, *122*(4), 1088–1093.

Verschuere, B., Crombez, G., De Clercq, A. & Koster, E. H. W. (2005). Psychopathic Traits and Autonomic Responding to Concealed Information in a Prison Sample. *Psychophysiology*, *42*(2), 239–245.

Vogt, B. A., Vogt, L., Farber, N. B. & Bush, G. (2005). Architecture and Neurocytology of Monkey Cingulate Gyrus. *The Journal of Comparative Neurology*, *485*(3), 218–239.

Volman, I., von Borries, A. K. L., Bulten, B. H., Verkes, R. J., Toni, I. & Roelofs, K. (2016). Testosterone Modulates Altered Prefrontal Control of Emotional Actions in Psychopathic Offenders. *ENeuro*, *3*(1), 1–12.

Wagner, N. J., Hastings, P. D. & Rubin, K. H. (2017). Callous-Unemotional Traits and Autonomic Functioning in Toddlerhood Interact to Predict Externalizing Behaviors in Preschool. *Journal of Abnormal Child Psychology*, *46*(7), 1439–1450.

Wagner, N. J., Mills-Koonce, R., Willoughby, M., Propper, C., Rehder, P. & Gueron-Sela, N. (2015). Respiratory Sinus Arrhythmia and Heart Period in Infancy as Correlates of Later Oppositional Defiant and Callous-Unemotional Behaviors. *International Journal of Behavioral Development*, *41*(1), 127–135.

Welker, K. M., Lozoya, E., Campbell, J. A., Neumann, C. S. & Carré, J. M. (2014). Testosterone, Cortisol, and Psychopathic Traits in Men and Women. *Physiology & Behavior*, *129*, 230–236.

Yang, Y., Raine, A., Lencz, T., Bihrle, S., LaCasse, L. & Colletti, P. (2005). Volume Reduction in Prefrontal Gray Matter in Unsuccessful Criminal Psychopaths. *Biological Psychiatry*, *57*(10), 1103–1108.

Yildirim, B. O. & Derksen, J. J. L. (2012). A Review on the Relationship between Testosterone and the Interpersonal/Affective Facet of Psychopathy. *Psychiatry Research*, *197*(3), 181–198.

6
PSYCHOLOGICAL FACTORS

Classifying biopsychosocial factors into one domain can be a major challenge because of the overlap each factor has with another. While this is a challenge when dedicating a chapter for each domain, this blurring of scientific disciplines is evidence that the biopsychosocial approach is imperative to understanding psychopathy. To provide an overview of the psychological correlates and predictors of psychopathy, this chapter is broken into four main sections. First, an overview is provided of the theory between childhood temperament and psychopathy, and the research linking childhood psychopathology with adult psychopathic traits. Second, a review will be conducted on how psychopathy is associated with personality traits and psychopathology using the "Big Five", and externalizing and internalizing psychiatric symptoms. Third, a discussion will be provided on the evidence linking psychopathy to cognitive function, including risk-taking and impulsivity, executive function, intelligence, emotional intelligence and facial expression recognition. Fourth, the chapter will conclude with a summary on the recent findings between moral attitudes and behaviors, and moral decision-making and psychopathy. The aim of this chapter is to provide the reader with an overview of the most prominent psychological correlates of psychopathy.

Temperament

Chapter 5 discussed the biological correlates of psychopathy, and several of these associations provide biological evidence that temperament is a risk factor in the development of psychopathy. However, as Fowles (2018) highlights, psychopathy may have many developmental pathways (equifinality), and even though early risk factors for psychopathy may be identified, these may lead to different outcomes (multifinality). This notion that there are multiple pathways to developing psychopathic traits highlights the complexity involved in understanding the development of psychopathy, which is probably one of the strongest arguments for the need of an integrative model, such as the biopsychosocial approach. The genetic and biological evidence presented in Chapters 4 and 5 supports the idea of a dual process or the dual pathway model of psychopathy. Based on the dual pathway model, interpersonal-affective psychopathic traits develop, in part, because of an under-active response to aversive and punitive stimuli. For example, a toddler who hits a peer to get a toy will be told off by the teacher. As a result, the toddler will become upset and feel sad (all of which are supported by a physiological feedback loop). The next time the toddler wants the toy, she has learned that hitting another child ends by getting in trouble and feeling bad, both emotionally and physiologically. In which case the toddler may try a different tactic that is more prosocial that will not lead to being punished and feeling bad. This prosocial approach may be supported through instruction and praise by the teacher. However, if the child has a "fearless temperament", which means she does not experience the negative emotional and physiological consequences (getting upset and feeling sad), then she will continue to hit a child every time she wants the toy because, after all, she got the toy.

Theory and research suggests the affective features of psychopathy in youth are associated with reward-sensitivity and being punishment insensitive (Frick, 2012; Frick & Viding, 2009; Frick & White, 2008; Hawes & Dadds, 2005). Thus, children higher on these traits will be more responsive to the positive outcomes (e.g., getting the toy) of the situation than any negative outcome (e.g., punishment). This fearless temperament and high reward sensitivity may lead to reinforcement of delinquent behavior. In contrast, impulsive-antisocial traits are associated with a temperament characterized as highly neurotic, disinhibition and a proneness to emotion dysregulation. Using the same situation above, the toddler sees a toy that she wants, and because toddlers are still learning ways of communicating, she may become frustrated that the other toddler is not giving up the toy. This frustration leads to anger and aggression. However, unlike the toddler with the fearless temperament, this toddler is more responsive to punishment and once emotions cool down they do feel guilty for the harm caused. Therefore, from an early age, temperament may be able to predict the development of psychopathic traits.

Indeed, research from adolescent and adult forensic samples has shown facet scores relate to different types of temperament. For example Snowden and Gray (2010) found higher Psychopathy Checklist – Revised (PCL-R) scores on the Interpersonal facet were associated with low harm avoidance, and higher scores on the Affective facet were associated with low reward dependence. Both the Lifestyle and Antisocial facets were related to high novelty seeking and low co-cooperativeness. Partially consistent results have been found in adolescent offenders. For instance, in a sample of 122 adolescent male offenders, Lennox and Dolan (2014) found Psychopathy Checklist: Youth Version (PCL:YV) total scores were positively associated with novelty seeking but negatively correlated with cooperativeness and harm avoidance. At the facet level, the Interpersonal and Antisocial facets were associated with lower harm avoidance, while the Lifestyle facet was associated with reward dependence and cooperativeness. Both of these studies suggest that individuals with interpersonal features of psychopathy are less concerned about uncertainty of situations and avoiding harm, while individuals with impulsive-antisocial feature of psychopathy are more likely to seek out novel situations and be socially intolerant and disinterested, unhelpful and revengeful. Unlike the results from the adolescent sample but similar to theories and research assessing callous-unemotional (CU) traits in youth, the Affective facet in male offenders was associated with being tough-minded, detached and independent, which results in a self-centered temperament uninfluenced by punishment. Collectively, theories and research indicate that childhood temperament may put youth at risk of developing psychopathy, and these temperamental characteristics, which are differently associated with facets of psychopathy, can be seen from childhood into adulthood.

Childhood psychopathology and psychopathic traits

Most clinicians and researchers agree that psychopathy develops from an early age (Kosson, Vitacco, Swogger & Steurwald, 2016). Indeed, adolescent psychopathy score on the PCL:YV remain stable into early adulthood using the PCL-R, and this is consistent for males and females (Hemphälä, Kosson, Westerman & Hodgins, 2015). However, there is active debate about how childhood psychopathic traits should be measured (Salekin, Andershed, Batky & Bontemps, 2018). Since before its introduction to the DSM-5, CU traits have become increasingly used as a single construct of psychopathic traits for youth. However, these traits map only onto the Affective facet of psychopathy in adults, which is why some researchers are averse to liken CU traits as a downward extension of psychopathy for youth (Bergstrøm & Farrington, 2018; Colins, Andershed, Salekin & Fanti, 2018; Salekin, 2016, 2017). A great deal of research has explored the clinical relevance of psychopathic traits in youth to assess risk and predict antisocial outcomes; however, there are only a few studies that test if psychopathic traits or CU traits in youth predict psychopathy into adulthood. Thus, arguably the debate centered on the best method of assessing psychopathic traits in youth (either CU traits or the full dimensional construct of psychopathy) cannot be definitively answered until more prospective studies are conducted.

The studies discussed here all come from the Pittsburgh Youth Study, which is a longitudinal study following over a thousand inner-city boys, which began in 1987; however, the sample sizes do vary in the following studies. In a sample of 271 boys, Lynam and colleagues (2007) found psychopathic traits at age 13 years (measured by the Child Psychopathy Scale; CPS) predicted adult Psychopathy Checklist: Screening Version (PCL:SV) scores at age 24 years, and Lynam and colleagues (2009) found psychopathic traits at age 7 remained stable through to 17 years in a cohort of 1500 participants. Using the Interpersonal-Callousness scale, Burke et al. (2007) showed Interpersonal-Callousness traits at age 10 to 12 years predicted factor 2 scores in adulthood, but not factor 1. These results have since been replicated by Hawes et al. (2017) who showed the Interpersonal-Callousness scale predicted adult total PCL:SV and factor 2 scores, but again, not factor 1. These results suggest that there may be a disconnect between the measure of interpersonal-affective traits in youth and interpersonal-affective traits in adults. However, when exploring the combination of psychopathic traits (interpersonal-affective) and conduct problems, Hawes et al. (2017) found boys who scored high on both constructs were at greatest risk of developing psychopathy into adulthood. Arguments have been made about incorporating antisocial behavior into the construct of psychopathy, suggesting the inclusion is a tautological measurement, yet, this research may support the assertion that antisocial behavior in youth is important for the development of psychopathic traits into adulthood.

Indeed, conduct problem behaviors have been important in predicting psychopathy into adulthood, even without the combination of psychopathic traits. A recent prospective study used teacher-reported childhood behaviors and personality traits at ages 6, 10 and 12 years old to see how they predicted adult psychopathy using the PCL-R at age 33 (Bamvita et al., 2017). In their male sample, Bamvita et al. (ibid.) found total PCL-R scores were predicted by childhood conduct problems, and when assessing the facet structure of the PCL-R, the authors found conduct problems predicted all four facets, while oppositional behaviors predicted the Interpersonal, Affective and Lifestyle facets. In addition, the Interpersonal facet was predicted by lower levels of anxiety, and the Lifestyle and Antisocial facets were predicted by inattention. Therefore, psychopathy and the facets were generally predicted by conduct problems and oppositional behaviors, with the most distinctive difference for interpersonal traits, which were predicted by low anxiety at age 6 years. Thus, the authors suggest low anxiety (as found in adult psychopaths; Newman & Schmitt, 1998) may be an early indicator of adult psychopathic personality (Bamvita et al., 2017), and in line with the PCL-R construct of psychopathy in adults, early behavior problems adds to the predictive model of adult psychopathy.

Although there is an active discussion that CU traits are downward extension of adult psychopathy, there is limited empirical support that CU traits are a robust predictor of psychopathy into adulthood. Instead, based on the limited evidence available, psychopathy in adulthood is most reliably predicted by the full construct of psychopathic traits, which includes an ongoing history of antisocial behaviors. Using the full dimensional approach, the prediction of adult psychopathy is stronger and more stable across youth development. Furthermore, not only does this construct better predict adult psychopathy, but it is also more predictive of future and stable conduct problems for boys and girls (Bergstrøm & Farrington, 2018; Colins et al., 2018).

Personality

Based on the Five-Factor Model of personality, normal personality consists of five domains – neuroticism (e.g., sensitive/nervous vs. secure/confident), extraversion (e.g., outgoing/energetic vs. solitary/reserved), openness (e.g., inventive/curious vs. consistent/cautious), agreeableness (e.g., friendly/compassionate vs. challenging/detached) and conscientiousness (e.g., efficient/organized vs. easy-going/careless). Research has demonstrated a strong relationship between psychopathy and the five-factor model of personality, and the most consistent associations with psychopathy are for lower agreeableness and conscientiousness, and these associations are found across different sample types and assessment tools (Lynam et al., 2005; Lynam & Miller, 2015; Miller & Lynam, 2003; Nigel et al., 2018; O'Boyle, Forsyth, Banks, Story & White, 2015; Ross, Benning, Patrick, Thompson & Thurston, 2009). Because of the close association between the five-factor model of personality and psychopathy, a five-factor trait-based model of psychopathy has been proposed (for a review see Lynam, Miller & Derefinko, 2017). Importantly, the five-factor model is differently related to the factor and facet structure of psychopathy.

Drawing from a sample of hospitalized male offenders diagnosed with personality disorders, individuals with a PCL-R score higher than 25 were lower on neuroticism than offenders with a PCL-R lower than 24 (Pereira, Huband & Duggan, 2008). No other significant psychopathic group differences were found for the five-factor model. However, when using the PCL-R as a continuous variable and assessing the factor structure more associations were found. PCL-R total scores were still related to lower neuroticism, but also to lower agreeableness. Factor 1 was negatively related to lower neuroticism and agreeableness, whereas factor 2 was associated with higher extraversion and lower agreeableness (ibid.). Thus, in personality disordered male offenders, factor 1 traits are related to a personality that is secure and confident, and challenging and detached, whereas factor 2 is related to a personality profile that is outgoing and energetic, and challenging and detached. Somewhat similar results have been found using the two-factor model of the Psychopathic Personality Inventory – Revised (PPI-R) in a forensic sample of male and female substance abusers. Nigel and colleagues (2018) found the Impulsive-Antisociality factor was positively associated with neuroticism, and negatively related to agreeableness and conscientiousness, while the Fearless-Dominance factor was negatively related to neuroticism, agreeableness, and positively associated with extraversion. In nonforensic samples using the Triarchic Psychopathy Measure (TriPM), Blagov and colleagues (2016) found the Boldness facet was related to higher extraversion and lower neuroticism, the Disinhibition facet was related to low conscientiousness and agreeableness, and the Meanness facet was related to lower extraversion, conscientiousness, agreeableness and openness. Although findings are generally consistent between psychopathy measures and forensic and non-forensic samples, there have been some cross cultural differences between psychopathy and the five-factor model (see Latzman et al., 2015).

One of the few studies to test the association between the five-factor model of personality and psychopathy using the four-facet model of the PCL-R in incarcerated women found the Interpersonal facet was negatively related to neuroticism and agreeableness, and positively related to extroversion. Further, the Antisocial facet was also negatively related to agreeableness, and both the Lifestyle and Antisocial facets were related to lower conscientiousness (Eisenbarth, Krammer, Edwards, Kiehl & Neumann, 2018). Thus, in general, the associations between the five-factor model and psychopathy are mostly consistent for men and women, although there are some reported sex differences. Similar to adults, the associations between the five-factor model and psychopathic traits for male and female youth are generally consistent. For example, using the Youth Psychopathic Trait Inventory (YPI) in a sample of adolescent males and females, Grandiose-Manipulate traits were associated with higher extraversion and lower agreeableness (Borroni, Somma, Andershed, Maffei & Fossati, 2014). Callous-unemotional traits for both males and females were associated with lower agreeableness and neuroticism, and the Impulsive-Irresponsibility facet was associated with low conscientiousness, agreeableness and higher extraversions. The only sex difference that did emerge was that males with higher Grandiose-Manipulative and CU traits were lower on conscientiousness, and this was not found for females (Borroni et al., 2014).

Externalizing and internalizing traits

General psychopathology typically falls into two broad dimensions, internalizing and externalizing. Using these psychopathological domains, research has revealed important distinctions in understanding the construct of psychopathy. For instance, in a sample of 1,741 offenders (17% female), Blonigen et al. (2010) assessed the relation between externalizing and internalizing traits with the PCL-R and PPI-R. The measure of internalizing traits included anxiety, anxiety-related disorders and depression, while the externalizing scale included antisocial features, aggression, drug problems and alcohol problems. The authors found the interpersonal-affective features on both the PCL-R and PPI-R were negatively associated with internalizing symptoms. In contrast, the antisocial features of psychopathy on both the PCL-R and PPI-R were positively associated with internalizing and externalizing. In a large sample of young adult males (M_{age} = 25 years), Neumann and Pardini (2014) found higher scores on the Self-Report Psychopathy Scale (SRP) Affective and Lifestyle facets and the YPI Impulsivity facet were related to greater externalizing. Internalizing was predicted by lower scores on the Affective facet and higher scores on the Lifestyle facet using the SRP, and high impulsivity on the YPI (ibid.). Thus, research indicates that there is a strong link between externalizing behaviors and psychopathy, but this is most consistent for the antisocial features of psychopathy. Furthermore, higher levels of internalizing symptoms are related to higher impulsive-antisocial features of psychopathy. There was a more general consensus that affective traits were a protective factor for internalizing symptoms. Indeed, these findings are consistent with research showing interpersonal-affective traits are associated with reduced genetic risk for internalizing psychopathology, while behavioral psychopathic traits are linked to an increased genetic risk for externalizing psychopathology (Blonigen, Hicks, Krueger, Patrick & Iacono, 2005).

Similar to internalizing symptoms, research linking Post-Traumatic Stress Disorder (PTSD) with psychopathy differ based on the dimensional construct. For example, in a large sample of combat-exposed National Guard and Reserve service members, interpersonal-affective traits were found to provide combat soldiers' increased resiliency to post-traumatic stress disorder (Anestis, Harrop, Green & Anestis, 2017). In contrast, factor 2 on the PCL:YV was positively associated with PTSD in a sample of 1,354 adolescent serious offenders (Tsang, 2018). Thus, factor 2 is most associated with higher externalizing and internalizing, as well as symptoms of PTSD. In contrast, factor 1 is protective for internalizing symptoms and susceptibility to PTSD in soldiers.

Suicidality

Cleckley (1941, 1984) stated that psychopaths often make threats of suicide, but these are typically done for attention, and more generally, psychopaths are immune to suicidality. However, there is a clear link between psychopathy and suicidality, but as discussed above, this link differs based on the factor structure of psychopathy. For instance, an early study including male inmates found factor 2 PCL-R scores were related to more extensive histories of suicide, while factor 1 was unrelated (Verona, Patrick & Joiner, 2001). In female inmates, factor 1 on the PCL-R was found to be a protective factor for past suicide attempts, whereas factor 2 was a risk factor (Verona, Hicks & Patrick, 2005). Drawing from a multi-sample including 17,111 adult and juvenile criminal offenders, forensic psychiatric patients and civil psychiatric patients, Douglas et al. (2006) also found a positive association between suicidality and factor 2, but not for factor 1. The positive association with factor 2 was largely explained by the Lifestyle facet over the Antisocial facet. However, in a civil psychiatric sample (Swogger, Conner, Meldrum & Caine, 2009) and a female offender sample (Kimonis et al., 2010) only the Antisocial facet was associated with suicidal behaviors.

Latzman et al. (2018) found suicidality in a community sample was positively associated with the TriPM Disinhibition facet, but in their student sample suicidality was positively associated with the Meanness facet. Consistent with forensic samples, the Boldness facet was a protective factor for suicidality in the student sample (ibid.). It is important to note, however, that using self-report in a sample of male offenders, neither Levenson Self-Report Psychopathy Scale (LSRP) factor 1 or 2 were directly associated with suicidal ideation (Pennington, Cramer, Miller & Anastasi, 2015). The authors did find that offenders who posed the greatest risk of suicidal ideation had the highest scores on both factor 2 and depression (ibid.). In summary, there is more evidence that suggests the interpersonal-affective features of psychopathy are either unrelated or are a protective factor for suicidality, while the antisocial and lifestyle features of psychopathy are related to a greater risk of suicidality, especially when factor 2 traits are accompanied by depression. Importantly, these findings are generalizable for men and women, and across sample types (e.g., forensic, community).

Impulsivity and risk-taking

There are several explanations why psychopathy is associated with risk-taking behaviors. The first is that individuals with psychopathic traits have low fear and are punishment insensitive. This failure to learn from a risky situation increases the cycle of risk-taking behaviors. Removing fear or concern from the possible consequences of risk-taking may make the act enjoyable and thrilling, especially because this behavior ends with a physical "reward" (e.g., profit from selling stolen property, physical thrill). Thus, psychopathy may be related to risk-taking simply because they enjoy it and reap rewards for doing so. A second explanation is impulsivity. Psychopathy is associated with impulsivity, and impulsive individuals engage in risky behaviors without thinking or realizing the consequences (Thomson, Towl & Centifanti, 2016; Vassileva, Georgiev, Martin, Gonzalez & Segala, 2011). Regardless of the rationale, there is ample evidence to support that psychopathy is related to risk-taking behavior. However, these two explanations may be unique to specific features of psychopathy.

Using a laboratory experiment called the Balloon Analogue Task in a mixed sample of offenders and people from the community, Snowden and colleagues (2017) found total scores on the TriPM were associated with behavioral risk-taking, and this was unique to the Boldness facet. This is partly expected because the Boldness facet includes insensitivity to punishment and remaining calm when under pressure. Therefore, the authors suggest people with these traits are not perturbed by being risky even if they fail (e.g., get caught). Exploring the association between psychopathic traits and types of risk-taking, Satchell et al. (2018) found Fearless-Dominance on the PPI-R predicted pro-social risk-taking behaviors, which may increase the successful manipulative tactics seen in psychopaths. The authors also found Self-Centered Impulsivity predicted ethical and health risk-taking, which have long-term antisocial outcomes. Lastly, Cold-Heartedness was found to be a "minimal" predictor of risk-taking (ibid., p. 168). Thus, it is evident that psychopathic traits are related to risk-taking, however, risk-taking associated with the interpersonal-affective features of psychopathy are generally related to the individual achieving an outcome or a goal (e.g., thrill, physical gain), whereas individuals high on impulsive-antisocial features of psychopathy engage in risk-taking that is high risk and characteristically impulsive, and thus, they act without thinking (Maes, Woyke & Brazil, 2018). Indeed, then, risk-taking based on the presence of specific psychopathic traits may reflect different cognitive abilities, with factor 2 associated with poor inhibitory control and impulsivity, while factor 1 risk-taking involves planned and directed cognitive control to achieve an outcome.

Executive function

Executive functioning can be defined as the self-regulation of emotion, thought and actions that aid cognitive flexibility, working memory and inhibitory control (Miyake et al., 2000). Although executive function is dependent on the integrity of neural systems of the prefrontal cortex (Séguin & Zelazo, 2005), executive function falls into the neuropsychological field. There is a longstanding association linking poor executive function with antisocial behavior in youth and adults (Morgan & Lilienfeld, 2000; Thomson & Centifanti, 2018). In contrast, the evidence linking poor executive function to psychopathy is mixed, which has led researchers to argue that executive function deficits are not specific to psychopathy, and instead, these deficits are found in people who are antisocial, regardless of their levels of psychopathic traits (Delfin, Andiné, Hofvander, Billstedt & Wallinius, 2018). However, these mixed findings may be due to the different types of populations being studied, such as youths and adults, prisoners and university students, as wells as different measures of psychopathy and executive function. Further, some studies include only a single measure of executive function (e.g., inhibition) and neglect the other domains (e.g., cognitive flexibility) or they fail to control for general intelligence, which is a different construct but shares substantial overlap (Friedman et al., 2006). Nevertheless, results indicate that when comparing groups of similarly antisocial individuals, with and without the presence of psychopathy, there is no significant difference in executive function (De Brito, Viding, Kumari, Blackwood & Hodgins, 2013; Dvorak-Bertsch, Sadeh, Glass, Thornton & Newman, 2007).

However, when comparing psychopaths with a criminal history to non-psychopathic healthy controls, the psychopathic group were found to have deficits in response inhibition (Krakowski et al., 2015). More recently though, Delfin and colleagues (2018) tested four executive function domains (cognitive flexibility, working memory, inhibition and planning and problem solving) in relation with the four-facet model of the PCL-R in a sample of 214 male violent offenders. The authors found that the most reliable evidence was that poor planning and problem solving was associated with the Antisocial and Lifestyle facets of psychopathy. This finding is also supported by earlier research on offenders, which showed factor 2 was associated with poor planning (Baskin-Sommers et al., 2015). Thus, based on the evidence to date, deficits in executive function are not typically found for individuals with affective and interpersonal features of psychopathy, which is somewhat expected as these traits are associated with drawn out cognitive processes and goal-directed behaviors. Any associations that are found between psychopathy and deficits in executive function are generally between the impulsive-antisocial features of psychopathy and inhibitory control and planning (Thomson et al., 2019). Thus, deficits in executive function linked to psychopathy are largely explained by the overlap with antisocial behavior, which has a strong association with poor executive function.

Intelligence

Cleckley (1941, p. 338) described psychopaths as having "good" intelligence, and Henderson (1939, p. 112) even went as far as to describe the creative psychopath as "near genius". However, since these clinical descriptions of psychopathy, the scientific testing of the link between psychopathy and intelligence has been limited.

Although the development of the Psychopathy Checklist – Revised (Hare, 2003) was based on Cleckley's clinical observations and criteria, Hare (ibid.) differed in his view of the links between psychopathy and intelligence. This was bolstered by research suggesting little relationship between PCL-R scores and intelligence (Hare & Neumann, 2008; Hart, Forth & Hare, 1990; Johansson & Kerr, 2005). However, intelligence plays an important role in psychopathy and offending. Psychopaths with higher intelligence typically start violent offending at a younger age (Johansson & Kerr, 2005), child molesters with higher levels of psychopathy and lower IQ are four times more likely to be reconvicted (Beggs & Grace, 2008), and adolescents with higher CU traits with high verbal intelligence engage in the higher levels of proactive aggression (Jambroes et al., 2018).

Using the dimensional construct of psychopathy, significant associations have been found with intelligence. For instance, higher scores on factor 2 and the Antisocial and Lifestyle facets are related to poorer performance on full-scale IQ (Heinzen, Köhler, Godt, Geiger & Huchzermeier, 2011; Neumann & Hare, 2008). In contrast, factor 1 and the Interpersonal facet are related to better performance on full-scale IQ and verbal intelligence (Nijman, Merckelbach & Cima, 2009; Vitacco, Neumann & Wodushek, 2008). It is important to note that research involving women is more mixed but this may be due to the limited number of studies and the broad scope of populations being tested. For example, in an Italian forensic inpatient sample of women, poorer performance on the Raven's Progressive Matrices was related to higher total scores on the PCL-R, as well as higher scores on all factors and facets (Spironelli, Segrè, Stegagno & Angrilli, 2014). In a sample of non-psychotic female offenders in the US, Vitale and colleagues (2002) found total PCL-R scores were related to lower intelligence for African Americans but not Caucasians, suggesting significant cultural differences in the link between psychopathy and intelligence. Furthermore, in a Bulgarian community sample, total PCL:SV and factor 1 and factor 2 scores were weakly related with lower intelligence (Bozgunov, Vasilev & Vassileva, 2014). A recent study including non-institutionalized women found LSRP factor 1 psychopathic traits were related to higher intelligence (Ben-Yaacov & Glicksohn, 2018). In a mixed sample of hospitalized and incarcerated violent female offenders from Finland, Weizmann-Henelius and colleagues (2004) found full-scale intelligence was unrelated to the PCL-R and the two factors. However, the authors found PCL-R total scores, factor 2, and the Lifestyle facet were related to lower verbal intelligence.

Studying psychopathy at the dimensional level has been important for understanding the relation with intelligence and so too has the study of intelligence across domains. For instance, research from a large US psychiatric sample has shown that verbal intelligence is positively related to interpersonal psychopathic traits (Vitacco, Neumann & Jackson, 2005), and this finding has since been supported by a German male prisoner sample (de Tribolet-Hardy, Vohs, Mokros & Habermeyer, 2014), and high-risk personality disordered female offenders (Mckeown & Thomson, in press). Therefore, when testing the relation between psychopathy and intelligence it seems beneficial to measure multiple measures of intelligence, as well as the dimensional construct of psychopathy. Collectively, these studies show antisocial and lifestyle psychopathic traits are typically related to lower intelligence, while the interpersonal features of psychopathy are more consistently related to higher verbal intelligence for men and women.

Emotional intelligence

Emotional intelligence consists of four branches: managing emotions, understanding emotions, facilitating thought using emotion and perceiving emotion (Mayer, Caruso & Salovey, 2016). Facial expression recognition will be discussed in the next section. These four branches are combined to assess experiential emotional intelligence (perceiving emotions and using emotion to facilitate thought) and strategic emotional intelligence (understanding emotion and managing emotion). A recent meta-analysis including 13 studies and 2,401 participants found total psychopathy scores (self-report and clinical) were related to poor emotional intelligence (Megías, Gómez-Leal, Gutiérrez-Cobo, Cabello & Fernández-Berrocal, 2018). Exploring associations at the dimensional level reveal important differences. Using an emotional ability-based assessment, male prisoners with higher levels of psychopathic traits demonstrated lower emotional intelligence (Ermer, Kahn, Salovey & Kiehl, 2012). However, when exploring the four emotional intelligence branches and the two-factor model of psychopathy, factor 2 was associated with deficits in global emotional intelligence and strategic emotional intelligence (both understanding emotions and managing emotions). Although it could be expected that factor 1 would be associated with poor emotional intelligence because of the emotional disconnect with others (e.g., lack of empathy and remorse), this was not found. A likely explanation may be that the personality features of psychopathy are intertwined with the need of having intact emotional intelligence in order to successfully manipulate people. The findings for factor 2 support assertions that these traits are associated with poor emotion regulation and recognizing emotions in others and oneself.

The result from a large ($n = 1,257$) nonclinical sample have shown total scores of psychopathic traits using the PPI-R were related to poor emotional intelligence (Watts et al., 2016). However, at the dimensional level Fearless-Dominance was found to be positively related to higher levels of emotional self-awareness, assertiveness, self-esteem and confidence in their ideas and beliefs. While Coldheartedness was associated with higher levels of emotional adjustment measures, but negatively associated with interpersonal emotional intelligence. In contrast, higher Self-Centered Impulsivity scores were related to poor emotional intelligence. Thus, psychopathic traits that involve manipulative and conning behaviors were related to better emotional intelligence, while those psychopathic traits associated with problems regulating emotions were linked to poor emotional intelligence.

A novel study by Ling, Raine, Gao and Schug (2018) found that lower emotional intelligence in incarcerated males fully mediated the link between psychopathy (PCL-R) and low autonomic social stress arousal, and this was consistent for factor 1, factor 2, and the Affective, Interpersonal and Lifestyle facets (partial mediation was observed for the Antisocial facet). Therefore, in this study poor emotional intelligence may explain why psychopathy is related to blunted physiological arousal. Similarly, poor ability to understand and manage emotions has been found to mediate the link between PPI-R Self-Centered Impulsivity scale and reactive and proactive aggression (Lanciano, Curci, Guglielmi, Soleti & Grattagliano, 2018).

In women, however, the results are somewhat different. In a sample of 228 female offenders, no significant associations were found for total PCL-R, factor 1 and factor 2 and emotional intelligence, both strategic and experiential (Edwards, Ermer, Salovey & Kiehl, 2018). But the authors found the Affective and Antisocial facets were correlated with poor strategic emotional intelligence; however, when controlling for IQ and age, only the Affective facet remained significant (ibid.). Thus, women higher on affective psychopathic traits demonstrate a poor ability to understand and manage emotions in themselves and others. Indeed, biological vulnerability to emotion dysregulation has been shown to moderate the link between affective psychopathic traits and reactive aggression in women (Thomson, Kiehl & Bjork, 2019).

In summary, the research to date has been mixed linking psychopathy to emotional intelligence. Most consistently though, is that poor emotional intelligence is associated with impulsive-antisocial psychopathic traits. When assessing the branches of emotional intelligence, interpersonal traits have been linked to better interpersonal emotional intelligence. In theory, these findings are logical, as individuals who display personality traits that involve charming, conning and manipulating other people may require good emotional intelligence.

Emotion recognition

Part of perceiving emotions is the ability to recognize facial expressions in others, which is a topic that has received a great deal of attention in the field of psychopathy. Psychopathic traits in youth and adults are associated with an atypical emotional function that may impede information processing. In particular, adults and youth with psychopathic traits have been found to display deficits in recognizing a range of facial expressions in others (Dawel, O'Kearney, McKone & Palermo, 2012), but this deficit seems to be more specific for fearful expressions. For instance, youth with high levels of CU traits and psychopathic traits have been found to have deficits in the recognition of fearful voices (Blair, Budhani, Colledge & Scott, 2005) and fearful facial and body expressions (Muñoz, 2009; Viding et al., 2012). Based on eye-tracking paradigms, research has found youth with psychopathic traits tend to focus less on the eyes when interpreting facial expressions, which is a key facial region for identifying emotion.

Somewhat similar findings have been reproduced in adults. For example, Dargis, Wolf and Koenigs (2018) found PCL-R factor 1 traits in male offenders were associated with poor recognition of fearful faces; however, unlike results in youth samples, fewer fixations on the eyes was largely explained by the Interpersonal facet, whereas poor fear emotion recognition was most strongly associated with the Affective facet. Gillespie and colleagues (2017) also found the TriPM Boldness facet was associated with less attention to the eyes in a sample of violent offenders. Some have speculated that this deficient recognition of fear in others may increase the psychopaths' propensity for cruel behaviors, which would make poor facial expression recognition a key target for interventions. Indeed, research by Dadds et al. (2006) has shown that youth with CU traits have improvement in recognizing facial expressions when they are instructed to look at the eyes during laboratory tasks, and in response to emotion recognition training (Dadds, Cauchi, Wimalaweera, Hawes & Brennan, 2012). However, more research is needed to assess the long-term effects of this intervention to see if recognition of fearful expressions impacts the development of psychopathic traits and antisocial behaviors into adulthood.

It is important to draw attention to the antithetical contribution of these findings to our understanding of psychopathy. On one hand, it is unsurprising that psychopathic traits are associated with poor facial expression recognition because of the link between psychopathy and impairments in the amygdala. But on the other hand, psychopaths are experts in the art of conning, manipulating and charming others. To expertly take advantage of people it is crucial to be able to read and gauge other people's emotions. Without the ability to pick up on social cues, such as facial expressions, the psychopath would be less successful at detecting the need to apply/adjust appropriate techniques to pacify and ease their victim. A possible explanation for the associations between facial expression recognition and psychopathy could be due to intelligence. For example, a recent study including a sample of 685 personality-disordered prisoners, it was found that poor intelligence explained the association between psychopathy (and the Affective facet) and the ability to recognize facial expressions (Igoumenou, Harmer, Yang, Coid & Rogers, 2017). Thus, when the authors accounted for intelligence, psychopathy was no longer related to deficits in emotion recognition. Furthermore, drawing from a university sample (which may provide a more homogeneous sampling for intelligence than clinical or forensic samples), factor 1 traits were positively related to accuracy in emotion recognition (specifically to fear), whereas factor 2 was associated with poor emotion recognition (Del Gaizo & Falkenbach, 2008). In support of the statement that psychopaths should be able to recognize emotions in others to successfully implement their destructive interpersonal tactics, a recent study has found proactive violent offenders were no different than a non-violent control group in emotion recognition, whereas reactively violent offenders performed worse than both the control group and proactive violent offenders (Philipp-Wiegmann, Rösler, Retz-Junginger & Retz, 2017). Indeed, reactive violence is associated with cognitive deficits, while proactive violence is not. Thus, individuals who use proactive violence, such as the prototypical psychopath, may have an intact ability to recognize social cues in others, which undoubtedly furthers the psychopath's predaciousness.

Psychopaths are notorious for picking up on and using peoples' weaknesses against them, and therefore it is only logical to expect them to be able to recognize vulnerable emotions too.

Besides intelligence being the reason why research is finding an association between psychopathy and poor emotion recognition (Igoumenou et al., 2017), there are several other possible explanations for the results, including variability in the ecological validity of facial expression tasks, which use static computer images or short video clips with no contextual information. But the most likely explanation is that psychopaths are goal-oriented. When manipulating other people, the psychopath is motivated by the success of the manipulation, thus, she is incentivized to pay particular attention to the individual's emotions to reciprocate accordingly. In sum, there is considerable evidence that psychopathic traits are related to poor emotion recognition, and this seems specific to the Affective facet in adults and CU traits in youth. However, more recent evidence has begun to shed light that this association is not as clear cut as some have argued, and these emotion recognition deficits may be due to more general cognitive deficits, such as poor intelligence. Much more research is needed in this area to fully understand if facial expression recognition is both a psychopathy-related deficit and a mechanism in the development of psychopathic personality.

Moral foundations

Given the psychopath's propensity for violent and criminal behavior, there is no surprise that psychopathic traits are related to impairments in moral attitudes and moral decision-making. Based on the moral foundations questionnaire (MFQ; Graham et al., 2011), there are five moral pillars: Harm/Care, Fairness/Reciprocity, Ingroup/Loyalty, Authority/Respect and Purity/Sanctity. Each foundation score reflects how much a person prioritizes a set of moral attitudes. A recent meta-analysis including 6 studies found total psychopathy scores were significantly related to less concern about harm to others, fairness, purity and respect for authority, with no significant relation with ingroup loyalty (Marshall, Watts & Lilienfeld, 2018). The effects are generally stronger for the fairness and harm foundations, and this is found using the PCL-R in prisoners and the LSRP and PPI-R in community and student samples (Aharoni, Antonenko & Kiehl, 2011; Efferson, Glenn, Remmel & Iyer, 2017; Gay, Vitacco, Hackney, Beussink & Lilienfeld, 2018; Glenn, Iyer, Graham, Koleva & Haidt, 2009). Thus, higher psychopathic traits are related to less concern about the well-being and equality of individuals and bettering injustices.

Differential associations are found for the factors and facets. Using the TriPM in a community sample, Boldness was associated with lower purity; Meanness was associated with lower concern for harm and fairness; Disinhibition was positively associated with fairness, but negatively associated with authority and purity (Almeida et al., 2015). Using the two-factor model of the LSRP, Efferson and colleagues (2017) found factor 1 was most negatively associated with harm, fairness and authority, and positively associated with in-group loyalty. Factor 2 was negatively associated with fairness, authority, in-group loyalty and purity, and positively associated with harm. However, when the authors statistically controlled for the nontarget factor, factor 1 was only related to lower concern for the harm of others, while factor 2 was associated with a greater concern for the harm of others. The authors did not find any significant differences for men and women. Using the PPI-R in nonclinical samples, higher Fearless-Dominance scores were related to lower concerns for fairness and preventing harm to others, and self-centered impulsivity was also associated with less concern for preventing harm to others but was also related to less purity (e.g., sanctity of body, mind and soul) and respect for authority (Gay et al., 2018). Finally, coldheartedness was related to less concern for purity, fairness and preventing harm to others (ibid.).

Collectively, this research suggests that individuals with psychopathic traits are not just immoral but that they display a specific set of moral attitudes (Aharoni et al., 2011), and these specific associations differ based on the presence of particular psychopathic traits. Specifically, the affective features of psychopathy were most consistently related to less concern about the well-being and equality of other people, while behavioral psychopathic traits were most consistently related to a lack of respect for authority, and these results were fairly consistent across clinical and self-report measures and clinical, forensic and community populations.

Moral decision-making

A popular method of understanding moral decision-making is called "sacrificial moral dilemmas". The premise is to understand the person's moral intuitions by asking the participants to make decisions based on moral contexts. Typically, the hypothetical task involves choosing to get involved by harming one person to save many more people. For instance, there is a runaway train and there is an option to divert the train onto another track. On the train's current track there are five people, on the other track there is one person. The participant must then decide to either (a) do nothing and save one person with the consequence of five people dying, or (b) push the lever to save the five people with the consequence that one person will die. Choosing to do nothing falls into the deontological moral judgment, whereby the moral decision is based on a duty-bound approach to decision-making. There is less emphasis on the outcome and more focus on what action is ethically right based on a set of rules or principles. For instance, based on the moral principles it is wrong to kill, thus, the moral decision should be to not push the lever (option a). In contrast, the rational decision, known as the "utilitarian" moral judgment, is the pursuit of good for the greatest number of people; in this scenario, the moral decision is to save the greatest number of lives (option b; push the lever). There are many versions of the moral dilemma, from smothering your crying baby to prevent enemy soldiers finding and killing you and your family, to stealing medication to save a family member, to harming a terrorist's son to deter the father from detonating a bomb and killing many people.

To date, there is mixed evidence linking psychopathy with a specific set of moral decision-making. For example, evidence from a Dutch sample of male psychiatric inmates found psychopaths ($n = 14$; PCL-R < 25) did not differ from non-psychopathic offenders on their moral decision-making (Cima, Tonnaer & Hauser, 2010). Similarly, in a small community sample, Glenn, Raine et al. (2009) found no association between PCL-R scores and moral decision-making. However, when Koenigs and colleagues (2012) compared low-anxious psychopaths (PCL-R > 30), high-anxious psychopaths (PCL-R > 30) and non-psychopaths on moral decision-making, they found low-anxious psychopaths had more utilitarian decisions for "personal" dilemmas that involved direct and intimate physical contact (e.g., pushing someone off a bridge to stop a runaway train from killing five people). High-anxious psychopaths did not differ in their decision-making for personal moral dilemmas than non-psychopaths. Thus, anxiety may reflect key phenotypic moderator in psychopathy. Both high-and low-anxious psychopaths were more likely to endorse actions for impersonal moral dilemmas, where harm or rule violation is indirect, such as pulling a switch to divert a runaway train car from hitting five people (Koenigs et al., 2012). An explanation of the mixed findings, proposed by Koenigs et al. (ibid.), is that Cima et al. (2010) and Glenn, Iyer et al. (2009) had poor methodology in sampling, resulting in very few participants who met the diagnostic criteria of being psychopathic (PCL-R > 30), whereas Koenigs et al. (2012) sample had an adequate representation of psychopaths meeting the PCL-R cut off score in their psychopathic group.

Several studies have been conducted on student samples using self-report measures, which may be more lenient in detecting subtle moral differences in non-forensic samples. For instance, students scoring high on the LSRP tend to make more utilitarian judgments, and while making the moral decision these individuals experience less unpleasantness (Pletti, Lotto, Buodo & Sarlo, 2017). Using the TriPM and PPI-R, Balash and Falkenbach (2018) found further support that psychopathic traits in undergraduate students were related to utilitarian judgments. On the TriPM, Meanness was associated with endorsing personal and impersonal utilitarian moral decisions, whereas Disinhibition was associated with only personal utilitarian moral decisions, and Boldness was not associated with either utilitarian moral decision. On the PPI-R, the authors found Fearless-Dominance, Self-Centered Impulsivity and Cold-Heartedness scales were related to utilitarian decision-making for personal decisions but not to impersonal.

Collectively, this research suggests psychopathic individuals do have a moral compass, and it is more often set to a utilitarian approach. However, as anyone who has worked with psychopaths knows, we must be diligent about the motivation, as well as the outcome. Logically, the utilitarian approach is to sacrifice one person in order to save many – thus, here is a free pass to *actively* hurt someone (e.g., push them off a bridge, smother a child). Because the utilitarian option is the only one to allow the participant to actively engage in hurting another person, it is very possible that saving many people is a consequence of the motivation to hurt a person (and get away with it). Psychopaths get a thrill from the crime they commit, they positively appraise using aggression, they get pleasure from hurting and dominating others, and they glibly recount and brag about the brutality. Therefore, it is completely plausible that psychopaths make the utilitarian moral judgment, not because they want to save more people but because they want to hurt one, especially as the other option is to sit idly by. However, this has not been tested empirically and is only speculation drawing from research in other fields (e.g., moral intuitions) and based on my clinical work with psychopaths. These individuals are opportunistic in their cruelty, and sometimes what we perceive as good or moral decisions and behaviors are just opportunities to camouflage cruel intentions.

Summary

This chapter has provided a general overview of psychological correlates and predictors of psychopathy. Overall, the results demonstrate that interpersonal-affective and impulsive-antisocial features of psychopathy relate differently to psychological risk factors, as they do with biological risk factors. This supports the assertion that there may be multiple pathways in the development of psychopathy, as well as the importance of assessing the dimensions of psychopathy (Salekin, 2017). The argument for this book is that a single research discipline is not adequate to fully explain the development of psychopathy. Indeed, one of the most expected psychological constructs to be predictive of psychopathy in adulthood would be psychopathic traits in youth. Yet, psychopathic traits in youth are not a robust predictor of adult psychopathy, and in some sense the findings are perplexing. For instance, interpersonal-callousness in adolescence only predicted impulsive-antisocial traits in adulthood and did not predict interpersonal-affective traits. The predictive model, however, does become strengthened when including multiple factors (e.g., conduct problems) in conjunction with psychopathic traits. Certainly, the combination of psychopathic traits with conduct problems has been shown to have greater importance for predicting antisocial outcomes and these seem to be true for the development of psychopathy. However, the limited associations between youth and adult psychopathic traits suggest there must be more factors at play in the development of psychopathy than just having psychopathic traits in adolescence.

In accordance with multifinality, youth may have similar risk factors (e.g., psychopathic traits) but these may lead to different outcomes, which may be contingent on underlying risk factors or subsequent exposure to risk factors. This suggests that the developmental model of psychopathy needs to become more dynamic and integrative. Given that psychopathy is made up of a constellation of personality and behavioral traits, which are driven by biopsychosocial factors, it is time to start recognizing that a more refined model of psychopathy will require integrating multidisciplinary practice. A refined model means not relying exclusively on one discipline (i.e., psychological). With the research presented so far in this book, there is clear reason to integrate biological indices of risk (e.g., neuroscience) in conjunction with psychological correlates (e.g., temperament) to help triangulate a more specific diagnosis of psychopathy. The biopsychosocial approach is the only model to accommodate this standard of practice. Integrating the biopsychosocial approach to produce a refined but inclusive model will help in understanding the mechanisms behind psychopathy, as well as identifying the multiple pathways for developing the disorder, which will ultimately lead to improved treatment.

Acknowledgments

Thank you to Dr. Jasmin Vassileva and Dr. Michael Vitacco for providing a valuable review of this chapter. Dr. Vassileva is an Associate Professor in the Departments of Psychiatry and Psychology at Virginia Commonwealth University. Her research focuses on personality and neurocognitive risk factors for the development of addiction and neurocognitive sequelae of chronic drug use and externalizing psychopathology. Dr. Vitacco is a Board-Certified Forensic Psychologist and Associate Professor of Psychiatry and Health Behavior at Augusta University. His research specialty includes biological mechanisms associated with psychopathy, risk assessment with forensic inpatients, empathy-related phenomenon and their association with psychopathic traits, and clinical issues relevant to the insanity defense.

References

Aharoni, E., Antonenko, O. & Kiehl, K. A. (2011). Disparities in the Moral Intuitions of Criminal Offenders: The Role of Psychopathy. *Journal of Research in Personality, 45*(3), 322–327.

Almeida, P. R., Seixas, M. J., Ferreira-Santos, F., Vieira, J. B., Paiva, T. O., Moreira, P. S. & Costa, P. (2015). Empathic, Moral and Antisocial Outcomes Associated with Distinct Components of Psychopathy in Healthy Individuals: A Triarchic Model Approach. *Personality and Individual Differences, 85*, 205–211.

Anestis, J. C., Harrop, T. M., Green, B. A. & Anestis, M. D. (2017). Psychopathic Personality Traits as Protective Factors against the Development of Post-Traumatic Stress Disorder Symptoms in a Sample of National Guard Combat Veterans. *Journal of Psychopathology and Behavioral Assessment, 39*(2), 220–229.

Balash, J. & Falkenbach, D. M. (2018). The Ends Justify the Meanness: An Investigation of Psychopathic Traits and Utilitarian Moral Endorsement. *Personality and Individual Differences, 127*, 127–132.

Bamvita, J.-M., Larm, P., Checknita, D., Vitaro, F., Tremblay, R. E., Côté, G. & Hodgins, S. (2017). Childhood Predictors of Adult Psychopathy Scores among Males Followed from Age 6 to 33. *Journal of Criminal Justice, 53*, 55–65.

Baskin-Sommers, A. R., Brazil, I. A., Ryan, J., Kohlenberg, N. J., Neumann, C. S. & Newman, J. P. (2015). Mapping the Association of Global Executive Functioning onto Diverse Measures of Psychopathic Traits. *Personality Disorders, 6*(4), 336–346.

Beggs, S. M. & Grace, R. C. (2008). Psychopathy, Intelligence, and Recidivism in Child Molesters: Evidence of an Interaction Effect. *Criminal Justice and Behavior, 35*(6), 683–695.

Ben-Yaacov, T. & Glicksohn, J. (2018). Intelligence and Psychopathy: A Study on Non-incarcerated Females from the Normal Population. *Cogent Psychology, 5*(1), 1–13.

Bergstrøm, H. & Farrington, D. P. (2018). Grandiose-Manipulative, Callous-Unemotional, and Daring-Impulsive: The Prediction of Psychopathic Traits in Adolescence and their Outcomes in Adulthood. *Journal of Psychopathology and Behavioral Assessment, 40*(2), 149–158.

Blagov, P. S., Patrick, C. J., Oost, K. M., Goodman, J. A. & Pugh, A. T. (2016). Triarchic Psychopathy Measure: Validity in Relation to Normal-Range Traits, Personality Pathology, and Psychological Adjustment. *Journal of Personality Disorders*, *30*(1), 71–81.

Blair, R. J. R., Budhani, S., Colledge, E. & Scott, S. (2005). Deafness to Fear in Boys with Psychopathic Tendencies. *Journal of Child Psychology and Psychiatry*, *46*(3), 327–336.

Blonigen, D. M., Hicks, B. M., Krueger, R. F., Patrick, C. J. & Iacono, W. G. (2005). Psychopathic Personality Traits: Heritability and Genetic Overlap with Internalizing and Externalizing Psychopathology. *Psychological Medicine*, *35*(5), 637–648.

Blonigen, D. M., Patrick, C. J., Douglas, K. S., Poythress, N. G., Skeem, J. L., Lilienfeld, S. O., . . . Krueger, R. F. (2010). Multimethod Assessment of Psychopathy in Relation to Factors of Internalizing and Externalizing from the Personality Assessment Inventory: The Impact of Method Variance and Suppressor Effects. *Psychological Assessment*, *22*(1), 96–107.

Borroni, S., Somma, A., Andershed, H., Maffei, C. & Fossati, A. (2014). Psychopathy Dimensions, Big Five Traits, and Dispositional Aggression in Adolescence: Issues of Gender Consistency. *Personality and Individual Differences*, *66*, 199–203.

Bozgunov, K., Vasilev, G. & Vassileva, J. (2014). Investigating the Association between Psychopathy and Intelligence in the Bulgarian Population. *Clinical and Consulting Psychology VI*, *1*(19), 1–6.

Burke, J. D., Loeber, R. & Lahey, B. B. (2007). Adolescent Conduct Disorder and Interpersonal Callousness as Predictors of Psychopathy in Young Adults. *Journal of Clinical Child and Adolescent Psychology: The Official Journal for the Society of Clinical Child and Adolescent Psychology, American Psychological Association, Division 53*, *36*(3), 334–346.

Cima, M., Tonnaer, F. & Hauser, M. D. (2010). Psychopaths Know Right from Wrong but Don't Care. *Social Cognitive and Affective Neuroscience*, *5*(1), 59–67.

Cleckley, H. (1941). *The Mask of Sanity*. St. Louis, MO: Mosby.

Cleckley, H. (1984). *The Mask of Sanity: An Attempt to Clarify Some Issues About the So-Called Psychopathic Personality*. St. Louis, MO: Mosby.

Colins, O. F., Andershed, H., Salekin, R. T. & Fanti, K. A. (2018). Comparing Different Approaches for Subtyping Children with Conduct Problems: Callous-Unemotional Traits Only Versus the Multidimensional Psychopathy Construct. *Journal of Psychopathology and Behavioral Assessment*, *40*(1), 6–15.

Dadds, M. R., Cauchi, A. J., Wimalaweera, S., Hawes, D. J. & Brennan, J. (2012). Outcomes, Moderators, and Mediators of Empathic-Emotion Recognition Training for Complex Conduct Problems in Childhood. *Psychiatry Research*, *199*(3), 201–207.

Dadds, M. R., Perry, Y., Hawes, D. J., Merz, S., Riddell, A. C., Haines, D. J., . . . Abeygunawardane, A. I. (2006). Attention to the Eyes and Fear-Recognition Deficits in Child Psychopathy. *British Journal of Psychiatry*, *189*(03), 280–281.

Dargis, M., Wolf, R. C. & Koenigs, M. (2018). Psychopathic Traits Are Associated With Reduced Fixations to the Eye Region of Fearful Faces. *Journal of Abnormal Psychology*, *127*(1), 43–50.

Dawel, A., O'Kearney, R., McKone, E. & Palermo, R. (2012). Not just Fear and Sadness: Meta-analytic Evidence of Pervasive Emotion Recognition Deficits for Facial and Vocal Expressions in Psychopathy. *Neuroscience & Biobehavioral Reviews*, *36*(10), 2288–2304.

De Brito, S. A., Viding, E., Kumari, V., Blackwood, N. & Hodgins, S. (2013). Cool and Hot Executive Function Impairments in Violent Offenders with Antisocial Personality Disorder with and without Psychopathy. *PLoS ONE*, *8*(6), e65566.

De Tribolet-Hardy, F., Vohs, K., Mokros, A. & Habermeyer, E. (2014). Psychopathy, Intelligence, and Impulsivity in German Violent Offenders. *International Journal of Law and Psychiatry*, *37*(3), 238–244.

Del Gaizo, A. L. & Falkenbach, D. M. (2008). Primary and Secondary Psychopathic Traits and Their Relationship to Perception and Experience of Emotion. *Personality and Individual Differences, 45*(3), 206–212.

Delfin, C., Andiné, P., Hofvander, B., Billstedt, E. & Wallinius, M. (2018). Examining Associations Between Psychopathic Traits and Executive Functions in Incarcerated Violent Offenders. *Frontiers in Psychiatry, 9*, 310.

Douglas, K. S., Herbozo, S., Poythress, N. G., Belfrage, H. & Edens, J. F. (2006). Psychopathy and Suicide: A Multisample Investigation. *Psychological Services, 3*(2), 97–116.

Dvorak-Bertsch, J. D., Sadeh, N., Glass, S. J., Thornton, D. & Newman, J. P. (2007). Stroop Tasks Associated with Differential Activation of Anterior Cingulate Do Not Differentiate Psychopathic and Non-psychopathic Offenders. *Personality and Individual Differences, 42*(3), 585–595.

Edwards, B. G., Ermer, E., Salovey, P. & Kiehl, K. A. (2018). Emotional Intelligence in Incarcerated Female Offenders with Psychopathic Traits. *Journal of Personality Disorders, 31*, 1–24.

Efferson, L., Glenn, A., Remmel, R. & Iyer, R. (2017). The Influence of Gender on the Relationship between Psychopathy and Five Moral Foundations. *Personality and Mental Health, 11*(4), 335–343.

Eisenbarth, H., Krammer, S., Edwards, B. G., Kiehl, K. A. & Neumann, C. S. (2018). Structural Analysis of the PCL-R and Relationship to Big Five Personality Traits and Parenting Characteristics in an Hispanic Female Offender sample. *Personality and Individual Differences, 129*, 59–65.

Ermer, E., Kahn, R. E., Salovey, P. & Kiehl, K. A. (2012). Emotional Intelligence in Incarcerated Men with Psychopathic Traits. *Journal of Personality and Social Psychology, 103*(1), 194–204.

Fowles, D. C. (2018). Temperament Risk Factors for Psychopathy. In C. J. Patrick (Ed.), *The Handbook of Psychopathy* (2nd ed., pp. 94–123). New York: Guilford.

Frick, P. J. (2012). Developmental Pathways to Conduct Disorder: Implications for Future Directions in Research, Assessment, and Treatment. *Journal of Clinical Child & Adolescent Psychology, 41*(3), 378–389.

Frick, P. J. & Viding, E. (2009). Antisocial Behavior from a Developmental Psychopathology Perspective. *Development and Psychopathology, 21*(4), 1111–1131.

Frick, P. J. & White, S. F. (2008). Research Review: The Importance of Callous-Unemotional Traits for Developmental Models of Aggressive and Antisocial Behavior. *Journal of Child Psychology and Psychiatry, and Allied Disciplines, 49*(4), 359–375.

Friedman, N. P., Miyake, A., Corley, R. P., Young, S. E., Defries, J. C. & Hewitt, J. K. (2006). Not All Executive Functions Are Related to Intelligence. Retrieved from http://jtoomim.org/brain-training/not all executive functions are related to intelligence.pdf

Gay, J. G., Vitacco, M. J., Hackney, A., Beussink, C. & Lilienfeld, S. O. (2018). Relations among Psychopathy, Moral Competence, and Moral Intuitions in Student and Community Samples. *Legal and Criminological Psychology, 23*(2), 117–134.

Gillespie, S. M., Rotshtein, P., Beech, A. R. & Mitchell, I. J. (2017). Boldness Psychopathic Traits Predict Reduced Gaze toward Fearful Eyes in Men with a History of Violence. *Biological Psychology, 128*, 29–38.

Glenn, A. L., Iyer, R., Graham, J., Koleva, S. & Haidt, J. (2009). Are All Types of Morality Compromised in Psychopathy? *Journal of Personality Disorders, 23*(4), 384–398.

Glenn, A. L., Raine, A., Schug, R. A., Young, L. & Hauser, M. (2009). Increased DLPFC Activity during Moral Decision-Making in Psychopathy. *Molecular Psychiatry, 14*(10), 909–911.

Graham, J., Nosek, B. A., Haidt, J., Iyer, R., Koleva, S. & Ditto, P. H. (2011). Mapping the Moral Domain. *Journal of Personality and Social Psychology*, *101*(2), 366–385.

Hare, R. D. (2003). *The Hare Psychopathy Checklist – Revised* (2nd ed.). Toronto, Ontario: Multi-Health Systems.

Hare, R. D. & Neumann, C. S. (2008). Psychopathy as a Clinical and Empirical Construct. *Annual Review of Clinical Psychology*, *4*(1), 217–246.

Hart, S. D., Forth, A. E. & Hare, R. D. (1990). Performance of Criminal Psychopaths on Selected Neuropsychological Tests. *Journal of Abnormal Psychology*, *99*(4), 374–379.

Hawes, D. J. & Dadds, M. R. (2005). The Treatment of Conduct Problems in Children With Callous-Unemotional Traits. *Journal of Consulting and Clinical Psychology*, *73*(4), 737–741.

Hawes, S. W., Byrd, A. L., Waller, R., Lynam, D. R. & Pardini, D. A. (2017). Late Childhood Interpersonal Callousness and Conduct Problem Trajectories Interact to Predict Adult Psychopathy. *Journal of Child Psychology and Psychiatry*, *58*(1), 55–63.

Heinzen, H., Köhler, D., Godt, N., Geiger, F. & Huchzermeier, C. (2011). Psychopathy, Intelligence and Conviction History. *International Journal of Law and Psychiatry*, *34*(5), 336–340.

Hemphälä, M., Kosson, D., Westerman, J. & Hodgins, S. (2015). Stability and Predictors of Psychopathic Traits from Mid-adolescence through Early Adulthood. *Scandinavian Journal of Psychology*, *56*(6), 649–658.

Henderson, D. K. (1939). *Psychopathic States*. New York: W. W. Norton & Company.

Igoumenou, A., Harmer, C. J., Yang, M., Coid, J. W. & Rogers, R. D. (2017). Faces and Facets: The Variability of Emotion Recognition in Psychopathy Reflects its Affective and Antisocial Features. *Journal of Abnormal Psychology*, *126*(8), 1066–1076.

Jambroes, T., Jansen, L. M. C., v.d. Ven, P. M., Claassen, T., Glennon, J. C., Vermeiren, R. R. J. M., . . . Popma, A. (2018). Dimensions of Psychopathy in Relation to Proactive and Reactive Aggression: Does Intelligence Matter? *Personality and Individual Differences*, *129*, 76–82.

Johansson, P. & Kerr, M. (2005). Psychopathy and Intelligence: A Second Look. *Journal of Personality Disorders*, *19*(4), 357–369.

Kimonis, E. R., Skeem, J. L., Edens, J. F., Douglas, K. S., Lilienfeld, S. O. & Poythress, N. G. (2010). Suicidal and Criminal Behavior among Female Offenders: The Role of Abuse and Psychopathology. *Journal of Personality Disorders*, *24*(5), 581–609.

Koenigs, M., Kruepke, M., Zeier, J. & Newman, J. P. (2012). Utilitarian Moral Judgment in Psychopathy. *Social Cognitive and Affective Neuroscience*, *7*(6), 708–714.

Kosson, D. S., Vitacco, M. J., Swogger, M. T. & Steurwald, B. L. (2016). Emotional Experiences of the Psychopath. In C. Gacono (Ed.), *The Clinical and Forensic Assessment of Psychopathy: A Practitioner's Guide* (pp. 73–95). London: Taylor & Francis.

Krakowski, M. I., Foxe, J., de Sanctis, P., Nolan, K., Hoptman, M. J., Shope, C., . . . Czobor, P. (2015). Aberrant Response Inhibition and Task Switching in Psychopathic Individuals. *Psychiatry Research*, *229*(3), 1017–1023.

Lanciano, T., Curci, A., Guglielmi, F., Soleti, E. & Grattagliano, I. (2018). Preliminary Data on the Role of Emotional Intelligence in Moderating the Link between Psychopathy and Aggression in a Nonforensic Sample. *Journal of Forensic Sciences*, *63*(3), 906–910.

Latzman, R. D., Megreya, A. M., Hecht, L. K., Miller, J. D., Winiarski, D. A. & Lilienfeld, S. O. (2015). Self-Reported Psychopathy in the Middle East: A Cross-National Comparison across Egypt, Saudi Arabia, and the United States. *BMC Psychology*, *3*(1), 37.

Latzman, R. D., Palumbo, I. M., Sauvigné, K. C., Hecht, L. K., Lilienfeld, S. O. & Patrick, C. J. (2018). Psychopathy and Internalizing Psychopathology: A Triarchic Model Perspective. *Journal of Personality Disorders*, *32*, 1–26.

Lennox, C. & Dolan, M. (2014). Temperament and Character and Psychopathy in Male Conduct Disordered Offenders. *Psychiatry Research*, *215*(3), 706–710.

Ling, S., Raine, A., Gao, Y. & Schug, R. (2018). The Mediating Role of Emotional Intelligence on the Autonomic Functioning – Psychopathy Relationship. *Biological Psychology*, *136*, 136–143.

Lynam, D. R., Caspi, A., Moffitt, T. E., Loeber, R. & Stouthamer-Loeber, M. (2007). Longitudinal Evidence that Psychopathy Scores in Early Adolescence Predict Adult Psychopathy. *Journal of Abnormal Psychology*, *116*(1), 155–165.

Lynam, D. R., Caspi, A., Moffitt, T. E., Raine, A., Loeber, R. & Stouthamer-Loeber, M. (2005). Adolescent Psychopathy and the Big Five: Results from Two Samples. *Journal of Abnormal Child Psychology*, *33*(4), 431–443.

Lynam, D. R., Charnigo, R., Moffitt, T. E., Raine, A., Loeber, R. & Stouthamer-Loeber, M. (2009). The Stability of Psychopathy across Adolescence. *Development and Psychopathology*, *21*(04), 1133.

Lynam, D. R. & Miller, J. D. (2015). Psychopathy from a Basic Trait Perspective: The Utility of a Five-Factor Model Approach. *Journal of Personality*, *83*(6), 611–626.

Lynam, D. R., Miller, J. D. & Derefinko, K. (2017). Psychopathy and Personality: An Articulation of the Benefits of a Trait-Based Approach. In C. Patrick (Ed.), *Handbook of Psychopathy* (2nd ed., pp. 259–280). New York: Guilford Press.

Maes, J. H. R., Woyke, I. C. & Brazil, I. A. (2018). Psychopathy-Related Traits and Decision-Making under Risk and Ambiguity: An Exploratory Study. *Personality and Individual Differences*, *122*, 190–194.

Marshall, J., Watts, A. L. & Lilienfeld, S. O. (2018). Do Psychopathic Individuals Possess a Misaligned Moral Compass? A Meta-Analytic Examination of Psychopathy's Relations with Moral Judgment. *Personality Disorders: Theory, Research, and Treatment*, *9*(1), 40.

Mayer, J. D., Caruso, D. R. & Salovey, P. (2016). The Ability Model of Emotional Intelligence: Principles and Updates. *Emotion Review*, *8*(4), 290–300.

Mckeown, A. & Thomson, N. D. (in press). Psychopathy and Intelligence in High-Risk Violent Women. *Journal of Forensic Psychiatry & Psychology*.

Megías, A., Gómez-Leal, R., Gutiérrez-Cobo, M. J., Cabello, R. & Fernández-Berrocal, P. (2018). The Relationship between Trait Psychopathy and Emotional Intelligence: A Meta-analytic Review. *Neuroscience & Biobehavioral Reviews*, *84*, 198–203.

Miller, J. D. & Lynam, D. R. (2003). Psychopathy and the Five-Factor Model of Personality: A Replication and Extension. *Journal of Personality Assessment*, *81*(2), 168–178.

Miyake, A., Friedman, N. P., Emerson, M. J., Witzki, A. H., Howerter, A. & Wager, T. D. (2000). The Unity and Diversity of Executive Functions and Their Contributions to Complex "Frontal Lobe" Tasks: A Latent Variable Analysis. *Cognitive Psychology*, *41*(1), 49–100.

Morgan, A. B. & Lilienfeld, S. O. (2000). A Meta-analytic Review of the Relation between Antisocial Behavior and Neuropsychological Measures of Executive Function. *Clinical Psychology Review*, *20*(1), 113–136.

Muñoz, L. C. (2009). Callous-Unemotional Traits Are Related to Combined Deficits in Recognizing Afraid Faces and Body Poses. *Journal of the American Academy of Child and Adolescent Psychiatry*, *48*(5), 554–562.

Neumann, C. S. & Hare, R. D. (2008). Psychopathic Traits in a Large Community Sample: Links to Violence, Alcohol Use, and Intelligence. *Journal of Consulting and Clinical Psychology*, *76*(5), 893–899.

Neumann, C. S. & Pardini, D. (2014). Factor Structure and Construct Validity of the Self-Report Psychopathy (SRP) Scale and the Youth Psychopathic Traits Inventory (YPI) in Young Men. *Journal of Personality Disorders*, *28*(3), 419–433.

Newman, J. P. & Schmitt, W. A. (1998). Passive Avoidance in Psychopathic Offenders: A Replication and Extension. *Journal of Abnormal Psychology*, *107*(3), 527–532.

Nigel, S. M., Dudeck, M., Otte, S., Knauer, K., Klein, V., Böttcher, T., . . . Streb, J. (2018). Psychopathy, the Big Five and Empathy as Predictors of Violence in a Forensic Sample of Substance Abusers. *The Journal of Forensic Psychiatry & Psychology*, *29*(6), 882–900.

Nijman, H., Merckelbach, H. & Cima, M. (2009). Performance Intelligence, Sexual Offending and Psychopathy. *Journal of Sexual Aggression*, *15*(3), 319–330.

O'Boyle, E. H., Forsyth, D. R., Banks, G. C., Story, P. A. & White, C. D. (2015). A Meta-Analytic Test of Redundancy and Relative Importance of the Dark Triad and Five-Factor Model of Personality. *Journal of Personality*, *83*(6), 644–664.

Pennington, C. R., Cramer, R. J., Miller, H. A. & Anastasi, J. S. (2015). Psychopathy, Depression, and Anxiety as Predictors of Suicidal Ideation in Offenders. *Death Studies*, *39*(1–5), 288–295.

Pereira, N., Huband, N. & Duggan, C. (2008). Psychopathy and Personality. An Investigation of the Relationship between the NEO-Five Factor Inventory (NEO-FFI) and the Psychopathy Checklist – Revised (PCL-R) in a Hospitalized Sample of Male Offenders with Personality Disorder. *Criminal Behaviour and Mental Health*, *18*(4), 216–223.

Philipp-Wiegmann, F., Rösler, M., Retz-Junginger, P. & Retz, W. (2017). Emotional Facial Recognition in Proactive and Reactive Violent Offenders. *European Archives of Psychiatry and Clinical Neuroscience*, *267*(7), 687–695.

Pletti, C., Lotto, L., Buodo, G. & Sarlo, M. (2017). It's Immoral, but I'd Do it! Psychopathy Traits Affect Decision-Making in Sacrificial Dilemmas and in Everyday Moral Situations. *British Journal of Psychology*, *108*(2), 351–368.

Ross, S. R., Benning, S. D., Patrick, C. J., Thompson, A. & Thurston, A. (2009). Factors of the Psychopathic Personality Inventory: Criterion-Related Validity and Relationship to the BIS/BAS and Five-Factor Models of Personality. *Assessment*, *16*(1), 71–87.

Salekin, R. T. (2016). Psychopathy in Childhood: Toward Better Informing the DSM-5 and ICD-11 Conduct Disorder Specifiers. *Personality Disorders*, *7*(2), 180–191.

Salekin, R. T. (2017). Research Review: What Do We Know about Psychopathic Traits in Children? *Journal of Child Psychology and Psychiatry*, *58*(11), 1180–1200.

Salekin, R. T., Andershed, H., Batky, B. D. & Bontemps, A. P. (2018). Are Callous Unemotional (CU) Traits Enough? *Journal of Psychopathology and Behavioral Assessment*, *40*(1), 1–5.

Satchell, L. P., Bacon, A. M., Firth, J. L. & Corr, P. J. (2018). Risk as Reward: Reinforcement Sensitivity Theory and Psychopathic Personality Perspectives on Everyday Risk-Taking. *Personality and Individual Differences*, *128*, 162–169.

Séguin, J. R. & Zelazo, P. D. (2005). Executive Function in Early Physical Aggression. In R. E. Tremblay, W. W. Hartup & J. Archer (Eds.), *Developmental Origins of Aggression* (pp. 307–329). New York: Guilford Press.

Snowden, R. J. & Gray, N. S. (2010). Temperament and Character as a Function of Psychopathy: Relationships between the Psychopathy Checklist – Revised and the Temperament and Character Inventory in a Sample of Personality Disordered Serious or Repeat Offenders. *Journal of Forensic Psychiatry & Psychology*, *21*(6), 815–833.

Snowden, R. J., Smith, C. & Gray, N. S. (2017). Risk Taking and the Triarchic Model of Psychopathy. *Journal of Clinical and Experimental Neuropsychology*, *39*(10), 988–1001.

Spironelli, C., Segrè, D., Stegagno, L. & Angrilli, A. (2014). Intelligence and Psychopathy: A Correlational Study on Insane Female Offenders. *Psychological Medicine*, *44*(1), 111–116.

Swogger, M. T., Conner, K. R., Meldrum, S. C. & Caine, E. D. (2009). Dimensions of Psychopathy in Relation to Suicidal and Self-Injurious Behavior. *Journal of Personality Disorders*, *23*(2), 201–210.

Thomson, N. D., Kiehl, K. A. & Bjork, J. M. (2019). Violence and aggression in young women: The importance of psychopathy and neurobiological function. *Physiology and Behavior, 201,* 130–138.

Thomson, N. D. & Centifanti, L. C. M. (2018). Proactive and Reactive Aggression Subgroups in Typically Developing Children: The Role of Executive Functioning, Psychophysiology, and Psychopathy. *Child Psychiatry & Human Development, 49*(2), 197–208.

Thomson, N. D., Vassileva, J., Kiehl, K., Reidy, D., Aboutanos, M., McDougle, R. & DeLisi, M. (2019). Which Features of Psychopathy and Impulsivity Matter Most for Prison Violence? New Evidence among Female Prisoners. *International Journal of Law and Psychiatry, 64,* 26–33.

Thomson, N. D., Towl, G. J. & Centifanti, L. C. M. (2016). The Habitual Female Offender Inside: How Psychopathic Traits Predict Chronic Prison Violence. *Law and Human Behavior, 40*(3), 257–269.

Tsang, S. (2018). Troubled or Traumatized Youth? The Relations Between Psychopathy, Violence Exposure, Posttraumatic Stress Disorder, and Antisocial Behavior Among Juvenile Offenders. *Journal of Aggression, Maltreatment & Trauma, 27*(2), 164–178.

Vassileva, J., Georgiev, S., Martin, E., Gonzalez, R. & Segala, L. (2011). Psychopathic Heroin Addicts Are Not Uniformly Impaired across Neurocognitive Domains of Impulsivity. *Drug and Alcohol Dependence, 114*(2–3), 194–200.

Verona, E., Hicks, B. M. & Patrick, C. J. (2005). Psychopathy and Suicidality in Female Offenders: Mediating Influences of Personality and Abuse. *Journal of Consulting and Clinical Psychology, 73*(6), 1065–1073.

Verona, E., Patrick, C. J. & Joiner, T. E. (2001). Psychopathy, Antisocial Personality, and Suicide Risk. *Journal of Abnormal Psychology, 110*(3), 462–470.

Viding, E., Sebastian, C. L., Dadds, M. R., Lockwood, P. L., Cecil, C. A. M., De Brito, S. A. & McCrory, E. J. (2012). Amygdala Response to Preattentive Masked Fear in Children with Conduct Problems: The Role of Callous-Unemotional Traits. *The American Journal of Psychiatry, 169*(10), 1109–1116.

Vitacco, M. J., Neumann, C. S. & Jackson, R. L. (2005). Testing a Four-Factor Model of Psychopathy and Its Association With Ethnicity, Gender, Intelligence, and Violence. *Journal of Consulting and Clinical Psychology, 73*(3), 466–476.

Vitacco, M. J., Neumann, C. S. & Wodushek, T. (2008). Differential Relationships Between the Dimensions of Psychopathy and Intelligence: Replication With Adult Jail Inmates. *Criminal Justice and Behavior, 35*(1), 48–55.

Vitale, J. E., Smith, S. S., Brinkley, C. A. & Newman, J. P. (2002). The Reliability and Validity of the Psychopathy Checklist – Revised in a Sample of Female Offenders. *Criminal Justice and Behavior, 29*(2), 202–231.

Watts, A. L., Salekin, R. T., Harrison, N., Clark, A., Waldman, I. D., Vitacco, M. J. & Lilienfeld, S. O. (2016). Psychopathy: Relations with Three Conceptions of Intelligence. *Personality Disorders: Theory, Research, and Treatment, 7*(3), 269–279.

Weizmann-Henelius, G., Viemerö, V. & Eronen, M. (2004). Psychopathy in Violent Female Offenders in Finland. *Psychopathology, 37*(5), 213–221.

7
SOCIAL FACTORS

Research on psychopathy has largely focused on biological correlates; yet social and environmental influences are a notable and important field of inquiry, especially because genetics research has demonstrated about half of the variance in psychopathy is explained by environmental factors. Indeed, understanding social risk factors is complimentary to biological and psychological disciplines as the three share much overlap. For instance, a child who has an antisocial parent who becomes incarcerated for a violent crime may be genetically vulnerable to develop antisocial psychopathic traits. This biological vulnerability coupled with the influence of having a parent incarcerated may spur the development of psychopathic traits, as parental incarceration has been shown to influence several risk factors for psychopathy, such as inhibiting the development of empathy and attachment, as well as increasing economic hardship and being placed in care. This single circumstance highlights the importance of a person-centered approach to understanding the development and correlates of psychopathy (Andershed, 2010). So far, this book has explored the role of genetics and the environment in the development of psychopathy, as well as biological and psychological risk factors. This chapter covers the main areas of research on social risk factors for psychopathic traits, drawing from research examining social risk during pregnancy into adulthood. First, a review will be conducted on the influence of prenatal and postnatal risk factors, dietary deficits, exposure to neurotoxins and poverty for predicting psychopathic traits in childhood and adolescence. Next, we shall explore the role of relationships including parenting and attachment styles, the influence of childhood maltreatment, antisocial parents, delinquent peers, and exposure to violence in the home and in the community. Collectively, these social risk factors contribute to the development of psychopathy, and interact with biological and psychological risk factors to differentiate developmental pathways of psychopathic traits.

Prenatal and postnatal risk factors

A great deal of research has established that exposure to toxins during pregnancy and birth complications pose future risk of violent behavior in childhood and adulthood (Yang & Raine, 2018). Yet, less research has explored this association in relation to psychopathy, and the literature that does exist suggests that not all violent behavior risk factors during the prenatal and postnatal period extend to psychopathy. During pregnancy, however, several notable risk factors of psychopathy have been found. The first is prenatal maternal stress. Prenatal maternal stress is typically measured across a range of situations and summed to form a total score. Examples of prenatal maternal stress include being a victim of crime, moving home, death of a family member, physical and mental health problems, poverty, loss of job, or having relationship difficulties. Maternal prenatal stress has been found to predict a fearless temperament in childhood (a precursor for callous-unemotional [CU] traits), and the development of CU traits in early adolescence (Barker, Oliver, Viding, Salekin & Maughan, 2011). Further, in a sample of 295 children from New York, self-report prenatal maternal stress was associated with higher scores on the Antisocial Process Screening Device (APSD) in children aged 8–10 years (Gao, Huang & Li, 2017). The authors found prenatal maternal stress was associated with all three facets on the APSD (CU traits, Grandiose-Manipulative and Daring-Impulsive), even after controlling for social adversity and sex. A possible explanation of this association is that high stress results in the greater exposure to cortisol during gestation impacting neurological development resulting in deficits in cognitive abilities (Huizink, Robles de Medina, Mulder, Visser & Buitelaar, 2003; LeWinn et al., 2009) and alterations in the development of infant temperament (Davis et al., 2007).

Another prenatal risk factor includes exposure to tobacco. In a sample of 177 clinic referred boys, prenatal tobacco exposure predicted Psychopathy Checklist – Revised (PCL-R) scores in early adulthood; however, this study found that this association was only significant for factor 1 and not factor 2 (Burke, Loeber & Lahey, 2007). This finding has since been supported by a longitudinal study involving 1,364 one-month-old infants who have been followed into adolescence. Beaver and colleagues (2010), showed prenatal exposure to cigarette smoke (maternal and environmental) predicted adolescent CU traits scores on the Youth Psychopathic Traits Inventory (YPI) at age 15 years old. However, the authors found this association was only significant for two-parent households, and not for single-parent households.

Birthing complications can cause damage to the structure and functioning of the brain, which in turn affects the development of behavior and personality (Eryigit Madzwamuse, Baumann, Jaekel, Bartmann & Wolke, 2015; Raine, Brennan & Mednick, 1997). Although obstetrical problems are linked to other psychiatric disorders and antisocial behavior (Arseneault, Tremblay, Boulerice & Saucier, 2002; de Haan et al., 2006), the same has not been found for psychopathy. For example, in a study involving 800 male offenders, Lalumière and colleagues (2001) found that psychopaths (PCL-R > 25) were significantly less likely to have birth complications (e.g., perinatal infection, cesarean section, asphyxia, anoxia, use of forceps/instruments during birth) when compared to non-psychopathic offenders (PCL-R < 24). The authors conclude that birth complications are more predictive of criminality that is not psychopathy-related. While this study is compelling, Chapter 5 provides ample evidence that psychopathy is marked by neurological dysfunction, and given that some forms of birthing complications may influence neural functioning (e.g., asphyxia) more than others (e.g., Cesarean section) much more research is needed before definitive conclusions can be drawn on the link between obstetrical problems and psychopathy.

A recently explored risk factor for psychopathy is the effects of breastfeeding. A longitudinal study including 2,500 adolescents from the National Longitudinal Study of Adolescent Health showed infants who were not breastfed were more likely to develop higher levels of psychopathic traits in adulthood (Jackson & Beaver, 2016). The authors' findings did not show infants who are weaned early were at greater risk of developing psychopathic traits in adulthood, which indicates that there was not a dosage effect of breastfeeding. Thus, the link between an infant not being breastfed and the development of adult psychopathy seems unrelated to the nutritional value of breastfeeding. Instead, the link could be because of other mechanisms, such as breastfeeding increasing maternal warmth (Gibbs, Forste & Lybbert, 2018) or mothers who live in poverty may have to work multiple jobs and are then unable to breastfeed. This area of research is still in its infancy, and the mechanisms of the link between breastfeeding and psychopathy need to be explored.

Diet (omega-3s)

Although the link between breastfeeding and psychopathy does not seem to be because of the nutritional value, there is evidence that a child's diet may influence psychopathic traits. Omega-3 polyunsaturated fatty acids (PUFAs) have received growing support for the link between brain functioning and violence. This research has tended to focus on three omega-3 fatty acids; (1) alpha-linolenic acid (ALA), (2) eicosapentaenoic acid (EPA) and (3) docosahexaenoic acid (DHA). Omega-3 is an essential fatty acid that cannot be synthesized in the human body and must, therefore, be obtained from the diet. ALA-rich foods include flaxseed, hemp, canola and walnuts. ALA is converted into DHA and EPA in the liver; however, this conversion is incomplete and dietary ALA is thought to have a small contribution on levels of DHA and EPA in humans (Bègue et al., 2018; Kalmijn et al., 2004). Instead, DHA and EPA are primarily absorbed from the diet, in particular cold-water oily fish species such as salmon, herring, trout and mackerel. There is substantial evidence that supports omega-3 as an integral contributor to neural development and function (Gajos & Beaver, 2016; Harris et al., 2009; Kalmijn et al., 2004; Thesing, Bot, Milaneschi, Giltay & Penninx, 2018). In general, omega-3 plays an important role in cell membrane elasticity and myelination, and is related to the functioning of dopaminergic and serotonergic systems, which influence neural signaling, mood and behavior (Bègue et al., 2018; Gajos & Beaver, 2016; Rogers, 2001). Having a low dietary intake of omega-3 influences neurological function, mood and personality. Although there has been a strong link between omega-3 and violence (Bègue et al., 2018; Corrigan et al., 1994; Hibbeln, 2001; Hibbeln, Ferguson & Blasbalg, 2006; Meyer et al., 2015), there have only been a few studies exploring the link with psychopathic traits. In a sample of youth with Attention Deficit Hyperactivity Disorder (ADHD), high CU traits were significantly associated with lower blood levels of omega-3s, and this was specific to EPA and a trend for DHA ($p = 0.054$; Gow et al., 2013). Using a randomized control design, Raine and colleagues (2015) assessed the influence of a 6-month treatment of an omega-3 daily supplement on psychopathic traits in 200 Mauritius youth (aged 8–16 years). Within the 6-month treatment period, both the placebo and omega-3 groups had a reduction in CU traits (measured on the parent-report APSD); however, unlike the placebo group, children in the omega-3 supplement group continued to see reductions in CU traits over the entire 12-month period (6 months after treatment). There were no significant changes for the Narcissism or Impulsive facets. Although the study of deficits in omega-3 as a developmental risk factor for psychopathic traits has only started to receive attention, the results thus far show that youth with CU traits may not receive sufficient omega-3 from their environment, as indexed by blood level samples, which may impact their cognitive functioning and ability to regulate emotions. Fortunately, as shown by Raine et al. (2015), providing omega-3 supplements may be an effective treatment to reduce CU traits at the biological level.

Lead exposure

As shown earlier in this chapter, exposure to toxins (e.g., tobacco) during pregnancy places children at greater risk of developing psychopathic traits. Thus, exposure to environmental toxins may be a significant contributor to the development of psychopathy. As discussed in Chapter 5, psychopathy is characterized by neurobiological dysfunction particularly in the frontal lobe. There is a link between early exposure to lead and deficits in frontal lobe function and structure (Bellinger, 2008), and exposure to lead has been found to increase childhood externalizing behavior and postnatal lead levels have been linked to a greater number of arrests in adulthood and violent behavior (Beckley et al., 2018; Boutwell et al., 2017; Wright et al., 2008). Regarding psychopathy, one of the few studies conducted has found higher blood levels of lead at age 6 years predicted Psychopathic Personality Inventory – Revised (PPI-R) total scores 13–18 years later (Wright, Boisvert & Vaske, 2009). The authors found that higher blood levels of lead were specifically linked to Machiavellian Egocentricity, Social Potency, Impulsive Nonconformity and Blame Externalization. But there was no association with Fearlessness nor Carefree Nonplanfulness. The authors suggest that although exposure to lead has drastically reduced since the 1970's, about 25% of youth in the US live in conditions where exposure to lead is prevalent (e.g., in paint, dust and soil around the home). Exposure to lead is more rampant in lower income families, and Wright et al. (2009) propose that exposure to this neurotoxin could explain the association between low socioeconomic status (SES) and criminality, and may, in part, explain the link between low SES and psychopathy.

Socioeconomic status

Although SES is typically included in research, it is mostly used as a control variable and rarely explored as a variable of interest in understanding psychopathy (Zwaanswijk, van Geel & Vedder, 2018). Drawing from one of the largest longitudinal studies to date, Farrington and Bergstrøm (2018) showed children (8–10 years old) who lived in a home of low family income, poor housing, and their parent had low occupational prestige had higher psychopathy scores on the PCL:SV at age 48. Although the authors did not assess the factor structure of psychopathy, these results suggest a fairly strong developmental link between childhood SES and adult psychopathy. However, there may be evidence which suggests this link is more specific to the Impulsive-Antisocial features of psychopathy rather than the Interpersonal-Affective features (Benning, Patrick, Hicks, Blonigen & Krueger, 2003; Hare, 2003; Harpur, Hare & Hakstian, 1989). This lends support to the assertion from genetics data, which shows that shared environmental influences, such as SES, play a small role in the development of Interpersonal-Affective features of psychopathy. Indeed, poverty may also have a negative impact on other social and environmental influences, such as increased exposure to lead and community violence, and because of high cost of fresh fish a reduced intake of omega-3.

Parenting

Unlike SES which influences the entire family, parenting may differ based on each child. A child who is more oppositional may receive a harsher parenting style than a sibling who is more docile. Indeed, Salihovic et al. (2012) found in a sample of 875 adolescents that psychopathic traits in youth influenced how parents parented, suggesting parental behavior can be reactive to a child's psychopathic features. Thus, while parenting has been considered a shared environmental factor, there is clear evidence to suggest parenting strategies/styles may be responsive to a specific child, and therefore child-dependent (Hawes, Dadds, Frost & Hasking, 2011; Larsson, Viding & Plomin, 2008; Muñoz, Pakalniskiene & Frick, 2011). Parenting strategies may then, in part, explain a developmental pathway of psychopathic traits in adulthood, which differ from sibling to sibling. Using retrospective reports, male prisoners who scored above 25 on the PCL-R recounted more experiences of negative and poorer parenting during childhood (e.g., indifference/neglect, parent–child and child–parent antipathy, more discipline and psychological abuse) than prisoners scoring below 25 on the PCL-R (Marshall & Cooke, 1999). Similar results have been found in female offenders, with psychopathic (PCL-R > 25) women having experienced more poorer parenting practices than non-psychopathic women (Forouzan & Nicholls, 2015), and this was specific to having fathers who had poor parenting practices. There were no significant associations between psychopathy and mothers' poor parenting practices.

Consistent results have been found in a community sample of males. Drawing data from the Cambridge Study in Delinquent Development, poor parental supervision at age 8 predicted higher PCL:SV scores at age 48, and this association was specific to factor 2 traits and not factor 1 (Farrington & Bergstrøm, 2018). Men and women from the island of Mauritius were found to have higher levels of self-report psychopathy scores if they had experienced lower quality of maternal care and paternal overprotection (Gao, Raine, Chan, Venables & Mednick, 2010). Similar to male offenders, female offenders higher on the PCL-R reported poorer parenting during childhood (Eisenbarth, Krammer, Edwards, Kiehl & Neumann, 2018). These included having a mother that was indifferent (e.g., ignoring, uncaring or uninterested) and abusive (unpredictable, verbally or physically abusive). At the facet level there were no significant associations found for the Interpersonal or Affective facets, but the Antisocial facet was related to having a mother or father that was indifferent, as well as a father that was abusive. The Lifestyle facet was associated with having an abusive mother. In a sample of 75 juvenile male offenders, higher PCL:YV scores were related to ineffective parenting practices (e.g., inconsistent discipline and poor monitoring/supervision); however, these associations were only found for Antisocial and Lifestyle facets, and not Interpersonal or Affective facets (Molinuevo, Pardo, González & Torrubia, 2014).

In contrast, prospective studies have shown CU traits in youth are associated with harsh parenting and low parental warmth (Fontaine, McCrory, Boivin, Moffitt & Viding, 2011; Kimonis, Cross, Howard & Donoghue, 2013; Waller et al., 2014). Recent evidence involving 662 twin pairs has shown encouraging results by demonstrating that high parental warmth and rewarding parenting may inhibit the genetic expression of CU traits (Henry et al., 2018). Parental warmth is also associated with lower scores on the YPI across all dimensions: Grandiose-Manipulative, Callous-Unemotional and Impulsive-Irresponsible (Ray, 2018). Fortunately, early parenting interventions that focus on maternal warmth have shown significant improvements in CU traits in youth as young as 3 years old (Kimonis et al., 2018).

Collectively, this research supports the notion that negative parenting styles, such as being uncaring, uninterested, physically and psychologically abusive contribute to the development of adult psychopathy but this association is most consistent for total psychopathy scores, and the Antisocial and Lifestyle facets but not the Interpersonal and Affective facets. This seems consistent for both men and women. These results stand in contrast to research showing the importance of parenting practices in the development of CU traits. Nevertheless, if CU traits are a downward extension of adult psychopathy there may be an opportunity to prevent the development of this disorder by implementing parenting interventions that improve parental warmth and rewarding parenting, which curb the genetic contribution to the disorder.

Attachment

Leading theories suggest psychopaths are unable to form authentic social bonds (Cleckley, 1941; Cooke, Hart, Logan & Michie, 2012; Hare, 2003; McCord & McCord, 1964), which may stem from dysfunctional early relationships. Indeed, the Clinical Assessment of Psychopathic Personality (CAPP) specifically incorporates Attachment as a domain (see Chapter 2), which includes symptoms of detachment, being uncommitted, unempathic and uncaring. Although attachment and psychopathic traits are largely studied in adult populations, attachment styles develop early based on childhood experiences with primary caregivers. These early experiences shape personality development and psychological adjustment, having lasting effects into adulthood (Bowlby, 1988).

The premise behind attachment theory is infants have an innate need to be in close proximity with their caregiver when distressed or threatened (Bowlby, 1988). Infants learn that certain behaviors (e.g., crying, smiling) lead to certain responses from caregivers (e.g., attention, soothing), which, by operant condition, infants and children learn to repeat the behaviors in order to get what they want/need (Ainsworth, 1964, 1979). Early relationships that support a secure attachment promote healthy emotional self-regulation through the infant expressing a need, and the caregiver being reliably available to meet these needs. Infants and children with a secure attachment are easily soothed when they become upset. A child who has grown up with a secure attachment with caregivers are they themselves more likely to become adults who promote secure attachment in their relationships (Bowlby, 1980, 1988). In contrast, an infant whose caregiver is inconsistent may resort to maximizing their distress cues in order to gain comfort from their caregiver, this is called an insecure-resistant attachment style (Ainsworth & Bell, 1970). This conditioning response results in the infant needing to reach a high state of distress in order to communicate their needs, and although these children display dependent and clingy behaviors they are difficult to soothe. A child who is raised by a caregiver who is insensitive to their needs (e.g., detached or emotionally unavailable) become physically and emotionally independent, and when they become distressed they do not seek out their caregiver; this is called an insecure-avoidant attachment style (Ainsworth, 1979; Ainsworth, Blehar, Waters & Wall, 1978).

Most research to date has studied psychopathy and attachment in student and community samples. Community-based studies have generally found the affective features of psychopathy (e.g., Levenson Self-Report of Psychopathy [LSRP] Callousness and the Triarchic Psychopathy Measure [TriPM] Meanness) relate to avoidant attachment, the Boldness scale on the TriPM negatively relates to insecure attachment, and the behavioral features positively relate to insecure attachment (Christian, Sellbom & Wilkinson, 2017). Similar results have been found in student samples, with TriPM Boldness scores negatively associated with attachment anxiety and attachment avoidance, TriPM Meanness scores were unrelated to attachment anxiety and positively related to attachment avoidance, and TriPM Disinhibition scores were positively related to both attachment anxiety and attachment avoidance (Craig, Gray & Snowden, 2013). Thus, affective features of psychopathy may, in part, stem from environments where the caregiver is often emotionally unavailable, resulting in the child becoming emotionally and physically independent. This may result in an adult attachment style that is detached and avoidant of close relationships. In contrast, behavioral features of psychopathy may stem from nonvalidating environments where the caregiver is inconsistent, resulting in the child developing poor emotion regulation capabilities, which as adults, leads to relationship instability and fear of abandonment.

The association between poor parental attachment has been found for adolescents too (Kosson, Cyterski, Steuerwald, Neumann & Walker-Matthews, 2002). Drawing from a sample of 51 male adolescent offenders, Flight and Forth (2007) found total PCL:YV, factor 2, and the Lifestyle facet were associated with poor paternal attachment, while no significant findings were evident for maternal attachment or peer attachment. A study involving male and female inpatient adolescents using self-and parent-report psychopathy scores found boys with dismissing and preoccupied attachment styles with their mothers and a dismissing attachment style with their fathers had higher levels of CU traits when compared to boys with a secure attachment style (Gambin, Wozniak-Prus & Sharp, 2018). In the same study, the authors found no significant associations between attachment styles and psychopathic traits in girls.

Research assessing CU traits and attachment have been mixed, with some finding an association with poor attachment (Bohlin, Eninger, Brocki & Thorell, 2012; Pasalich, Dadds, Hawes & Brennan, 2012) while others do not (Wright, Hill, Sharp & Pickles, 2018). A possible reason for the inconsistent results could be explained by variations in youth with CU traits. For instance, studies exploring the primary (high CU and low anxiety) and secondary (high CU and high anxiety) CU variants have found youth with the secondary CU profile were more often characterized by either disorganized or avoidant attachment styles, whereas those youth with the primary CU variant were mostly characterized by the secure attachment style (Cecil, McCrory, Barker, Guiney & Viding, 2018). This study highlights the importance of child-centered research for understanding developmental pathways for psychopathic traits.

Prior research has shown that poor attachment can be a result of childhood maltreatment (Cyr, Euser, Bakermans-Kranenburg & Van Ijzendoorn, 2010). Indeed, Cleckley (1984) suggested that psychopaths fail to develop a moral compass because of emotional neglect (i.e., lack of affective experiences), also indicating that childhood maltreatment may be important in the development of the disorder.

Maltreatment

There are five types of maltreatment, and these include emotional abuse, physical abuse, emotional neglect, physical neglect and sexual abuse. Weiler and Widom

(1996) conducted one of the earliest longitudinal studies to assess the influence of overall childhood maltreatment on the development of psychopathy into adulthood. The study involved 652 children who were abused and/or neglected during 1967 to 1971, these children were matched with a non-abused/neglected control group ($n = 489$). The follow-up assessments occurred almost 20 years after the childhood victimization. The results showed children who were abused and/or neglected had higher PCL-R scores, and this was found for both men and women. Exploring types of abuse/neglect and the dimensional construct of psychopathy suggest these associations are stronger for factor 2 traits, which are most often associated with emotional and physical abuse and neglect. In a sample of 183 male offenders, Dargis et al. (2016) found psychopathy scores on the PCL-R were related to childhood abuse. Again, factor 2 traits were related to emotional abuse and neglect, and physical abuse. At the facet level, only the Antisocial facet was associated with overall childhood trauma and physical abuse. No associations were found for sexual abuse, nor between factor 1 (and Interpersonal or Affective facets) and childhood maltreatment. This is consistent with prior findings in male prisoners (see Poythress, Skeem & Lilienfeld, 2006). Based on this research, childhood abuse is only associated with the Impulsive-Antisocial features of psychopathy, and is unrelated to the Interpersonal-Affective features. This finding is somewhat consistent cross-culturally using PCL-R derived measures. For instance, in a sample of Mauritius men and women, Gao et al. (2010) found childhood abuse was related to Self-Report Psychopathy Scale (SRP) total scores and factor 2 scores, but not factor 1. However, a study from an Italian sample of 78 violent male offenders found emotional abuse was related to high scores on PCL-R factor 1, factor 2, and the Affective and Lifestyle facets, and not associated with the Interpersonal or Antisocial facets.

Somewhat similar results have been found in student samples using self-report measures. Watts et al. (2017) assessed the association between the 3-facet model of the LSRP, the PPI-R, and childhood trauma in 1169 students. The study showed the PPI-R Fearless Dominance was unrelated to childhood maltreatment, whereas PPI-R Self-Centered Impulsivity, PPI-R Coldheartedness, LSRP Antisocial and LSRP Callousness were positively related to abuse/neglect. Except for LSRP Callousness, which was not associated with sexual or emotional abuse, most of the associations between the PPI-R and LSRP dimensions did not differ based on the type of maltreatment (e.g., emotion, physical, sexual).

Drawing from a community sample of adults, those who reported high levels on the Meanness facet of the TriPM experienced childhood emotional neglect, and those scoring high on the Boldness facet reported less emotional abuse and neglect, while those scoring high on the Disinhibition facet were more likely to report emotional and physical abuse, and emotional and physical neglect (Durand & De Calheiros Velozo, 2018). There are several explanations of the mixed findings between measures and populations being tested. The most compelling explanation is due the close link between childhood maltreatment and antisocial behavior. As discussed in Chapter 2, some measures of psychopathy include antisocial behavior within their construct (e.g., PCL-R), while others do not (e.g., TriPM). Therefore, studies using PCL-R derived scales find Impulsive-Antisocial features are best predicted by childhood maltreatment, while Interpersonal-Affective features are unrelated. This may suggest that any association between Interpersonal-Affective features of psychopathy and childhood maltreatment is explained by antisocial behavior. This is illustrated by the studies including personality-focused measures such as the PPI-R or TriPM (and to some degree the LSRP), which finds some personality features are associated with childhood trauma. Yet, accounting for antisocial behavior by comparing criminal non-psychopaths to criminal psychopaths, Marshall and Cooke (1999) found no differences in histories of childhood maltreatment.

In support of this assertion, studies in youth that have focused on the construct of CU traits have found a positive association with childhood maltreatment but this association differs based on the subtypes of CU traits. Specifically, this research has shown that youth with low CU traits and high conduct problems suffer from more emotional, physical and sexual abuse, and emotional and physical neglect compared to youth with high CU traits and high conduct problems (Cecil et al., 2018; Kimonis, Fanti, Isoma & Donoghue, 2013). This finding supports Karpman's (1941) early theory that there are two variants or subtypes of psychopathy (primary and secondary), and secondary psychopaths develop the disorder largely because of the environment, especially from childhood abuse and neglect. This work falls in line with that discussed on adult psychopathic traits, which typically finds a stronger association between childhood maltreatment and Impulsive-Antisocial psychopathic features.

Antisocial parents

Although there is evidence to suggest antisocial behavior can be hereditary from parent to child (Rosenström et al., 2017), we cannot ignore the environmental influence that having a parent who engages in criminal activities has on the development of particular psychopathic traits. Having an antisocial parent influences a host of risk factors, including those discussed in this chapter. For instance, having a parent incarcerated may impact developing a secure attachment, which in turn may affect the development of empathy (Thomson, Kuay, Baron-Cohen & Towl, 2018). Further, having a parent incarcerated will inevitably influence the availability of financial resources and some children are forced to live with other relatives or in foster care (Mumola, 2000; Thomson et al., 2018). In addition to the knock-on effects of having an antisocial parent increasing other well-known risk factors, another consideration is that having an antisocial parent may provide a home-life where antisocial behavior is normalized and encouraged. Indeed, social learning theory suggests children learn as both an observer and as an active participant that antisocial behavior can be rewarding (e.g., physical gain, parental praise, dominance). Thus, there are many reasons why antisocial parents may contribute to the development of psychopathic traits in their children.

The research conducted to date has shown a link between parent antisociality and the development of psychopathic traits in their offspring. For example, boys who had either a mother or father with a criminal history (e.g., conviction or criminal record) had higher total PCL-R scores at age 34 years (Bamvita et al., 2017) and age 48 years (Farrington & Bergstrøm, 2018). At the facet level, boys who had a mother with a criminal conviction were more likely to have higher scores on the Interpersonal and Affective facets at age 34 years (Bamvita et al., 2017), whereas boys who had a father with a criminal conviction had higher Lifestyle facet scores at age 34. Boys with a father who had a higher number of violent crimes were more likely to have higher Antisocial and Affective facet scores at age 34 years (ibid.). These results suggest that parental antisocial behavior may influence the development of psychopathic traits, and in particular having a mother with a criminal conviction greatly impacted the interpersonal-affective features of psychopathy but not the impulsive-antisocial features. In contrast, having a father involved in the criminal justice system predicted both impulsive-antisocial psychopathic traits, as well as affective psychopathic traits.

Peer delinquency

Although delinquent peers may not cause psychopathy, there is evidence that peers can exacerbate psychopathic tendencies. In the same way that Fred West surrounded himself with like-minded people, where sexual and physical abuse was normalized, antisocial peers may support the stability of psychopathic behaviors (Pardini & Loeber, 2008). Research has demonstrated youth who have higher levels of CU traits and total psychopathy scores throughout adolescence tend to have more delinquent peers (Backman, Laajasalo, Jokela & Aronen, 2018; Byrd, Hawes, Loeber & Pardini, 2018; Fontaine et al., 2011; Kimonis, Frick & Barry, 2004; Muñoz, Kerr & Besic, 2008). However, research exploring the dimensional construct of psychopathy (including antisocial psychopathic traits) shows delinquent peers do not always predict affective psychopathic traits over time.

Data from the Pittsburgh Youth Study has shown higher scores on the PCL:SV Interpersonal and Antisocial facets at age 24 was best predicted by the interaction of higher psychopathy scores at age 13 and greater peer delinquency (Lynam, Loeber & Stouthamer-Loeber, 2008). This indicates that having delinquent peers may increase the stability of specific psychopathic traits through adolescence into adulthood. Ray's (2018) longitudinal sample of 1,354 serious violent offenders showed peer delinquency at age 14.5 years was related to higher levels of all facets on the YPI. However, peer delinquency was partly responsible for CU traits remaining stable into early adulthood, and recent research has shown friendship quality (e.g., support and closeness) is a protective factor of CU traits (Backman et al., 2018). Overall, the research so far demonstrates that youth who have peers that engage in antisocial behavior are more likely to remain high in psychopathic traits throughout the adolescent period. At the dimensional level, this seems to be most consistent for the affective features of psychopathy; however, when the psychopathy models include antisocial psychopathic traits, such as the PCL:SV, peer delinquency does not predict the stability of CU traits, and rather it predicts the Interpersonal and Antisocial facets.

Exposure to violence

In the same way peer delinquency and antisocial parents contribute to the development of psychopathic traits, there is evidence that being exposed to community and family violence may increase the risk of psychopathy. This development of psychopathic traits may be a coping mechanism to dealing with a harsh environment, as well as adjusting to community norms. In a mixed prisoner and community sample of adults, self-report psychopathic traits total scores and all four facets were found to be related to higher levels of exposure to childhood community violence (Debowska, Boduszek, Dhingra, Kola & Meller-Prunska, 2015). Exposure to violence also occurs within the home, and similar to community violence, exposure to domestic violence has been associated with higher PCL-R scores in male offenders, and this association was strongest for the interpersonal-affective features of psychopathy (Dargis & Koenigs, 2017).

Research including adolescent samples is fairly conclusive in linking exposure to violence with psychopathic traits; however, findings are mixed based on the dimensions being tested. Drawing from a sample of 147 incarcerated adolescents (13.5% female) aged 15–17 years old, Schaft and colleagues (2013) found exposure to community violence was positively related to total PCL:YV scores and the Interpersonal, Lifestyle and Antisocial facets, but not the Affective facet. The authors found the same facets were related to witnessing community violence; however, all four facets were related to being a victim of community violence. In contrast, Kimonis et al. (2008) demonstrated exposure to community violence in a sample of detained adolescents was positively related to CU traits, whereas in a longitudinal study, exposure to violence in a sample of serious delinquent adolescents was related to higher Grandiose-Manipulate scores on the YPI at age 14.5 years, and youth who continued to be exposed to violence had more stable Grandiose-Manipulative traits into early adulthood (Ray, 2018). Therefore, it may be that growing up in an environment and having continued exposure to violence may result in a stable increase of psychopathic traits, as a coping mechanism to adverse conditions (ibid.).

The combination of psychopathic traits and exposure to violence also puts individuals at greater risk for severe antisocial behaviors. Debowska et al. (2015) found the combination of high levels of psychopathic traits, particularly the Affective facet, and exposure to violence increases positive attitudes towards sexual offending, which may put these individuals at greater risk of future violence. Recently, in an adolescent sample, Baskin-Sommers and Baskin (2016) found the link between exposure to community violence and later violence was mediated by total psychopathy scores on the YPI. Relatedly, CU traits association with aggressive behavior has been found to be mediated by exposure to community violence (Walters, 2018). In sum, exposure to violence seems to be an important risk factor for the development of psychopathic traits, and these effects are seen in adolescents and adults. Further, regardless of the direction of effect, the combination of exposure to violence and psychopathic traits places an individual at greater risk for future violence.

Summary

This chapter has presented evidence that social factors contribute to the development of psychopathic traits in youths and adults. These risk factors occur across the lifespan and can promote specific facets of psychopathy. A large proportion of this research establishes that the family environment plays a major role in the development of psychopathy, and these environments are not necessarily family-wide (e.g., SES) but are child-specific (e.g., parenting, attachment, maltreatment). Indeed, it is hard not to recognize how these social risk factors may be intertwined with each other, as well as with biological and psychological factors too. Before birth, social factors influence the biological processes predisposing youth to developing psychopathic traits. Exposure to maternal stress and neurotoxins, and poor nutrition (lack of omega-3), have been found to predict psychopathic traits later in life. Once a child is born, parents have the unique opportunity to shape their child. Unfortunately, some children are exposed to poor parenting practices, maltreatment, and exposure to violence in the community and in their home. These all contribute to the development of psychopathy. Indeed, having a parent who is antisocial may biological predispose a child to being antisocial too, but it is also difficult to ignore the social influences of having an antisocial parent that may exacerbate the genetic vulnerability (e.g., social learning of antisocial behavior, normalizing psychopathic and criminal behavior). Also, whether children with psychopathic traits seek out like-minded peers or delinquent peers promote the stability of psychopathic traits in their friends, there is no question that being exposed to peers who are antisocial increases the risk of psychopathic behaviors. Although this chapter provides a broad scope of social risk factors, there remains a scarcity of research on this biopsychosocial domain. Even so, it is undeniable that social factors contribute to the development of psychopathy, and in conjunction with the biological and psychological risk factors discussed so far in this book, we will begin to form a more complete person-centered understanding of developmental pathways of psychopathy.

Acknowledgments

Thank you to Dr. Henriette Bergstrøm and Dr. Hue San Kuay for their valuable review. Dr. Bergstrøm CPsychol, AFBPsS, is a lecturer and the programme leader for the BSc (Hons) Criminal Psychology in the Department of Social Sciences at the University of Derby. Her main research interests are within the field of Developmental and Life-Course Criminology, and mainly on the development of psychopathy. Dr. Kuay is a psychologist and lecturer at Universiti Sains Malaysia, and her research interests include understanding the mechanisms of family-level aggression.

References

Ainsworth, M. (1964). Patterns of Attachment Behavior Shown by the Infant in Interaction with His Mother. *Merrill-Palmer Quarterly of Behavior and Development*, *10*(1), 51–58.

Ainsworth, M. (1979). Infant–Mother Attachment. *American Psychologist*, *34*(10), 932–937.

Ainsworth, M. & Bell, S. M. (1970). Attachment, Exploration, and Separation: Illustrated by the Behavior of One-Year-Olds in a Strange Situation. *Child Development*, *41*(1), 49–67.

Ainsworth, M., Blehar, M. C., Waters, E. & Wall, S. (1978). *Patterns of Attachment: A Psychological Study of the Strange Situation*. Hillsdale, NJ: Erlbaum.

Andershed, H. (2010). Stability and Change of Psychopathic Traits: What Do We Know? In R. T. Salekin & D. R. Lynam (Eds.), *Handbook of Child and Adolescent Psychopathy* (pp. 233–250). New York: Guilford Press.

Arseneault, L., Tremblay, R. E., Boulerice, B. & Saucier, J.-F. (2002). Obstetrical Complications and Violent Delinquency: Testing Two Developmental Pathways. *Child Development*, *73*(2), 496–508.

Backman, H., Laajasalo, T., Jokela, M. & Aronen, E. T. (2018). Interpersonal Relationships as Protective and Risk Factors for Psychopathy: A Follow-Up Study in Adolescent Offenders. *Journal of Youth and Adolescence*, *47*(5), 1022–1036.

Bamvita, J.-M., Larm, P., Checknita, D., Vitaro, F., Tremblay, R. E., Côté, G. & Hodgins, S. (2017). Childhood Predictors of Adult Psychopathy Scores Among Males Followed from Age 6 to 33. *Journal of Criminal Justice*, *53*, 55–65.

Barker, E. D., Oliver, B. R., Viding, E., Salekin, R. T. & Maughan, B. (2011). The Impact of Prenatal Maternal Risk, Fearless Temperament and Early Parenting on Adolescent Callous-Unemotional Traits: A 14-Year Longitudinal Investigation. *Journal of Child Psychology and Psychiatry, and Allied Disciplines*, *52*(8), 878–888.

Baskin-Sommers, A. R. & Baskin, D. (2016). Psychopathic Traits Mediate the Relationship Between Exposure to Violence and Violent Juvenile Offending. *Journal of Psychopathology and Behavioral Assessment*, *38*(3), 341–349.

Beaver, K. M., DeLisi, M. & Vaughn, M. G. (2010). A Biosocial Interaction between Prenatal Exposure to Cigarette Smoke and Family Structure in the Prediction of Psychopathy in Adolescence. *Psychiatric Quarterly*, *81*(4), 325–334.

Beckley, A. L., Caspi, A., Broadbent, J., Harrington, H., Houts, R. M., Poulton, R., . . . Moffitt, T. E. (2018). Association of Childhood Blood Lead Levels With Criminal Offending. *JAMA Pediatrics*, *172*(2), 166.

Bègue, L., Zaalberg, A., Shankland, R., Duke, A., Jacquet, J., Kaliman, P., . . . Bushman, B. J. (2018). Omega-3 Supplements Reduce Self-Reported Physical Aggression in Healthy Adults. *Psychiatry Research*, *261*, 307–311.

Bellinger, D. C. (2008). Neurological and Behavioral Consequences of Childhood Lead Exposure. *PLoS Medicine*, *5*(5), e115.

Benning, S. D., Patrick, C. J., Hicks, B. M., Blonigen, D. M. & Krueger, R. F. (2003). Factor Structure of the Psychopathic Personality Inventory: Validity and Implications for Clinical Assessment. *Psychological Assessment*, *15*(3), 340–350.

Bohlin, G., Eninger, L., Brocki, K. C. & Thorell, L. B. (2012). Disorganized Attachment and Inhibitory Capacity: Predicting Externalizing Problem Behaviors. *Journal of Abnormal Child Psychology*, *40*(3), 449–458.

Boutwell, B. B., Nelson, E. J., Qian, Z., Vaughn, M. G., Wright, J. P., Beaver, K. M., . . . Rosenfeld, R. (2017). Aggregate-Level Lead Exposure, Gun Violence, Homicide, and Rape. *PLOS ONE*, *12*(11), e0187953.

Bowlby, J. (1980). *Loss: Sadness and Depression. Attachment and Loss (vol. 3)*. London: Hogarth Press.
Bowlby, J. (1988). *A Secure Base: Parent–Child Attachment and Healthy Human Development*. New York: Basic Books.
Burke, J. D., Loeber, R. & Lahey, B. B. (2007). Adolescent Conduct Disorder and Interpersonal Callousness as Predictors of Psychopathy in Young Adults. *Journal of Clinical Child and Adolescent Psychology: The Official Journal for the Society of Clinical Child and Adolescent Psychology, American Psychological Association, Division 53*, 36(3), 334–346.
Byrd, A. L., Hawes, S. W., Loeber, R. & Pardini, D. A. (2018). Interpersonal Callousness from Childhood to Adolescence: Developmental Trajectories and Early Risk Factors. *Journal of Clinical Child & Adolescent Psychology*, 47(3), 467–482.
Cecil, C. A. M., McCrory, E. J., Barker, E. D., Guiney, J. & Viding, E. (2018). Characterising Youth with Callous–Unemotional Traits and Concurrent Anxiety: Evidence for a High-Risk Clinical Group. *European Child & Adolescent Psychiatry*, 27(7), 885–898.
Christian, E., Sellbom, M. & Wilkinson, R. B. (2017). Clarifying the Associations between Individual Differences in General Attachment Styles and Psychopathy. *Personality Disorders: Theory, Research, and Treatment*, 8(4), 329–339.
Cleckley, H. (1941). *The Mask of Sanity*. St. Louis: Mosby.
Cleckley, H. (1984). *The Mask of Sanity: An Attempt to Clarify Some Issues About the So-Called Psychopathic Personality*. St. Louis: C.V. Mosby Co.
Cooke, D. J., Hart, S. D., Logan, C. & Michie, C. (2012). Explicating the Construct of Psychopathy: Development and Validation of a Conceptual Model, the Comprehensive Assessment of Psychopathic Personality (CAPP). *International Journal of Forensic Mental Health*, 11(4), 242–252.
Corrigan, F., Gray, R., Strathdee, A., Skinner, R., Rhijn, A. Van & Horrobin, D. (1994). Fatty Acid Analysis of Blood from Violent Offenders. *The Journal of Forensic Psychiatry*, 5(1), 83–92.
Craig, R. L., Gray, N. S. & Snowden, R. J. (2013). Recalled Parental Bonding, Current Attachment, and the Triarchic Conceptualisation of Psychopathy. *Personality and Individual Differences*, 55(4), 345–350.
Cyr, C., Euser, E. M., Bakermans-Kranenburg, M. J. & Van Ijzendoorn, M. H. (2010). Attachment Security and Disorganization in Maltreating and High-Risk Families: A Series of Meta-analyses. *Development and Psychopathology*, 22(1), 87.
Dargis, M. & Koenigs, M. (2017). Witnessing Domestic Violence during Childhood is Associated with Psychopathic Traits in Adult Male Criminal Offenders. *Law and Human Behavior*, 41(2), 173–179.
Dargis, M., Newman, J. & Koenigs, M. (2016). Clarifying the Link between Childhood Abuse History and Psychopathic Traits in Adult Criminal Offenders. *Personality Disorders*, 7(3), 221–228.
Davis, E., Glynn, L., Schetter, C., Hobel, C., Chicz-Demet, A. & Sandman, C. (2007). Prenatal Exposure to Maternal Depression and Cortisol Influences Infant Temperament. *Journal of the American Academy of Child & Adolescent Psychiatry*, 46(6), 737–746.
De Haan, M., Wyatt, J. S., Roth, S., Vargha-Khadem, F., Gadian, D. & Mishkin, M. (2006). Brain and Cognitive-Behavioural Development after Asphyxia at Term Birth. *Developmental Science*, 9(4), 350–358.
Debowska, A., Boduszek, D., Dhingra, K., Kola, S. & Meller-Prunska, A. (2015). The Role of Psychopathy and Exposure to Violence in Rape Myth Acceptance. *Journal of Interpersonal Violence*, 30(15), 2751–2770.

Durand, G. & De Calheiros Velozo, J. (2018). The Interplay of Gender, Parental Behaviors, and Child Maltreatment in Relation to Psychopathic Traits. *Adults Who Showed the Greatest Tendency for Impulsive Behavior, Irresponsibility and Hostility Were Also the More Likely to Report Experiencing Emotional and Physical Abuse and Neglect as a Child.*, *83*, 120–128.

Eisenbarth, H., Krammer, S., Edwards, B. G., Kiehl, K. A. & Neumann, C. S. (2018). Structural Analysis of the PCL-R and Relationship to Big Five Personality Traits and Parenting Characteristics in an Hispanic Female Offender Sample. *Personality and Individual Differences*, *129*, 59–65.

Eryigit Madzwamuse, S., Baumann, N., Jaekel, J., Bartmann, P. & Wolke, D. (2015). Neuro-cognitive Performance of Very Preterm or Very Low Birth Weight Adults at 26 Years. *Journal of Child Psychology and Psychiatry*, *56*(8), 857–864.

Farrington, D. P. & Bergstrøm, H. (2018). Family Background and Psychopathy. In C. J. Patrick (Ed.), *The Handbook of Psychopathy* (2nd ed., pp. 354–379). New York: Guilford Press.

Flight, J. I. & Forth, A. E. (2007). Instrumentally Violent Youths: The Roles of Psychopathic Traits, Empathy, and Attachment. *Criminal Justice and Behavior*, *34*(6), 739–751.

Fontaine, N. M. G. G., McCrory, E. J. P., Boivin, M., Moffitt, T. E. & Viding, E. (2011). Predictors and Outcomes of Joint Trajectories of Callous–Unemotional Traits and Conduct Problems in Childhood. *Journal of Abnormal Psychology*, *120*(3), 730–742.

Forouzan, E. & Nicholls, T. L. (2015). Childhood and Adolescent Characteristics of Women with High versus Low Psychopathy Scores: Examining Developmental Precursors to the Malignant Personality Disorder. *Journal of Criminal Justice*, *43*(4), 307–320.

Gajos, J. M. & Beaver, K. M. (2016). The Effect of Omega-3 Fatty Acids on Aggression: A Meta-analysis. *Neuroscience & Biobehavioral Reviews*, *69*, 147–158.

Gambin, M., Wozniak-Prus, M. & Sharp, C. (2018). Attachment and Psychopathic Traits in Inpatient Female and Male Adolescents. *Comprehensive Psychiatry*, *81*, 73–80.

Gao, Y., Huang, Y. & Li, X. (2017). Interaction between Prenatal Maternal Stress and Autonomic Arousal in Predicting Conduct Problems and Psychopathic Traits in Children. *Journal of Psychopathology and Behavioral Assessment*, *39*(1), 1–14.

Gao, Y., Raine, A., Chan, F., Venables, P. H. & Mednick, S. A. (2010). Early Maternal and Paternal Bonding, Childhood Physical Abuse and Adult Psychopathic Personality. *Psychological Medicine*, *40*(6), 1007–1016.

Gibbs, B. G., Forste, R. & Lybbert, E. (2018). Breastfeeding, Parenting, and Infant Attachment Behaviors. *Maternal and Child Health Journal*, *22*(4), 579–588.

Gow, R. V., Vallee-Tourangeau, F., Crawford, M. A., Taylor, E., Ghebremeskel, K., Bueno, A. A., . . . Rubia, K. (2013). Omega-3 Fatty Acids Are Inversely Related to Callous and Unemotional Traits in Adolescent Boys with Attention Deficit Hyperactivity Disorder. *Prostaglandins, Leukotrienes and Essential Fatty Acids (PLEFA)*, *88*(6), 411–418.

Hare, R. D. (2003). *The Hare Psychopathy Checklist – Revised* (2nd ed.). Toronto, Canada: Multi-Health Systems.

Harpur, T. J., Hare, R. D. & Hakstian, A. R. (1989). Two-Factor Conceptualization of Psychopathy: Construct Validity and Assessment Implications. *Psychological Assessment: A Journal of Consulting and Clinical Psychology*, *1*(1), 6–17.

Harris, W. S., Mozaffarian, D., Lefevre, M., Toner, C. D., Colombo, J., Cunnane, S. C., . . . Whelan, J. (2009). Towards Establishing Dietary Reference Intakes for Eicosapentaenoic and Docosahexaenoic Acids. *The Journal of Nutrition*, *139*(4), 804S–819S.

Hawes, D. J., Dadds, M. R., Frost, A. D. J. & Hasking, P. A. (2011). Do Childhood Callous-Unemotional Traits Drive Change in Parenting Practices? *Journal of Clinical Child and Adolescent Psychology: The Official Journal for the Society of Clinical Child and Adolescent Psychology, American Psychological Association, Division 53, 40*(4), 507–518.

Henry, J., Dionne, G., Viding, E., Vitaro, F., Brendgen, M., Tremblay, R. E. & Boivin, M. (2018). Early Warm-Rewarding Parenting Moderates the Genetic Contributions to Callous-Unemotional Traits in Childhood. *Journal of Child Psychology and Psychiatry, 59*(12), 1282–1288.

Hibbeln, J. R. (2001). Seafood Consumption and Homicide Mortality: A Cross-national Ecological Analysis. *World Review of Nutrition and Dietetics, 88*, 41–46.

Hibbeln, J. R., Ferguson, T. A. & Blasbalg, T. L. (2006). Omega-3 Fatty Acid Deficiencies in Neurodevelopment, Aggression and Autonomic Dysregulation: Opportunities for Intervention. *International Review of Psychiatry, 18*(2), 107–118.

Huizink, A. C., Robles de Medina, P. G., Mulder, E. J. H., Visser, G. H. A. & Buitelaar, J. K. (2003). Stress during Pregnancy is Associated with Developmental Outcome in Infancy. *Journal of Child Psychology and Psychiatry, and Allied Disciplines, 44*(6), 810–818.

Jackson, D. B. & Beaver, K. M. (2016). The Association between Breastfeeding Exposure and Duration, Neuropsychological Deficits, and Psychopathic Personality Traits in Offspring: The Moderating Role of 5HTTLPR. *Psychiatric Quarterly, 87*(1), 107–127.

Kalmijn, S., van Boxtel, M. P. J., Ocke, M., Verschuren, W. M. M., Kromhout, D. & Launer, L. J. (2004). Dietary Intake of Fatty Acids and Fish in Relation to Cognitive Performance at Middle Age. *Neurology, 62*(2), 275–280.

Karpman, B. (1941). On the Need of Separating Psychopathy into Two Distinct Clinical Types: The Symptomatic and the Idiopathic. *Journal of Criminal Psychopathology, 3*, 112–137.

Kimonis, E. R., Cross, B., Howard, A. & Donoghue, K. (2013). Maternal Care, Maltreatment and Callous-Unemotional Traits among Urban Male Juvenile Offenders. *Journal of Youth and Adolescence, 42*(2), 165–177.

Kimonis, E. R., Fanti, K. A., Isoma, Z. & Donoghue, K. (2013). Maltreatment Profiles Among Incarcerated Boys With Callous-Unemotional Traits. *Child Maltreatment, 18*(2), 108–121.

Kimonis, E. R., Fleming, G., Briggs, N., Brouwer-French, L., Frick, P. J., Hawes, D. J., … Dadds, M. (2018). Parent-Child Interaction Therapy Adapted for Preschoolers with Callous-Unemotional Traits: An Open Trial Pilot Study. *Journal of Clinical Child & Adolescent Psychology*, doi: 10.1080/15374416.2018.1479966

Kimonis, E. R., Frick, P. J. & Barry, C. T. (2004). Callous-Unemotional Traits and Delinquent Peer Affiliation. *Journal of Consulting and Clinical Psychology, 72*(6), 956–966.

Kimonis, E. R., Frick, P. J., Muñoz, L. C. & Aucoin, K. J. (2008). Callous-Unemotional Traits and the Emotional Processing of Distress Cues in Detained Boys: Testing the Moderating Role of Aggression, Exposure to Community Violence, and Histories of Abuse. *Development and Psychopathology, 20*(2), 569–589.

Kosson, D. S., Cyterski, T. D., Steuerwald, B. L., Neumann, C. S. & Walker-Matthews, S. (2002). The Reliability and Validity of the Psychopathy Checklist: Youth Version (PCL:YV) in Nonincarcerated Adolescent Males. *Psychological Assessment, 14*(1), 97–109.

Lalumière, M. L., Harris, G. T. & Rice, M. E. (2001). Psychopathy and Developmental Instability. *Evolution and Human Behavior, 22*(2), 75–92.

Larsson, H., Viding, E. & Plomin, R. (2008). Callous–Unemotional Traits and Antisocial Behavior. *Criminal Justice and Behavior, 35*(2), 197–211.

LeWinn, K. Z., Stroud, L. R., Molnar, B. E., Ware, J. H., Koenen, K. C. & Buka, S. L. (2009). Elevated Maternal Cortisol Levels during Pregnancy Are Associated with Reduced Childhood IQ. *International Journal of Epidemiology, 38*(6), 1700–1710.

Lynam, D. R., Loeber, R. & Stouthamer-Loeber, M. (2008). The Stability of Psychopathy From Adolescence Into Adulthood. *Criminal Justice and Behavior*, *35*(2), 228–243.

Marshall, L. A. & Cooke, D. J. (1999). The Childhood Experiences of Psychopaths: A Retrospective Study of Familial and Societal Factors. *Journal of Personality Disorders*, *13*(3), 211–225.

McCord, W. M. & McCord, J. (1964). *The Psychopath: An Essay on the Criminal Mind*. Princeton, NJ: Van Nostrand.

Meyer, B. J., Byrne, M. K., Collier, C., Parletta, N., Crawford, D., Winberg, P. C., . . . Grant, L. (2015). Baseline Omega-3 Index Correlates with Aggressive and Attention Deficit Disorder Behaviours in Adult Prisoners. *PLOS ONE*, *10*(3), e0120220.

Molinuevo, B., Pardo, Y., González, L. & Torrubia, R. (2014). Memories of Parenting Practices are Associated with Psychopathy in Juvenile Male Offenders. *The Journal of Forensic Psychiatry & Psychology*, *25*(4), 495–500.

Mumola, C. (2000). *Incarcerated Parents and Their Children*. Washington, DC: Bureau of Justice Statistics.

Muñoz, L. C., Kerr, M. & Besic, N. (2008). The Peer Relationships of Youths With Psychopathic Personality Traits: A Matter of Perspective. *Criminal Justice and Behavior*, *35*(2), 212–227.

Muñoz, L. C., Pakalniskiene, V. & Frick, P. J. (2011). Parental Monitoring and Youth Behavior Problems: Moderation by Callous-Unemotional Traits over Time. *European Child & Adolescent Psychiatry*, *20*(5), 261–269.

Pardini, D. A. & Loeber, R. (2008). Interpersonal Callousness Trajectories across Adolescence: Early Social Influences and Adult Outcomes. *Criminal Justice and Behavior*, *35*(2), 173–196.

Pasalich, D. S., Dadds, M. R., Hawes, D. J. & Brennan, J. (2012). Attachment and Callous-Unemotional Traits in Children with Early-Onset Conduct Problems. *Journal of Child Psychology and Psychiatry*, *53*(8), 838–845.

Poythress, N. G., Skeem, J. L. & Lilienfeld, S. O. (2006). Associations among Early Abuse, Dissociation, and Psychopathy in an Offender Sample. *Journal of Abnormal Psychology*, *115*(2), 288–297.

Raine, A., Brennan, P. & Mednick, S. A. (1997). Interaction between Birth Complications and Early Maternal Rejection in Predisposing Individuals to Adult Violence: Specificity to Serious, Early-Onset Violence. *American Journal of Psychiatry*, *154*(9), 1265–1271.

Raine, A., Portnoy, J., Liu, J., Mahoomed, T. & Hibbeln, J. R. (2015). Reduction in Behavior Problems with Omega-3 Supplementation in Children Aged 8–16 Years: A Randomized, Double-Blind, Placebo-Controlled, Stratified, Parallel-Group Trial. *Journal of Child Psychology and Psychiatry, and Allied Disciplines*, *56*(5), 509–520.

Ray, J. V. (2018). Developmental Patterns of Psychopathic Personality Traits and the Influence of Social Factors among a Sample of Serious Juvenile Offenders. *Journal of Criminal Justice*, *58*, 67–77.

Rogers, P. J. (2001). A Healthy Body, a Healthy Mind: Long-Term Impact of Diet on Mood and Cognitive Function. *The Proceedings of the Nutrition Society*, *60*(1), 135–143.

Rosenström, T., Ystrom, E., Torvik, F. A., Czajkowski, N. O., Gillespie, N. A., Aggen, S. H., . . . Reichborn-Kjennerud, T. (2017). Genetic and Environmental Structure of DSM-IV Criteria for Antisocial Personality Disorder: A Twin Study. *Behavior Genetics*, *47*(3), 265–277.

Salihovic, S., Kerr, M., Özdemir, M. & Pakalniskiene, V. (2012). Directions of Effects between Adolescent Psychopathic Traits and Parental Behavior. *Journal of Abnormal Child Psychology*, *40*(6), 957–969.

Schraft, C. V., Kosson, D. S. & McBride, C. K. (2013). Exposure to Violence within Home and Community Environments and Psychopathic Tendencies in Detained Adolescents. *Criminal Justice and Behavior, 40*(9), 1027–1043.

Thesing, C. S., Bot, M., Milaneschi, Y., Giltay, E. J. & Penninx, B. W. J. H. (2018). Omega-3 and Omega-6 Fatty Acid Levels in Depressive and Anxiety Disorders. *Psychoneuroendocrinology, 87,* 53–62.

Thomson, N. D., Kuay, H. S., Baron-Cohen, S. & Towl, G. J. (2018). The Impact of Maternal Incarceration on Their Daughter's Empathy. *International Journal of Law and Psychiatry, 56,* 10–16.

Waller, R., Gardner, F., Viding, E., Shaw, D. S., Dishion, T. J., Wilson, M. N. & Hyde, L. W. (2014). Bidirectional Associations between Parental Warmth, Callous Unemotional Behavior, and Behavior Problems in High-Risk Preschoolers. *Journal of Abnormal Child Psychology, 42*(8), 1275–1285.

Walters, G. D. (2018). Exposure to Violence as a Mediator of the CU–Aggression Relationship: on the Importance of Establishing the Causal Direction of Variables in a Path Analysis. *Exposure to Violence as a Mediator of the CU–Aggression Relationship: On the Importance of Establishing the Causal Direction of Variables in a Path Analysis, 40,* 169–179.

Watts, A. L., Donahue, K., Lilienfeld, S. O. & Latzman, R. D. (2017). Gender Moderates Psychopathic Traits' Relations with Self-Reported Childhood Maltreatment. *Personality and Individual Differences, 119,* 175–180.

Weiler, B. L. & Widom, C. S. (1996). Psychopathy and Violent Behaviour in Abused and Neglected Young Adults. *Criminal Behaviour and Mental Health, 6*(3), 253–271.

Wright, J. P., Boisvert, D. & Vaske, J. (2009). Blood Lead Levels in Early Childhood Predict Adulthood Psychopathy. *Youth Violence and Juvenile Justice, 7*(3), 208–222.

Wright, J. P., Dietrich, K. N., Ris, M. D., Hornung, R. W., Wessel, S. D., Lanphear, B. P., . . . Rae, M. N. (2008). Association of Prenatal and Childhood Blood Lead Concentrations with Criminal Arrests in Early Adulthood. *PLoS Medicine, 5*(5), e101.

Wright, N., Hill, J., Sharp, H. & Pickles, A. (2018). Maternal Sensitivity to Distress, Attachment and the Development of Callous-Unemotional Traits in Young Children. *Journal of Child Psychology and Psychiatry, 59*(7), 790–800.

Yang, Y. & Raine, A. (2018). The Neuroanatomical Bases of Psychopathy: A Review of Brain Imaging Findings. In C. Patrick (Ed.), *The Handbook of Psychopathy* (2nd ed., pp. 380–400). New York: Guilford Press.

Zwaanswijk, W., van Geel, M. & Vedder, P. (2018). Socioeconomic Status and Psychopathic Traits in a Community Sample of Youth. *Journal of Abnormal Child Psychology, 46*(8), 1643–1649.

8
THE BIOPSYCHOSOCIAL MODEL OF PSYCHOPATHY

Psychopathy has been proposed to be a "purely biological epiphenomenon" (Canavero, 2014, p. 2). However, based on the vast body of literature published to date, there is clear evidence that the development of psychopathy is more complex and, based on the empirical research summarized in this volume, biological, psychological and social risk factors all contribute to the progression of psychopathy. Thus, psychopathy has become recognized by the scientific community as a biopsychosocial disorder (Bergstrøm & Farrington, 2018; Dawson, Segrave & Carter, 2016; Paris, 1998). Continuing to implement an integrative and multidisciplinary approach is essential for understanding psychopathy and how it is treated. The biopsychosocial approach was first introduced more than 60 years ago (Grinker, 1956). However, until recently psychopathy has been researched from discipline specific perspectives, with a lack of integration. This research has been important and resulted in a great deal of understanding of the correlates of psychopathy, especially from the biological and psychological perspective. The strong foundation of research provides an important platform for the next step of integrating these findings to provide a richer understanding in the development of psychopathy. It is clear that there are multiple pathways that children develop psychopathic traits into adulthood, and it is only by integrating multidisciplinary practice that these pathways will be fully understood.

Indeed, at the core of psychopathy, behavioral genetics shows genetics explains 40–60% of psychopathy, while molecular genetics suggests this figure is too generous and the contribution is at most 20%. Both of these figures show that psychopathy is a disorder that is partly influenced by risk factors after the point of conception. Thus, as researchers and clinicians it is imperative to take a person-centered view of psychopathy across the lifespan. Taking this approach will help refine prevention methods before psychopathy fully develops and intervention methods for those with the disorder.

Although the biopsychosocial model emphasizes a multidisciplinary approach to research, to date there remains a scarcity of research exploring the interactive effects from at least two of biopsychosocial domains. However, what does exist shows that there is value in exploring these associations. For example, using longitudinal data from the Cambridge Study in Delinquent Development, Auty, Farrington and Coid (2015) found the link between father psychopathy levels (Psychopathy Checklist: Screening Version; PCL:SV), and a son's factor 1 scores was mediated by the father having employment difficulties, whereas the transmission of factor 2 scores was mediated by fathers' problems with accommodation and employment, and history of drug use. The transmission of psychopathy from father to daughter was only mediated by employment problems for factor 1 and factor 2. This study demonstrates that heritability of psychopathy for both men and women is, in part, contingent on exposure to social risk factors. This is encouraging, as employment difficulties are easily identified and can be targeted on a larger scale, which may reduce the transmission of psychopathic traits from parent to child.

Economic hardship can cause stress, especially when pregnant. As discussed in Chapter 7, maternal prenatal stress has been linked to psychopathic traits in children. However, this association seems to be contingent on biological vulnerabilities. Gao, Huang and Li (2017) explored the interaction between autonomic nervous system activity (heart rate) and prenatal maternal stress to predict psychopathy scores in 295 children (8–10 years old). The authors found children who were less physiologically aroused during data collection (a potential biomarker for fearlessness; Raine, 2005) who had mothers that experienced high stress during pregnancy had the highest scores on parent-report of Callous-Unemotional (CU) traits, Daring-Impulsive traits and Grandiose-Manipulative traits. The authors note that through the release and transmission of cortisol, maternal stress during pregnancy may impact neurological development in key brain regions associated with social behavior. Further, the hypo-arousal associated with psychopathy may be a product of exposure to high levels of prenatal cortisol, which is a product of the mother being exposed to high levels of stress. Thus, it may be possible to prevent, or at least reduce, the development of psychopathic traits in children by implementing a wrap-around case management service for pregnant women who are experiencing high levels of stress. Indeed, early screening of pregnant mothers for stress is a manageable task, given the frequent visits with health professionals. Another study using the biopsychosocial approach, conducted by Ling, Raine, Gao and Schug (2018), tested the link between low autonomic arousal and psychopathy in a community sample of 156 men. The authors proposed and found that psychopathy (PCL-R) was best predicted by the combination of low autonomic arousal and poor emotional intelligence. Drawing from Chapters 5 and 6, both poor emotional intelligence and low physiological arousal are associated with psychopathic traits; yet, it is the combination of the two which best predict psychopathy across all facets (Interpersonal, Affective, Lifestyle and Antisocial). The authors note that because emotional intelligence is malleable, it may be a key mechanism to target to reduce the biological vulnerability of psychopathy.

There are two disparate theories of how social risk factors influence biological risk factors for antisocial behavior, which may apply to psychopathy. The first is that antisocial behavior is made worse when social and biological risk factors are combined, and this may not just be additive effects but also because social risk factors may make the biological risk factor even more detrimental (Glenn & Raine, 2014). In contrast, Raine's (2002) "social push hypothesis" suggests biological factors will become more pronounced when there is a lack of social risk factors (e.g., poor parenting style, poverty, peer delinquency). The social push hypothesis suggests individuals from adverse social environments will become antisocial, regardless of their biological predisposition, whereas an individual without these social risk factors will only become antisocial if there are biological risk factors. Based on the research conducted so far, both theories could be applied to specific features of psychopathy, and both theories highlight the importance of the environment in conjunction with biology.

Expanding on these theories, this book proposes and supports prior assertions (Farrington, 2006; Paris, 1998) that the development of psychopathy is dynamic and there is not a single developmental pathway. Instead, the development of psychopathy is contingent on the full biopsychosocial model (see Figure 8.1). That is, biological (including genetics), psychological and social factors all contribute to the development of psychopathy. Further, there is likely to be an additive and multiplicative effect of the biopsychosocial factors. This means the more risk factors a person has the greater likelihood there is to developing psychopathy. Further, the interaction between biopsychosocial risk factors may greatly amplify the risk. An additional consideration of the biopsychosocial approach is that a protective factor in one domain (e.g., social) may act as a suppressor for a risk factor in another domain (e.g., biological). Thus, even with a genetic predisposition it is possible that social or psychological factors can reduce the development of psychopathy. To illustrate the model, two brief and notably categorical case studies are used: the *genetically vulnerable child* and the *environmentally vulnerable child*.

The genetically vulnerable child

A child with the genetic vulnerability to psychopathy will only develop high levels of psychopathy as an adult if the respective social, psychological and additional biological risk factors are present. However, if the child is raised in a home that nurtures "normative" and protective social and psychological factors, such as positive parenting, a father who is employed, peers who are not delinquent and prosocial adult role models (e.g., teachers) who praise positive behaviors, she will be less likely develop clinically significant levels of psychopathy in adulthood. It is also important to note that not having a negative risk factor can in itself be considered a protective factor. Thus, without the combination of biopsychosocial risk the genetic expression of psychopathy may be suppressed. This can be the same for any one of the biopsychosocial domains. This suppression effect over time may continue to shape biopsychosocial vulnerabilities and protective factors. Therefore, the stability of this suppression is contingent on maintaining protective factors and minimizing risk factors throughout the child's development. Over time, this biopsychosocial interaction will perpetuate and begin to shape the individuals' life circumstances; she will be less likely to be exposed to and seek out social risk factors (e.g., exposure and normalization of an antisocial environment), less likely to engage in risky behaviors leading to physical injury and be more likely to develop psychological protective factors (e.g., emotional intelligence), thus, digressing from the developmental risk of psychopathy.

Indeed, because the child is genetically vulnerable to psychopathy, certain characteristics of psychopathy are likely to emerge. Further, because these characteristics may be considered positive in certain scenarios some personality traits may be reinforced by caregivers, peers and teachers as they have value in society (e.g., confidence and boldness, charming behaviors, being goal-directed and strong-willed) and business (e.g., utilitarian decision-making, grandiosity and persuasive). It is also possible that these psychopathy-related genes may increase the child's risk of neurobiological deficits (e.g., *ROBO2*) and, therefore, she may have challenges in certain cognitive functions. However, because of the contribution of both social and psychological protective factors (and additional biological protective factors), it would be unlikely that the individual would develop the full cluster of psychopathic symptoms. The biopsychosocial model lends itself particularly well to psychopathy. As discussed throughout this book, psychopathy consists of a constellation of personality and behavioral features. Thus, rather than a single risk factor predicting these various symptoms, it is more compelling that multiple risk factors contribute to the development of each symptom or small cluster of closely related symptoms. This is why many risk factors are shared between psychopathy and other similar disorders.

The environmentally vulnerable child

In contrast, a child who is the victim of adverse social risk factors (e.g., maltreatment, low SES, exposure to delinquent peers and community violence) but does not carry the genes will not develop the full symptomology of psychopathy. This is because the genetic predisposition contributes significantly to the development of the disorder, especially to the personality and neurobiological features. Instead, and consistent with early theories (e.g., Karpman, 1948) and research, these risk factors will increase the likelihood of developing psychopathic-like behaviors (e.g., antisociality, emotion dysregulation, impulsivity and risk-taking). Indeed, without the early biological contribution to the disorder the behavior, personality and temperament features are more likely to resemble Antisocial Personality Disorder, rather than the core features of psychopathy (e.g., interpersonal-affective traits). Thus, in order for psychopathy to develop, the full biopsychosocial risk factors must be present, and in this case, not having the genetic disposition equates to having a biological protective factor.

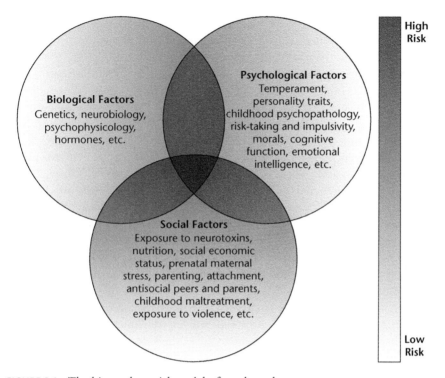

FIGURE 8.1 The biopsychosocial model of psychopathy

The biopsychosocial model of psychopathy and the research presented in this volume suggest that the biopsychosocial approach is essential to understanding both the development and retrogression of psychopathy. Therefore, the importance of the biopsychosocial approach extends beyond the realm of research and becomes integral to treatment and clinical practice.

Biopsychosocial model and treatment of psychopathy

The study and treatment of psychopathy is a public health issue. As discussed in Chapters 1–3, people with psychopathy pose high risk for criminal behavior, and are responsible for a significant proportion of crime. Further, the psychopath's crimes are more likely to be gratuitously violent, but they are also opportunistic and indiscriminate. Once convicted, psychopaths continue their illegal and violent behavior behind bars, emerging as inmate leaders and chronically violent prisoners. To make matters worse, psychopathic offenders more often get shorter prison sentences and parole early. Once released from prison or the inpatient facility, psychopathic individuals are more likely to continue their criminal careers and eventually become reconvicted – starting the perpetual cycle again. Therefore, prison provides a unique opportunity to provide treatment for these high-risk individuals. We know through clinical practice and empirical research that deterrents and punishment do not work on psychopaths, so unless forensic institutions start to incorporate targeted interventions specifically for psychopathic individuals we will continue to witness the wrath of the psychopath.

Since the earliest clinical conceptions of psychopathy, it has become widely accepted that treatment outcomes are bleak for the psychopath (Lewis, 2018; Polaschek & Skeem, 2018). However, this is largely based on regurgitation of conjecture and poor treatment design (e.g., use of psychoactive substances). Actually, more recent (and ethical) research has shown that levels of psychopathy do not influence the outcome of treatment for inpatients (Skeem, Monahan & Mulvey, 2002) and prisoners (Wong, Gordon, Gu, Lewis & Olver, 2012). Salekin (2002) conducted a review of 42 treatment studies and found a 62% success rate for cognitive behavioral therapy (CBT), a 59% success rate for psychoanalysis and an 88% success rate for a combination of CBT and insight-oriented approach (Lewis, 2018), which are promising numbers given the high level of risk these people pose. It is important to note too that none of these interventions were specifically designed and validated to target psychopathic traits. Another limitation to research exploring treatment efficacy for psychopathy is that they assess change based on the PCL-R. As discussed in Chapter 2, the construct of the PCL-R is considered less dynamic than more recent personality-based models of psychopathy (e.g., the Comprehensive Assessment of Psychopathic Personality; CAPP). A dynamic model would likely be more sensitive to change in response to treatment, therefore it will be interesting to see how interventions influence psychopathic traits using these dynamic assessments of psychopathic personality.

Within therapy it is essential to form a therapeutic alliance to achieve change, and this is done through establishing a therapeutic bond. Indeed, individuals higher on affective features of psychopathy are emotionally detached, which would suggest patients higher on these traits would fail to develop a bond with the therapist (DeSorcy, Olver & Wormith, 2017). Yet, in a sample of 111 male offenders, 85% of men scoring above 25 on the PCL-R developed a strong working alliance with their primary therapists and completed treatment (ibid.). Most interventions are developed to target harmful and illegal behaviors (e.g., violence), rather than focusing on treating interpersonal-affective psychopathic traits. To target risk factors that are more quickly responsive to treatment is good reason to employ this practice when prison resources are limited. Further, as Sewall and Olver (2018, p. 2) state, "it is not illegal to be an unpleasant person, but it is clearly illegal to commit a violent sexual assault". Yet, the interpersonal-affective traits of psychopathy bring challenges to treatment, such as manipulative and coercive behaviors, being disruptive, attention seeking, antagonizing patients and staff, as well as increasing the risk of the patient/client to drop out of treatment (ibid.). Therefore, the aim of most intervention strategies is to manage and tolerate these personality features to keep the individual in treatment, allowing enough time for the intervention to address impulsive-antisocial psychopathic traits, which will reduce the risk of illegal behaviors (ibid.).

With growing support that psychopathy is characterized as a biopsychosocial disorder, treatment approaches will also need to become aligned with the recent research and adopt a multidisciplinary approach to target biological, psychological and social risk factors. Indeed, this approach will likely result in more effective treatment. However, in order to accomplish this, researchers and clinicians will need to develop a treatment protocol specifically for psychopathic traits (as is being done in youth with CU traits; see Kimonis et al., 2018).

There is a misconception that a biological risk factor is unchangeable, and that if psychopathy is a biologically based disorder there is nothing that can be done to treat the disorder. As we have seen throughout this book, the development of psychopathy is influenced by biological risk factors but these may be contingent on psychological and social risk factors. This is important, because the biopsychosocial approach to psychopathy provides a more optimistic treatment view of these traits, regardless of the biological associations. That is, risk of psychopathy can be reduced by targeting at least one of the biopsychosocial domains, because each risk factor may have a subsequent effect on another risk factor, regardless of the domain. A biopsychosocial treatment model does not suggest every patient needs a brain scan or psychophysiological assessment, because research is continuing to provide information that psychopathy is associated with certain biological risk factors. Thus, this knowledge is acquired by practicing science-informed care. For example, generally, psychopathic traits are associated with prefrontal cortex (PFC) dysfunction, and this brain region plays an integral role in inhibitory control. Therefore, PFC dysfunction may partly explain the behavioral impulsivity associated with psychopathy. In which case, an intervention designed for individuals with psychopathic traits may incorporate neurocognitive training targeting inhibition. Indeed, research has found in older adults that inhibition training not only influences inhibitory control but also increases cortical thickness in parts of the PFC (Kühn et al., 2017). Similarly, factor 2 traits are associated with a biological vulnerability to emotion dysregulation. A psychopathy intervention may also choose to target this risk factor by introducing a meditation component, which has been shown to positively influence biomarkers of emotion dysregulation (e.g., respiratory sinus arrhythmia; Krygier et al., 2013). These brief examples of evidence demonstrate that biological risk factors can be malleable to intervention; however, the targeted intervention component must be pertinent to the risk factors of psychopathy. Therefore, the merging of research into clinical practice is essential. Overall, there is more evidence to be optimistic about the treatment of psychopathy, and as these new measures and specific treatment methods become developed and introduced it will only be a matter of time before an effective intervention for psychopathy becomes established.

Conclusion and future directions

The biopsychosocial model was established over 40 years ago, and since this time it has been held as the gold-standard for research practice. Today, the biopsychosocial approach has been integrated into practitioner guides by the National Health Service for offender management (National Offender Management Service, 2015), proposed as an important approach for treating high-risk offenders (Walton, Ramsay, Cunningham & Henfrey, 2017), and become a central theory to understanding violence (Hoffer, Hargreaves-Cormany, Muirhead & Meloy, 2018). This volume highlights that the biopsychosocial approach should be used as the central model for understanding the development of psychopathy. Researchers in field of psychopathy have largely urged the importance of integrating a multidisciplinary approach to understand the development of psychopathy, but still very few studies have tested the interactive associations across the biopsychosocial domains. Fortunately, researchers have made substantial headway exploring the individual role of biological, psychological and social risk factors, which has, collectively, provided a deeper understanding into the etiology of psychopathy and provides support that psychopathy is a biopsychosocial disorder. Indeed, with all the evidence from each discipline it is a natural step in progression to become more integrative in our study designs. In Chapter 1 we reviewed the strengths of the biopsychosocial model by discussing the criticisms. One of the main criticisms is that the biopsychosocial model is too broad. However, as we have seen throughout this book, the scientific evidence suggests that expecting a simple explanation of the development of psychopathy is just not going to happen. Instead, a disorder as complex as psychopathy, which encompasses a system of personality and behavioral traits, will only be fully understood by integrating a multidimensional approach to include genetics, biological, psychological and social factors. The value of the biopsychosocial approach is that it removes disciplinary boundaries and promotes multidisciplinary research and innovation – at its core the biopsychosocial approach is a dynamic tactic suitable for the next stage of advancements in understanding psychopathy.

References

Auty, K. M., Farrington, D. P. & Coid, J. W. (2015). Intergenerational Transmission of Psychopathy and Mediation via Psychosocial Risk Factors. *The British Journal of Psychiatry: The Journal of Mental Science, 206*(1), 26–31. doi: 10.1192/bjp.bp.114.151050

Bergstrøm, H. & Farrington, D. P. (2018). Grandiose-Manipulative, Callous-Unemotional, and Daring-Impulsive: the Prediction of Psychopathic Traits in Adolescence and their Outcomes in Adulthood. *Journal of Psychopathology and Behavioral Assessment, 40*(2), 149–158. doi: 10.1007/s10862-018-9674-6

Canavero, S. (2014). Criminal Minds: Neuromodulation of the Psychopathic Brain. *Frontiers in Human Neuroscience, 8*, 124. doi: 10.3389/fnhum.2014.00124

Dawson, A., Segrave, R. A. & Carter, A. (2016). Curing Psychopathy: Just Activate the Amygdala? *AJOB Neuroscience, 7*(3), 164–166. doi: 10.1080/21507740.2016.1225847

DeSorcy, D. R., Olver, M. E. & Wormith, J. S. (2017). Working Alliance and Psychopathy. *Journal of Interpersonal Violence*, online first. doi: 10.1177/0886260517698822

Farrington, D. P. (2006). Family Background and Psychopathy. In C. J. Patrick (Ed.), *Handbook of Psychopathy* (pp. 229–250). New York: Guilford.

Gao, Y., Huang, Y. & Li, X. (2017). Interaction between Prenatal Maternal Stress and Autonomic Arousal in Predicting Conduct Problems and Psychopathic Traits in Children. *Journal of Psychopathology and Behavioral Assessment*, *39*(1), 1–14. doi: 10.1007/s10862-016-9556-8

Glenn, A. L. & Raine, A. (2014). *Psychopathy: An Introduction to Biological Findings and Their Implications*. New York: New York University Press.

Grinker, R. R. (1956). *Toward a Unified Theory of Human Behavior*. Oxford: Basic Books.

Hoffer, T., Hargreaves-Cormany, H., Muirhead, Y. & Meloy, J. R. (2018). Meloy's Biopsychosocial Model of Violence. In *Violence in Animal Cruelty Offenders. SpringerBriefs in Psychology* (pp. 17–19). Cham: Springer. doi: 10.1007/978-3-319-91038-3_6

Karpman, B. (1948). The Myth of the Psychopathic Personality. *American Journal of Psychiatry*, *104*(9), 523–534. doi: 10.1176/ajp.104.9.523

Kimonis, E. R., Fleming, G., Briggs, N., Brouwer-French, L., Frick, P. J., Hawes, D. J., . . . Dadds, M. (2018). Parent-Child Interaction Therapy Adapted for Preschoolers with Callous-Unemotional Traits: An Open Trial Pilot Study. *Journal of Clinical Child & Adolescent Psychology*, online first. doi: 10.1080/15374416.2018.1479966

Krygier, J. R., Heathers, J. A. J., Shahrestani, S., Abbott, M., Gross, J. J. & Kemp, A. H. (2013). Mindfulness Meditation, Well-being, and Heart Rate Variability: A Preliminary Investigation into the Impact of Intensive Vipassana Meditation. *International Journal of Psychophysiology*, *89*(3), 305–313. doi: 10.1016/J.IJPSYCHO.2013.06.017

Kühn, S., Lorenz, R. C., Weichenberger, M., Becker, M., Haesner, M., O'Sullivan, J., . . . Gallinat, J. (2017). Taking Control! Structural and Behavioural Plasticity in Response to Game-Based Inhibition Training in Older Adults. *NeuroImage*, *156*, 199–206. doi: 10.1016/J.NEUROIMAGE.2017.05.026

Lewis, M. (2018). Treatment of Psychopathy: Conceptual and Empirical Review. *Journal of Criminological Research, Policy and Practice*.

Ling, S., Raine, A., Gao, Y. & Schug, R. (2018). The Mediating Role of Emotional Intelligence on the Autonomic Functioning – Psychopathy Relationship. *Biological Psychology*, *136*, 136–143. doi: 10.1016/j.biopsycho.2018.05.012

National Offender Management Service. (2015). *Working with Offenders with Personality Disorder A Practitioners Guide*. London: National Offender Management Service.

Paris, J. (1998). A Biopsychosocial Model of Psychopathy. In T. Millon, M. Simonsen, M. Birket-Smith & R. D. Davis (Eds.), *Psychopathy: Anti-social, Criminal and Violent Behavior* (pp. 277–287). New York: Guilford Press.

Polaschek, D. L. & Skeem, J. L. (2018). Treatment of Adults and Juveniles with Psychopathy. In C. J. Patrick (Ed.), *The Handbook of Psychopathy* (2nd ed., pp. 710–731). New York: Guildford.

Raine, A. (2002). Biosocial Studies of Antisocial and Violent Behavior in Children and Adults: A Review. *Journal of Abnormal Child Psychology*, *30*(4), 311–326. doi: 10.1023/A:1015754122318

Raine, A. (2005). The Interaction of Biological and Social Measures in the Explanation of Antisocial and Violent Behaviour. In D. Stoff & E. J. Susman (Eds.), *Developmental Psychobiology Aggression* (pp. 13–42). New York: Cambridge University Press.

Salekin, R. T. (2002). Psychopathy and Therapeutic Pessimism: Clinical Lore or Clinical Reality? *Clinical Psychology Review*, *22*(1), 79–112.

Sewall, L. A. & Olver, M. E. (2018). Psychopathy and Treatment Outcome: Results from a Sexual Violence Reduction Program. *Personality Disorders: Theory, Research, and Treatment*, *10*(1), 59–69. doi: 10.1037/per0000297

Skeem, J. L., Monahan, J. & Mulvey, E. P. (2002). Psychopathy, Treatment Involvement, and Subsequent Violence among Civil Psychiatric Patients. *Law and Human Behavior*, *26*(6), 577–603. doi: 10.1023/A:1020993916404

Walton, J. S., Ramsay, L., Cunningham, C. & Henfrey, S. (2017). New Directions: Integrating a Biopsychosocial Approach in the Design and Delivery of Programs for High Risk Services Users in Her Majesty's Prison and Probation Service. *Advancing Corrections: Journal of the International Corrections and Prison Association*, *3*, 21–47.

Wong, S. C. P., Gordon, A., Gu, D., Lewis, K. & Olver, M. E. (2012). The Effectiveness of Violence Reduction Treatment for Psychopathic Offenders: Empirical Evidence and a Treatment Model. *International Journal of Forensic Mental Health*, *11*(4), 336–349. doi: 10.1080/14999013.2012.746760

INDEX

5-HTT 69–70, 72

abuse 11–12; emotional 131–132; physical 131–132, 134; psychological 128; sexual 131–313; verbal 49
ACC (anterior cingulate cortex) 80, 81–82, 85
ADHD (Attention Deficit Disorder) 70, 72, 127
aggression 29–30, 49–50, 83, 90, 101, 105, 116; physical 42, 48; predatory 48; proactive 49–50, 83, 109; psychological 46; psychotic 48; reactive 49–50, 90, 111
aggression subtypes 40, 50
amygdala 79–85, 90–91, 112
ANKK1 gene 69
anterior cingulate cortex *see* ACC
antisocial parents 12, 124, 133, 135–136
antisocial peers 134, 147
Antisocial Personality Disorder *see* ASPD
anxiety 9, 19, 24, 27, 29, 89, 103, 115
APSD (Antisocial Process Screening Device) 32
ASPD (Antisocial Personality Disorder) 19, 27–31, 33, 62–63, 69, 146
assault 23, 39–40, 42–43, 47, 51; aggravated 42; sexual 39–40, 42, 44, 148
attachment 23–24, 49, 124, 130–131, 136, 147
attachment styles 124, 130–131
AVPR1A 71–72

birth complications 125–126
Borderline Personality Disorder (BPD) 27–28, 33
brain injury, traumatic 10, 12–13
breastfeeding 126

Callous-Unemotional (CU) 13, 31–32, 60–63, 70, 102, 125, 144
candidate genes 68
CAPE (Clinical Assessment of Prosocial Emotions) 31–32
CAPP (Comprehensive Assessment of Psychopathic Personality) 23–24, 49, 130, 148
CD (Conduct Disorder) 30–31
childhood abuse 69, 131–133
childhood maltreatment 124, 131–133, 147
childhood psychopathology and psychopathic traits 102
childhood temperament 100–102
childhood trauma 132–133
child molesters 45, 109
Cleckley, H. 20–21, 29, 34, 106, 108–109, 130–131
cognitive behavioral therapy (CBT) 148
Comprehensive Assessment of Psychopathic Personality *see* CAPP
COMT 69–70
Conduct Disorder *see* CD
conduct problems 30–31, 35, 70, 89, 103, 116
cortisol 9, 89–90, 125, 144

Index

CPS (Childhood Psychopathy Scale) 32
CPTI (Child Problematic Traits Inventory) 32
CU *see* Callous-Unemotional

DAT1 68
diet 126
discipline, inconsistent 129
Dissocial Personality Disorder 27–29
DNA 66–67
dopamine 68–69
DRD1 68
DRD2 68–69
DSM-5 (*Diagnostic and Statistical Manual of Mental Disorders*) 27–31, 102

emotion recognition 111–113
emotional intelligence 100, 110–111, 144, 146–147
empathy 3, 13, 18–19, 22, 31, 70, 80, 82, 110, 124, 133
equifinality 100
executive functioning 79, 107–108
exposure, maternal stress and neurotoxins 126, 136
exposure, prenatal tobacco 125
externalizing traits 105

family environment 136
family violence 135
fatty acids, polyunsaturated 126–127
fearless temperament 101, 125
female offenders 39–41, 47, 106, 109, 111
females 39, 64–65, 68, 90, 102, 105
FFM (Five Factor Model) 68, 72

Gage, Phineas 79–80
genetics 57–77, 143, 145, 147, 150; behavioral 8, 57–65, 143; molecular 58, 65–71, 143
genome-wide association *see* GWA
genome-wide complex trait analysis *see* GWCTA
GWA (genome-wide association) 66–67, 76
GWCTA (genome-wide complex trait analysis) 67

heart rate 86, 144
heart rate variability (HRV) 85
Henderson, D. K. 18–20, 29, 108
heritability 62, 65, 67, 71, 144
homicide 39–42, 50–51
hormones 89–91, 147
HPA (hypothalamus–pituitary–adrenal) axis 89

ICD-10 27–29
ICU (Inventory of Callous-Unemotional Traits) 31–32
impression management 13, 23, 25
impulsivity 107
intelligence 20, 100, 108–109, 112–113
internalizing traits 105–106
intimate partner violence *see* IPV
IPV (intimate partner violence) 40, 45–47

Karpman, B. 19–20, 133, 146

LPE (Limited Prosocial Emotions) 30–31
LSRP (Levenson Self-Report Psychopathy Scale) 26

malingering 3
MAOA 57, 69–70
Mask of Sanity, The 20
maternal warmth 126, 129
moral attitudes 100, 113–116
moral decisions 114–116
moral dilemmas 114–115
moral foundations 113

nervous system: autonomic 79, 84, 87, 89; parasympathetic 78, 84, 87; peripheral 84; sympathetic 84, 86
neuroimaging 79, 89
neuroticism 19, 103–105
nutrition 126, 147

offenders 9, 2, 50, 104–108
omega-3 126–128, 136
oxytocin 70, 74–75

PAPA (Psychopathic Processing and Personality Assessment) 27
parental warmth 60, 129–130
parenting 13, 58–59, 65, 73, 124, 128–130, 136, 147
PCL-R (Psychopathy Checklist-Revised) 21–22
PDM-2 (The Psychodynamic Diagnostic Manual), 27, 29
peers 52, 59–60, 64–65, 73, 101, 134, 136, 145–46; delinquent 124, 134, 136, 146
perinatal infection 126
PFC (prefrontal cortex) 79–80, 83, 85, 149; anterior 90; dorsolateral 81; medial 80
Pinel, Philippe 18
Post-Traumatic Stress Disorder *see* PTSD
PPI *see* psychopathic personality inventory

PPTS (Psychopathic Personality Traits Scale) 26
prenatal maternal stress 125, 144
prenatal and postnatal risk factors 125–126
prison and inpatient violence 47
prisoners 40, 83, 87, 108, 113, 147, 148; female 43, 47; male 40, 110, 128, 132
psychodynamic 29
PPI-R (Psychopathic Personality Inventory – Revised) 26
psychopathic states 18
psychopaths: primary and secondary 19–20
PTSD (Post-Traumatic Stress Disorder) 106

respiratory sinus arrhythmia (RSA) 85, 149
risk-taking 85, 100, 107, 146–147
robbery 40, 42–44
ROBO2 66, 146

school shootings 13
serotonin 69
sex differences: genetics 61, 64–65, 68, 105
sexual offending 44–45
skin conductance 84–86
socioeconomic status 59, 128
sociopathy 27–29

SRP-4 (Self-Report Psychopathy Scale) 25
startle potentiation 88–89
suicidality 78, 106

TaqIA 68
testosterone 89–91
theft 43
Theophrastus 17
toddlers 59, 61–62, 64, 87, 101
treatment of psychopathy 147–149
TriPM (Triarchic Psychopathy Measure) 26
twin studies 58, 60–65, 67, 71–72

verbal intelligence 109
violence 1, 3, 8, 19–20, 33, 39–43, 45–47, 49–51, 126–127, 135–136; domestic 43, 135; exposure to 124, 135–136, 147; extra-familial 46; female 48; intimate partner 40, 45–47, 55; proactive 112; reactive 112; sexual 45–46
violent crime 3–4, 38–51, 124, 134
violent recidivism 48–49, 55

YPI (Youth Psychopathic Traits Inventory) 32

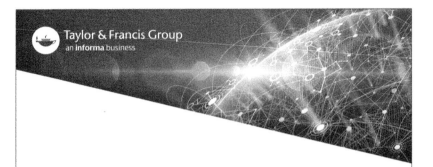